A CONTINUITY OF
SHARI'A

A CONTINUITY OF SHARI'A

POLITICAL AUTHORITY AND HOMICIDE IN THE NINETEENTH CENTURY

BRIAN WRIGHT

The American University in Cairo Press
Cairo   New York

First published in 2023 by
The American University in Cairo Press
113 Sharia Kasr el Aini, Cairo, Egypt
One Rockefeller Plaza, 10th Floor, New York, NY 10020
www.aucpress.com

ISBN 978 1 649 03262 1

Library of Congress Cataloging-in-Publication Data

Names: Wright, Brian (Professor of Islamic Studies), author.
Title: A continuity of shari'a : political authority and homicide in the nineteenth
    century / Brian Wright.
Identifiers: LCCN 2022034807 | ISBN 9781649032621 (hardback) |
    ISBN 9781649032638 (epub) | ISBN 9781649032645 (pdf)
Subjects: LCSH: Homicide (Islamic law)—Influence. | Murder (Islamic law) |
    Homicide—Law and legislation—Egypt. | Homicide—Law and legislation—Turkey. |
    Homicide—Law and legislation—India.
Classification: LCC KBP4050 .W75 2022 | DDC 345/.167025—dc23/eng/20220929

1 2 3 4 5   27 26 25 24 23

Designed by Westchester Publishing Services

For all those searching for the shari'a

Contents

Note on Abbreviations, Cases, and Transliteration

Abbreviations

CM	Ceride-ye Mahakim, Ottoman Empire
FB	*Fatawa* of Muhammad al-Banna, Grand Mufti of Egypt (d. 1896)
FM	*al-Fatawa al-Mahdiya* of Muhammad al-Mahdi, Grand Mufti of Egypt (d. 1897)
EPC	Egyptian Penal Code of 1883
HC Nwp	High Court of India, Northwestern Provinces
IPC	Indian Penal Code of 1860
OPC	Ottoman Penal Code of 1858
NA Ben	Reports of the Nizamut Adawlut, Bengal
NA Nwp	Reports of the Nizamut Adawlut, North-Western Provinces
SCC	Supreme Court of India, Cases

Citing Cases and Statutes

For published case records from Muslim jurisdictions, I have used the following format:

Case Name (Year of Publication) Series Name, Volume Number, Court Location, Page Number.

Example:

Sumadhan v. Roopun (1853) NA Nwp 1 Bareilly 311.

Cases and statutes cited from modern jurisdictions (such as Britain and the United States) follow standard citation styles.

Transliteration and Translation

All non-English terms are transliterated according to the standards of the American University in Cairo Press and taken from their source language of Arabic, Ottoman Turkish, Persian, or Urdu. Translations of primary sources are those of the author unless otherwise noted.

Preface

My journey in developing the idea for this book began when I first studied Islamic law in Cairo in 2007. I was fresh out of an undergraduate program and excited to jump back into the world that I had gotten a taste of a few years earlier, when I was studying abroad. At the Sibawayh Center, one of my main teachers, Ustaz Sayed Fathy, suggested that I use an introductory text in the Shafi'i school as a practical application of the grammar studies that I had become convinced were a frustrating and endless pursuit. Having practically grown up in a Texas law office, I was immediately drawn to this new realm of study, and within a few weeks I found myself confidently wading through detailed rules for ablution, prayer, and fasting.

During one of our lunchtime breaks, I asked the other teachers in the center about modern Egyptian law and what connection it had to what I was studying. "There is no connection," one teacher responded. "Everything in Egypt today is French law *(qanun faransi)*." I was confused. It made sense that some aspects of the law were geared toward the individual, like what kind of water had to be used for ablution. But surely other things, like commercial and criminal law, remained connected to the Islamic legal tradition, albeit adapted to modern circumstances. I asked sarcastically, "So why then do we bother studying this, if it is all French today anyway?" The teacher's response was solemn and straightforward: "Because one day the shari'a will be applied, and all this will become relevant again." From that moment on, the question of what had happened to the shari'a stuck in my mind.

At the next stop on my journey, I met Professor Muhammad Serag at the American University in Cairo. I had studied in Egypt for almost three years, and I wanted to more formally dedicate my life to the study of Islamic law. Before I started my MA program, I had been carefully reading through the multilevel seventeenth-century commentary on Shafi'i law known as

Qaliubi and ʿUmayra. I brought the first two volumes to my first meeting with Professor Serag. After hearing my questions about modern Egyptian law, he politely suggested that I change my reading habits and gave me a copy of *Masadir al-ḥaqq fi al-fiqh al-islami* by ʿAbd al-Razzaq al-Sanhuri.

Through the work of al-Sanhuri, I began to truly love and respect Islamic law. That book was the answer to the questions that had troubled me for years. Finally, here was someone who grasped the nuances of both the traditional and modern legal traditions. He could point out problems and provide solutions, and he possessed a sense of agency in dealing with the law that I felt was absent in so many people, who were resigned to making comments like *"qanun faransi"* and hoping that classical Islamic law would return one day. It was also with the help of Professor Serag that I began to see Islamic law as, in his words, a "legal system." Consisting of the work of jurists, muftis, judges, and governments, Islamic law was (and still is) not fundamentally different from common or civil law and must be approached as such.

My final stage came when I lived in Lucknow, India, during the first six months of 2014, before I headed to Montreal for my PhD. I studied the Hanafi school of jurisprudence at a Sufi shrine *(dargah)* next to my residence and was interested in seeing how Islamic law was approached in this non-Arab, minority context in which people were still grappling with the aftermath of British colonialism. One day, sitting with a colleague at breakfast, I was thumbing through Dinshaw Mulla's *Principles of Mahomedan Law.* My friend, who was finishing his studies at Nadwat al-ʿUlama at the time, looked at the book and said, "You know that isn't *really* Islamic law." "How so?" I asked. "Well," he replied, "Islamic law ended with the British, as it can only come from the *ʿulama.*"

As I would discover as soon as I reached Montreal and explored the secondary literature, this was not an isolated view. In India, I was faced with the same position that I had initially found in Egypt. Despite centuries of dynamic interpretation, the law of Islam was now relegated by many people to the annals of history. This view of the shariʿa continues to be shared across the spectrum of academic viewpoints and includes Muslims, Orientalists, and even Western critics of Orientalism. Moreover, it makes most attempts to discuss Islamic law a project for historians and ethnographers, with little room for modern lawyers and legal specialists. Finally, seeing the shariʿa in this way also means that much of Islamic law is locked in the past. The only way to access it is to comb through works of jurisprudence *(fiqh)* that, at least in the Hanafi tradition, have largely come to an end since the works of the early nineteenth-century Syrian jurist Muhammad Amin b. 'Abidin.

This book, therefore, is not intended to be purely a work of history. Indeed, it is based on the introduction of penal codes in the nineteenth century and is a technical analysis of how the Islamic law of homicide was adapted and understood by local actors during the colonial period. However, it is also an attempt to provide Muslims with a new way to look at the colonial and postcolonial periods. If Islamic law is indeed a legal system applicable in all times and places, it must be subject to change. The frustration that many of my colleagues and I face when looking at the development of modern legal systems in the Muslim world can be overcome with newly charted pathways that give the shari'a a place in the contemporary world.

Acknowledgments

Although I have already mentioned some of my influences in the preface, I have also enjoyed the company of many dear friends along the way, in Abu Dhabi, Cairo, Lucknow, Istanbul, and Montreal. In their own way, each person has been critical to the development of this book and has helped shape me as a person and student of knowledge. Specifically, I want to mention again Ustaz Sayed Fathy, my first teacher of Islamic law at the Sibawayh Center in Cairo, and Professor Muhammad Serag at the American University in Cairo. Their wisdom, guidance, and support have been invaluable, and I continue to value their friendship today. I would also like to acknowledge other colleagues, mentors, and interlocutors for their input and willingness to consider my arguments: Professor Ahmad Atif Ahmad, Professor Saiyad Nizamuddin Ahmad, Nasser Dumairiyyah, Osama Eshera, Ian Greer, Ashutosh Kumar, Ibrahim Mansur, Munther al-Sabbagh, and Temel Ucuncu.

The great libraries and archives that I have had the honor of visiting are also deserving of praise, as is their librarians' selfless and tireless work—which goes unnoticed in too many academic works. I would therefore like to thank the librarians at the Institute of Islamic Studies at McGill University, the Süleymaniye Library and Ottoman Archives in Istanbul, the al-Azhar Library in Cairo, the Shibli Nu'mani Library of Nadwat al-'Ulama in Lucknow, the Khuda Baksh Library in Patna, the Rampur Raza Library in Rampur, the library of Dar al-'Ulum Deoband, and the National Archives of India in Bhopal.

I would also like to thank the faculty and staff of the Institute of Islamic Studies at McGill University and the members of my dissertation defense committee. My co-supervisors, Professor Pasha Khan at McGill University and Professor Iza Hussin at the University of Cambridge, provided valuable corrections and forced me to think more deeply about the implications of my dissertation. Some readers will undoubtedly find the thesis presented in this book controversial, and the criticisms of my dissertation defense committee have helped me better shape my ideas. Research for this book was partially funded by a Graduate Mobility Award from McGill University, which enabled me to travel to Turkey in the summer of 2017, and a graduate funding package from the Institute of Islamic Studies. As this work has developed from a dissertation to its current form, sincere thanks are also due to the American University in Cairo Press and the peer reviewers who provided support and valuable suggestions for improvement.

Finally, I would like to thank my mother, Karla Wright, and my sister, Lauren Little, for their support and patience throughout this process.

Introduction

During the 1870s, in the northern Indian district of Hamirpur, a region close to the current borders of the states of Uttar Pradesh and Madhya Pradesh and at the confluence of the Betwa and Yamuna Rivers, villagers were under constant threat from a criminal named Lalooa. While committing one of his most daring acts, Lalooa shot and killed a police constable. In response, the police called on provincial authorities to issue an order for Lalooa's capture dead or alive, offering the incredible sum of a thousand rupees to anyone who assisted in his capture. The government agreed and authorized the police to hang posters in the surrounding villages but ordered them not to use the phrase "dead or alive," an order that the police did not obey. A few months later, Lalooa came upon a man named Aman and asked him for food. Recognizing the criminal from the posters, Aman gave Lalooa some food and told him to wait while he went to fetch more. Aman ran back to his village, where he informed his friends—a lumber merchant named Umrao, a police constable named Mahomed Nawaz, and another friend named Nund Kishore—that he knew Lalooa's whereabouts. The four men hatched a plan to capture Lalooa and turn him in for the reward. Nund Kishore picked up a sword, and the group returned to where Lalooa was eating.

As Lalooa finished his meal, Aman gave the signal to attack, and Nund Kishore struck Lalooa on the back of his neck with the sword. Lalooa started to run away, but Nund Kishore swung his sword again, severing Lalooa's hand as he raised it to block the attack. Aman and Nund Kishore then struck Lalooa four more times until they confirmed that he had died. Mahomed Nawaz, who had been watching the events from afar, came forward and raised his sword to strike another blow but was stopped by Aman and Nund Kishore, who said that the job was done.

The four villagers were then brought in front of the local magistrate, who charged them with abetment of murder—believing that because they had brought swords with them, their intent was clearly to kill and not merely capture Lalooa. The sessions judge[1] agreed in the case of Aman and Nund Kishore and sentenced them to one year of prison each, while the other two were acquitted because they had not actively participated in the events. Aman and Nund Kishore appealed the ruling, arguing that they believed that the reward was for the capture of Lalooa dead or alive. Therefore, they claimed that they should not be held criminally responsible for his death.

In the final judgment, the High Court of the Northwestern Provinces held that the actions of the defendants fell under the third exception to Section 302 of the Indian Penal Code of 1860, which stated: "Culpable homicide is not murder if the offender, being a public servant or aiding a public servant acting for the advancement of public justice, exceeds the powers given to him by law and causes death by doing an act which he, in good faith, believes to be lawful and necessary for the due discharge of his duty as such public servant and without ill-will towards the person whose death is caused."[2] As a result, the court reduced the charge to one of "culpable homicide not amounting to murder"[3] and reduced the sentences to four months of simple imprisonment.[4]

The events of this case illustrate several essential elements of law in British India, the most important of which was the role of the state. Why were the defendants brought to court at all, much less charged with abetment of murder? Were they not merely following the orders of the provincial authorities who wanted Lalooa brought to justice dead or alive? The answers to these questions lie in the colonial state's fear of vigilantism and threats to its power to administer justice. Had they allowed the defendants to go free, the courts would have set an example encouraging others in search of a reward to attack criminals, leading to chaos. To deter future offenders and prevent the application of the "dead or alive" standard in other cases, the courts felt that they had to act and therefore charged the defendants with homicide.

Additionally, was the presence of a sword, a deadly weapon by any measure, sufficient for the magistrate and sessions judge to establish murderous intent? Clearly, the appellate judges thought so, but they differed as to whether they should consider that the defendants acted on the belief that they were doing so with the state's approval. The judges should have sentenced the men to execution or life in prison, the punishment set out in Section 302 of the code.[5] Instead, the judges chose to sentence the men to merely one year in jail. In its final judgment, the High Court followed the lower court's concerns but found another way to solve the problem of intent. Rather than focus on the presence of a deadly weapon, the judges used an exception to Section 302 wherein defendants found to be acting "for the advancement of public justice" could have their sentence lessened to culpable homicide, the prescribed punishment for which was "imprisonment of either description for a term which may extend to ten years."[6] The High Court chose one of the shortest periods of punishment available, only four months for each man.

A final element of interest in this case was the degree of shared responsibility between the defendants. Why were the two other defendants acquitted so easily, even though they had both conspired with Aman and Nund Kishore to commit the crime? According to Section 107 of the code, abettors were those who "engage with one or more person or persons in any conspiracy for the doing of that thing, if an act or illegal omission takes place in pursuance of that conspiracy, and in order to the doing of that thing."[7] Both Mahomed Nawaz and Umrao conspired to capture Lalooa and were present during the attack. Moreover, Mahomed Nawaz went so far as to raise his sword to strike another deadly blow but was stopped at the last minute by the two main defendants. On this point, the lower courts seem to have once again relied upon the idea that Mahomed Nawaz and Umrao were acting honestly in the interests of the state. The two men did not take part in the murder and, therefore, could have intended merely to capture Lalooa, although the two other defendants attacked and killed him.

Would the outcome have been different if the circumstances of the case had occurred under the jurisdiction of shari'a following the understandings of the Hanafi school, the dominant legal tradition in northern India before the arrival of the British? If the points of the case raised above are analyzed, the ruling would have been the same. On the first point, under the Islamic system individuals do not have the right to take the law into their own hands, a principle established during the time of the Prophet Muhammad.[8] Violators of this principle could be charged with spreading corruption in the land (*fasad fi al-ard*) and unlawful warfare (*hiraba*) and could be subject to execution, crucifixion, cutting off of their hands and feet from opposite sides, or exile.[9] On the second point, jurists of the Hanafi school would have seen the presence of a deadly weapon—the swords—as evidence of intent to commit the highest category of intentional murder (*qatl 'amd*).

The defendants would therefore be subject to execution, the severest punishment available. Finally, on the third point, since all defendants conspired together to capture Lalooa, they could have all been held responsible for his death. However, given that only Aman and Nund Kishore enacted the blows that directly caused the death, only they would be subject to punishment.

Beyond these points of substantive law, what can be said about the larger question of the state's role in the prosecution of crime? Under the Hanafi system—and indeed all schools of jurisprudence—cases of homicide and personal injury (*qisas*) were constructed by jurists as crimes against not the state but the victim's family. It would have been the responsibility of the family members to bring the defendants to court and request retaliation in the form of execution or the payment of blood money (*diya*), although they could choose to forgive the defendants altogether. The British colonial state, taking that right of prosecution away from the family, fundamentally changed how homicide was treated in India, acting contrary to juristic (*fiqhi*) norms.

This change in the state's role and the legal interventions made by the colonial authorities in the nineteenth century have led observers to suggest that the Indian Penal Code of 1860 (IPC) marked the end of Islamic law's influence in the criminal system. According to Scott Kugle, for example, the code "legislated into oblivion many of the overtly Islamic facets of the law" and was part of a colonial project that was "wresting political power away from Muslims."[10] Radhika Singha has described this project as a "despotism" that strove to "sweep away what has been described as an Anglo-Muhammadan construct, assembled over the preceding half-century from various modifications of the Islamic law, supplemented by [British East India] Company regulations, and clarified by various 'constructions' and circular orders."[11]

This view is not unique to the Indian context and is part of a larger argument within the historiography of Islamic law that sees the introduction of penal codes in the second half of the nineteenth century as the end of shari'a's influence in criminal law. According to the argument, through codification, the reduction of the role of jurists (*fuqaha'*; sing., *faqih*), and the direct implementation of laws from Europe, the Islamic system that had dominated for centuries was sidelined. Wael Hallaq framed this argument most strongly with his "demolish and replace" thesis, noting: "The demise of the *sharī'a* was ensured by the strategy of 'demolish and replace': the weakening and final collapse of educational *waqf*s, the *madrasa*, positive

Islamic law, and the *shari'a* court was [*sic*] made collateral, diachronically correlational, and causally conjoined with the introduction of state finance, Western law schools, European codes, and a European court system."[12] As a result, by 1900, "the shari'a in the vast majority of Muslim lands had been reduced in scope of application to the area of personal status, including child custody, inheritance, gifts, and to some extent, *waqf*."[13] Writing specifically on criminal law, Rudolph Peters argued that the impact of Westernization and the desires of centralizing and modernizing states resulted in reforms that eventually "eclipsed" *fiqh* constructions of criminal punishments to create "effective and rational tools for disciplining its subjects, tools that are applied by a rational bureaucracy (in the Weberian sense) through impersonal procedures."[14]

When we look at the content of the new codes and the role of local actors in their development and application, an interesting phenomenon becomes visible. Instead of directly opposing the modern state, Muslim jurists discussed the state's role in the development of law and gave states legitimacy to enact new laws to achieve greater justice for their populations through the classical Islamic legal category of political authority *(siyasa)*. Those who developed the codes had training in Islamic law and sought to comply with Islamic legal understandings. In the content of the laws, concepts and definitions matched those developed in the Hanafi school. Even in the case of India, where the penal code was drafted and implemented by a British colonial law commission that had no input from Muslim scholars, the rules of the Hanafi school continued to influence legal decisions, making the Indian Penal Code the closest of the new codes to the rules as constructed in Hanafi works of jurisprudence. In the Ottoman Empire and Egypt, when the codes did depart from Hanafi rules, results were still in line with those found in other schools—most notably, the Maliki school.

Therefore, the penal codes of the nineteenth century have much more to do with Islamic law than not. Far from being a divergence from Islamic law, the codes should be seen as a convergence of Islamic juristic discourse, European influence, and local custom, all of which came together to create the new codes and form the foundations of the legal systems that would serve each jurisdiction's needs. This process was not clear-cut, and within each convergence some debates needed to be carefully navigated. For example, jurists who formed Islamic criminal law theory before the implementation of the new codes had to balance their desire to achieve the absolute justice of God through the application of punishment with their keen awareness of the human failure to reach that justice. Thus, they incorporated a strong sense of doubt when applying the most extreme penalties. Likewise, in European law, jurists in the nineteenth century debated whether it was best for society to deter criminals through the implementation of harsher punishments or to err on the side of caution and impose lighter penalties that could reform criminals and help address the deeper social factors that drove them to commit the crime in the first place.[15]

This book, therefore, studies the development and content of new penal codes in three different nineteenth-century Muslim jurisdictions and examines how they dealt with the crime of homicide: the Ottoman Penal Code of 1858, the Indian Penal Code of 1860, and the Egyptian Penal Code of 1883. By investigating the role of local actors in the development and implementation of the codes, it attempts to challenge the thesis that the shari'a came to an end in the nineteenth century and adds to a growing body of literature that incorporates the evolving role of the state in the definition of the shari'a.

Before the main topic is addressed, it is necessary to discuss the recent historiography of Islamic law, which gave rise to the thesis that this book seeks to challenge, the importance of focusing on homicide, and the comparative approach using the cases of Egypt, India, and the Ottoman Empire.

The End of the Shari'a

The argument that the role of the shari'a in these Muslim jurisdictions ended in the nineteenth century rests on the following points:

1. Codification is antithetical to Islamic law.

With its multiple schools and methods of interpretation, the Islamic legal tradition is pluralistic by its very nature. Works of *fiqh* are not law codes but reflect open, discursive, and sometimes contradictory interactions among scholars.[16] The differing opinions developed within each school were viewed as equally valid. If a scholar's judicial reasoning *(ijtihad)* met the formal requirements, it was accepted as religiously legitimate for Muslims to follow. The differences between scholars are a "mercy" from God, according to an oft-cited statement falsely attributed to the Prophet,[17] and in practice, such differences often worked in favor of litigants. According to Hallaq, "In pre-modern shari'a, the individual Muslim had the freedom to choose among the schools, in whole or in part, but he or she was bound to whichever school [was] chosen for a transaction."[18]

During the nineteenth century, the introduction of new codes removed that intrinsic diversity and selected singular points of legislation that were to be applied in a particular geographical region (read: nation-state). Codification was a "deliberate choice in the exercise of political and legal power" that fundamentally altered the nature of Islamic law and restricted the freedom of juristic interpretation.[19]

However, others have pointed out that codification projects are not new to Islamic legal history and noted that there have always been efforts to restrict the diversity of laws applied in a particular jurisdiction. For example, Mohammad Fadel argued that the development of abbreviated jurisprudential texts—known as *Mukhtasar* literature—in the seventh to the thirteenth centuries helped create a set of uniform rules that would make legal outcomes in the courts more certain.[20] Building on this idea, Ahmed Fekry Ibrahim suggested that this rise of legal certainty and the limitation of opinions constituted an epistemological shift toward codification and that Islamic law, following what is referred to as the "closing of the gates of *ijtihad*," came much closer to the codified civil law system.[21] Finally, Anver Emon has argued that the uneasiness about the process of codification does not adequately account "for the disaggregated nature of the state, the indeterminacy of codified law, and the various sites (state-based and otherwise) in which people experience the law."[22]

Therefore, labeling codification as antithetical to Islamic law ignores the complex legal realities of those taking part in and subject to codification projects in the Muslim world. As will be seen in the rest of this book, new legal elites such as Nazeer Ahmed and Muhammad Qadri Basha embraced the concept of codification and worked with the state to create codes. When it came to applying the codes, the results were usually in line with Islamic understandings, and when they differed, actors such as Khalil Rif'at—an explainer of the Ottoman Penal Code—found no problem in placing the elements of the new penal code squarely within the Islamic tradition.

This book also considers whether codification should be seen as part of a broader global trend. During the nineteenth century, many nation-states took up codification projects, although the reasons for and results of such projects varied. When speaking of the Ottoman Empire, Avi Rubin has suggested that the thesis of codification of the law as a form of Westernization is untenable. For example, the development of the Ottoman Civil Code of 1877, known as the *Mecelle-i Ahkam-ı Adliye*, represented both an acceptance of the global idea of a civil code exemplified in the Napoleonic Code of 1804 and the development of a unique interpretation of Islamic law, and the *Mecelle-i Ahkam-ı Adliye* became known as one of the most outstanding achievements of nineteenth- and even twentieth-century Middle Eastern law.[23] Therefore, it is essential to understand that the codification processes in the jurisdictions covered in this book were part of a larger trend in legal development, one not necessarily in contradiction with the shari'a.

2. Islamic law is the domain of jurists *(fuqaha')*.

Before the implementation of the new codes and the rise in the power of the state, the law was debated and understood through works of jurisprudence *(fiqh)* constructed by jurists *(fuqaha')*, who had legal and religious legitimacy. Political actors such as caliphs, sultans, and their local counterparts had nothing more than enforcement power. For Hallaq, "interference [of the political authority] in the legislative processes, in the determination of legal doctrine, and in the overall internal dynamics of the law was nearly, if not totally, absent."[24]

In the nineteenth century, the focus shifted to the state, with rulers and their legislatures becoming responsible for creating new laws. Students and practitioners of the law were now trained in schools and colleges that drew their legitimacy from the state rather than God. Even the shari'a courts, the main centers of justice in the Muslim world, were replaced with non-shari'a courts such as the Nizamiye system in the Ottoman Empire[25] and the Native Courts (al-Mahakim al-Ahliya) in Egypt.[26]

However, others have pointed out that throughout Islamic history, the state was always present in the law-making process. Guy Burak has argued that through the creation of what he calls the "dynastic law" of the sultans during the Ottoman period, the state was "able to regulate the structure of the [Hanafi] school and its doctrine."[27] Samy Ayoub has built on this premise, showing that the state regularly influenced Hanafi legal discussions during the seventeenth and eighteenth centuries. He argues that the incorporation of state orders "was made possible by a turn in Hanafi legal culture that embraced the indispensability of the state in the law-making process."[28]

At the enforcement level, the state used its discretionary power— defined through political authority *(siyasa)* to implement punishment when deemed necessary—whether or not juristic discourse sanctioned such a penalty. For example, when speaking about the role of the market inspector *(muhtasib)* in Cairo, Kristen Stilt saw that in Islamic law, "Choices about how to use the power of *siyasa* are inherently discretionary, but, once examined closely, so are choices about the use of *fiqh*."[29]

The most relevant work that has sought to reexamine the state's role in developing the law in the nineteenth century is that of Khaled Fahmy. In his book on the introduction of forensic medicine into the Egyptian context, Fahmy argued, "The shari'a that was implemented in nineteenth-century Egypt derived its flexibility and adaptability from coupling *fiqh* with *siyasa*."[30] Although Fahmy's narrative ends with the establishment of the Mixed and Native Courts, this book uses his framework and takes it further into the remainder of the nineteenth century with the implementation of the new codes. The trend that Fahmy speaks of within Egyptian law—calling for political actors to increase their authority in the law to further the application of justice—was widespread and can be traced across the Muslim world. Additionally, as chapters 3–5 of this book will show, the content of the codes was aligned with *fiqh* understandings. Even at what some might consider points of departure from the shari'a, such as the state's role in prosecuting homicide in place of the victim's family, the explainers of the codes justified this shift in Islamic terms. Clearly, they believed that they were continuing what Fahmy would describe as the "coupling" of *siyasa* and *fiqh*.

3. The content of the new codes are copies of foreign laws and legal systems.

In its content, the law as constructed by jurists before the nineteenth century is viewed as the interaction of jurists with two types of sources: those from which the law may be derived (the Qur'an and Sunna) and those through which the law may be derived (legal reasoning, interpretation, or consensus).[31] Through these tools, jurists expounded upon laws and legal principles that rested on the ultimate authority of God through His message and messenger. If they chose to depart from the texts, it was only to handle the most necessary cases *(darura)*, provide for the fulfillment of an important public good *(maslaha)*, or cope with the inevitable collapse of society *(fasad al-zaman)*.[32]

Laws were drawn from very different sources during the nineteenth century, directly inspired by the European tradition. When speaking about the Ottoman penal code, Gabriel Baer remarked that during the second half of the nineteenth century, "the French code was adopted—lock, stock and barrel."[33] Peters has modified this thesis by stating that the code retained a connection with the shari'a since its introduction, as well as later articles on the treatment of homicide, referred to rulings derived from *fiqh* discourse. However, according to Peters, the connection stopped there, with the 1858 code "clearly of French inspiration, especially in its structure, system, and general notions," and with many articles being direct translations from the French Code of 1810.[34] In the Egyptian case, however, Peters is more explicit in his belief in the removal of Islamic influence. "In 1883/1889," he argues, "Islamic criminal law was totally abolished in Egypt. Only the rule that death sentences must be approved by the State Mufti provides a reminder of the role Islamic criminal law once played in the Egyptian legal system."[35]

One way that recent scholarship has sought to approach the issue of the importation of foreign laws has been to see the new codes as based upon local and national interests. Tobias Heinzelmann, when speaking about the Ottoman code, suggested that the Penal Code of 1858 was an implementation of French law within an Ottoman legal context. Using what he called an "amalgamation of traditional rhetorics," Heinzelmann argued that the state used Islamic language to legitimize the adoption of French law.[36] Fahmy put forth a similar argument for the Egyptian context, arguing that European legal categories were synthesized locally to facilitate "the desire of the khedives and their sultans (together with their numerous European advisors) to introduce in their respective realms a society that was disciplined and controlled—and hence efficient and productive."[37]

In the case of Indian law, however, the view of the Penal Code of 1860 has changed little since the work of Joseph Schacht. He argued that the colonial period created a mixed form of law that was a "result of the symbiosis of Islamic and of English legal thought," but this was wholly superseded by British-inspired codes in the second half of the nineteenth century.[38] Writing in 1993, Michael Anderson remarked that "by 1875, new colonial codes had displaced the Anglo-Muhammadan law in all subjects except family and certain property transactions."[39] When speaking about the development of British influence, Bernard Cohn noted that the reforms of the Indian judicial system in the second half of the nineteenth century resulted in "English law as the law of India."[40] Finally, in the application of the law, the Indian Supreme Court has recently echoed the same sentiments, noting that the principal architect of the Indian Penal Code, Lord Thomas Babington Macaulay, drew upon the French Code of 1810, Edward Livingston's Louisiana Code, English common law, and the British Royal Commission's 1843 Draft Code.[41] As a result, in Indian legal historiography, the underlying narrative is clear: the Penal Code of 1860 was a colonial product that had little to do with previous local understandings.

It is because the view of the penal codes of the nineteenth century continues to dominate both the academic and juristic discourse that this book investigates the development, content, and implementation of the new penal codes, challenging the thesis of Westernization and arguing that Islamic norms continued to form the basis of the law. Though it is crucial not to ignore or belittle the influence of colonialism and its impact on the Muslim world, it is also important to give a voice to those local actors who worked in the field of legal change or on the sidelines. Muslim muftis, jurists, and translators played a critical role throughout this process and were instrumental in every phase of reform. Other scholars such as Iza Hussin have already begun this process and argued that more attention should be given to local elites in the formation of the law.[42] Speaking specifically about the construction of legal codes in Malaysia, Egypt, and India, Hussin holds that each code was produced "between local and British elites, invoking Islamic law and incorporating elements of ethnic and Islamic identity: the content and form of these codes continue to represent Islam in the state in each case."[43] As a result, she advocates for a modification of Hallaq's thesis of "demolish and replace," replacing it with one of "occupy and renovate."[44]

Although Hussin warns of the power differential between local elites and colonial influence, the fact that she shows that some local actors supported and worked toward the development of these codes should not be ignored. During this period, Muslims were influenced by the West and nonetheless believed that their work was fulfilling the goal of Islamic law: to provide justice. In their view, justice could be achieved only by implementing a uniform criminal system that placed the state at the head of the prosecution. As will be seen in chapter 6 of this book, it was not until the rise of anticolonial movements at the end of the nineteenth and the beginning of the twentieth centuries, along with the legal views that they espoused, that we see new conceptions of the shari'a limited to the *fiqh* that laid the groundwork for viewing state-led codification as marking the "end of the shari'a."

Homicide as a Point of Convergence

Discussing the rules related to homicide places this book at the heart of the convergence of forces in the nineteenth century reflected in the new penal codes. How homicide was defined and categorized, its intent established, and the degree of criminal responsibility to which murderers could be held accountable were determined by an equilibrium between numerous opposing forces. Should the definition of homicide be restricted so that fewer perpetrators are subject to execution? Or do society's circumstances necessitate a broader implementation of execution that will deter people from committing homicide? How should a court determine the true intent of a killer? What happens when multiple individuals participate in the same crime? Should they all be judged equally or based upon their specific actions? At what point can a child or mentally incapacitated person be held responsible for killing another person? These and other questions were at the heart of legal discussions, and actors in the nineteenth century grappled with different answers to these questions in their attempt to construct law. As will be seen throughout this book, Muslims and non-Muslims alike came to similar conclusions.

The issue of homicide is also relevant for the broader discussion of Islamic law because it straddles the boundary between personal and state crime and highlights the long-standing conflicts between state power and jurisprudence. For example, works of jurisprudence constructed homicide as a crime against the victim's family members and, in theory, left prosecution and retribution to them. However, throughout history, political actors used their authority to execute and imprison murderers because their actions threatened general safety. In India, for example, the Mughal state often encouraged (and sometimes forced) members of the victim's family to sign what was called a *razinama*—a statement that they were content (*radi*) with a settlement. This was reportedly to help ensure a more lenient punishment and avoid execution, as the family forfeited its rights to retribution in court (*qisas*).[45]

In the nineteenth century, as the state became the central player in the formation and implementation of the law, this conflict reached its climax, and penal codes enshrined the prosecution of homicide as primarily in the hands of state authorities. Chapter 3 highlights the tension between the desire of jurists to lessen punishment through what has been called the doubt canon and the state's wish to punish murderers when it felt that by doing so it was protecting the public interest. In the nineteenth century, scholars working with the penal codes accepted and justified this shift not as being in line with the rulings of the jurists but rather as meeting the general Qur'anic goal of putting a halt to revenge killings and achieving justice. Understanding the dynamics involved in the shift in the laws of homicide is critical to evaluating the relationship of these laws to the shari'a and helps frame debates within Islamic law. The fact that there was a conflict between the state and jurists' desires also helps observers problematize the narrative about the end of the shari'a and integrate other documents, sources of law, and viewpoints into the discussion.

The Shared Fates of India, Egypt, and the Ottoman Empire

Vastly different in their histories and legal dynamics, India, Egypt, and the Ottoman Empire nonetheless share several factors that make a comparison of their criminal law systems salient and fruitful. For example, before the development of their current legal systems, each jurisdiction was dominated by Hanafi legal discourse. The Ottoman Empire is the best known for this, as it designated the Hanafi the official legal school of the empire and imposed its interpretation of the law on its many provinces, including Egypt.[46] In northern India, the Mughal Empire also followed the Hanafis, and significant works in the school—such as the *al-Fatawa al-'alamgiriya*—were constructed within the Mughal context. Although there was always a powerful Shafi'i influence along the western shore of the Indian subcontinent, particularly in what is now the state of Kerala, the Hanafi school (implemented and developed by the Mughals) remained dominant throughout most of the subcontinent, particularly in the north.

Also, in the second half of the nineteenth century, each of these jurisdictions developed new penal codes and placed them at the heart of reforming their legal systems. Additionally, each of these codes is considered the benchmark of modernization and the main point of departure from Islamic law. The Ottoman Empire began this with its Penal Code of 1858, and the Indian Penal Code of 1860 soon followed. Although the Egyptians started the process of codification in their criminal law with Muhammad 'Ali's *Qanun al-Filaha* in 1830,[47] they did not institute a complete domestic penal code until the creation of the Mixed Courts in 1875. The codes developed for the Mixed Courts represented a significant development in the country's application of criminal justice. However, their content is often considered not to have had a long-standing influence on the Egyptian legal system as a whole. The Mixed Courts were held in Cairo, Alexandria, and Mansoura and were intended to handle cases that involved foreign nationals.[48] Most Egyptians were not subject to a unified criminal system until the establishment of the Native Courts in 1883, and a new penal code was introduced in the same year. The Mixed and Native Courts continued to work side by side until 1949—when they were merged into the new National Court system, which remains in effect today.

Where these jurisdictions differ is in the role and impact of colonialism. At one extreme, the central Ottoman provinces of Anatolia were never officially colonized until after World War I. After first experiencing colonialism with the short-lived French occupation (1798–1801), Egypt became semi-independent from the Ottoman Empire under Governor Muhammad 'Ali and his descendants, a state that lasted until the British occupied the country in 1882. At the opposite end of the spectrum, in India the British East India Company began expanding its influence beyond commerce in the middle of the eighteenth century, winning administrative control of Bengal in 1757 following the Battle of Plassey. After briefly sharing power with the Mughal-appointed naib, the Company became solely responsible for the court system and the prosecution of criminals in the first months of 1758. In the following century, the Company continued to expand its power into new areas. By the middle of the nineteenth century, it controlled most of the Indian subcontinent's court system. Following the Uprising of 1857, the British Crown took complete control of all territories previously administrated by the Company, and by 1858 India had officially become the so-called jewel in the crown of the British Empire—which it remained until the end of colonial rule, in 1947. Thus, the colonial experience differed across the jurisdictions covered in this book: Anatolia was never occupied in the nineteenth century, Egypt was occupied only in that century's last few decades, and India was under complete colonial control by the middle of the century.

The degree of difference in these jurisdictions' colonial experience is the greatest obstacle to making a fair comparison between their legal systems. The impact of colonial influence, expressed as a change in the dynamics of power of a given jurisdiction, should not be underestimated. In India, for example, the changes brought to the subcontinent by British rule fundamentally changed the way that colonized people thought about and expressed themselves. In the language of the judiciary, for example, during the Mughal period, the official language was Persian, with most scholarly works written in and accessed through Arabic. Although the British initially accepted that paradigm, they eventually changed it to promote English following the Education Act of 1835—whose architect (Macaulay, the same colonial officer who would draft the Indian Penal Code of 1860) remarked that there was a need to change Indian society by creating "a class of persons, Indian in blood and colour, but English in taste, in opinions, in morals, and in intellect."[49] In Egypt, the development of the Penal Code of 1883 was done in the shadow of a newly established British occupation, following the failed revolution of Ahmad 'Urabi just one year earlier.[50] The new British administrator, Evelyn Baring (Lord Cromer), influenced the development of the criminal system so that it violently punished offenders, creating new methods of supervision and control.[51]

However, what is important to note (and as will be seen throughout the subsequent chapters of this book) is that despite this difference, India, Egypt, and the Ottoman Empire dealt with similar issues in criminal law and came to the same conclusions, with Islamic concerns still at the heart of their new laws. Many of the actors (whether Muslim in the Ottoman Empire and Egypt or non-Muslim in India) felt that introducing a uniform criminal code was the best way to handle the needs of their legal systems. Each new code struggled with the growing influence of European norms and a local context defined by Islamic and Hanafi law. Even in India, where most of the population was Hindu, Islamic legal discussions played an important role. As will be seen in chapter 1, many British administrators saw themselves as continuing in the footsteps of the Mughal or Islamic legal tradition. They made gradual changes to the system until the introduction of the Indian Penal Code of 1860. They sought the help of Muslim scholars, translated Islamic legal texts, and employed muftis in their courts—who acted as local verifiers who would make sure that their rulings received the backing of local religious custom. Within the code, as chapters 3–5 show, Islamic juristic opinions on homicide continued to dominate. Finally, following the introduction of the Penal Code of 1860, this process continued, with Muslim actors working as advocates and pleaders within the appellate courts and translating and commenting on the code in local languages.

A Question of Terms: Shari'a versus Law

When approaching the critical historical period of legal transformation, which this book seeks to observe, understanding the inherent conflict between the terms *shari'a* and *law* becomes essential.[52] For some scholars, such as Hallaq, to make the term "law" reflect what the shari'a meant in the premodern period would require "so many omissions, additions, and qualifications that we would render the term itself largely, if not entirely, useless."[53] However, an alternative view argues for describing the shari'a as a legal system. It labels what the shari'a produced as law and considers the shari'a as not so different from legal systems developed in the West. According to Mathias Rohe, all legal systems share several essential features: for example, "their self-image is that of being the guiding concept of society. The idea of justice immanent in them is meant to set standards."[54] In Rohe's view, each legal system is also "integrated within a social context and influenced by it to a significant degree."[55]

Muhammad Serag, a professor of Islamic studies at the American University in Cairo, presented a similar view. For him, the shari'a must be understood as a legal system (*nizam qanuni*) that is guided by principles such as "justice, freedom, and equality" and that acts as a guiding philosophy to fit the needs of modern society. Methodologically, the Islamic legal system is "the science of extracting the rules of the shari'a *(al-ahkam)* from their sources"—the traditional definition of the fundamentals of jurisprudence *(usul al-fiqh)*—combined with "the mechanisms for implementing these rules in practical reality through legislation and the judiciary."[56]

To refer to the shari'a as the law or legal system of Islam is therefore not as problematic as envisioned by Hallaq. Of course, the shari'a takes a more extensive view than that of state law in that, for example, it regulates what is viewed today as private and spiritual areas of life (such as prayer and fasting), in which the modern nation-state has little interest. However, that should not prohibit the shari'a from also being understood as a legal system, nor should it render an analysis of a particular topic within that system (such as homicide) less critical, simply because it does not cover the entirety of the social interactions that take place within the shari'a's structure.

Therefore, this book advocates for a view of the shari'a that is closer to the views of Rohe and Serag than that of Hallaq. However, that framework does not entail a dismissal of the work of Hallaq or a complete departure from his vision of the shari'a. The integration of multiple sources and the reliance on actors other than jurists (including muftis, contemporary law reformers, and litigants in cases) are explicitly intended to achieve a closer understanding of the broader social framework within which these legal changes were taking place. Those sources should define how the shari'a was perceived during the second half of the nineteenth century and how those actors understood the inner workings of their changing legal environments.

Defining the Shariʻa

In the early decades of the twentieth century, the shariʻa became a rallying cry for Muslim anticolonial movements, with Islamist groups calling for a reapplication of *sharʻi* rules. As a result, in the second half of the century, states such as Brunei, Iran, and Pakistan and semiautonomous regions in Nigeria and Indonesia sought to reshape their legal systems to address that call and apply what they understand as the law of God. In addition, other movements that seek similar changes continue elsewhere in places such as Egypt.

Key to these legal reform programs is the criminal punishments of Islam, including the amputation of a hand for stealing, lashing and stoning for adultery, and death for murder. However, in jurisdictions where these new systems have been implemented, most observers have noted that they bear little resemblance to the laws applied before the nineteenth century. For these movements, the reimplementation of the shariʻa is mainly symbolic or "an expression of cultural and political assertion against Western hegemony."[57]

For observers like Hallaq, the impact of colonial influence represented an epistemological shift in the legal system. The new judiciary process, relying on the power of the modern state rather than the absolute authority of God, meant that the shariʻa could no longer be understood as operative in these jurisdictions. The "form" of the state, as Hallaq has argued, is based on five distinct yet inseparable properties: "(1) its constitution as a historical experience that is fairly specific and local (European); (2) its sovereignty and the metaphysics to which it has given rise; (3) its legislative monopoly and the related feature of monopoly over so-called legitimate violence; (4) its bureaucratic machinery; and (5) its cultural-hegemonic engagement in the social order, including its production of the national subject."[58] The content of the law produced and practiced within the state is, in Hallaq's view, immaterial. And whether controlled by "liberals, socialists, communists, oligarchs, or any such brand," the essential form of the modern state cannot be changed.[59]

The question at hand is how to judge whether or to what extent an epistemic shift has occurred. For Hallaq, whose definition of the shariʻa is based on the works of *fiqh*, the law's outcome in both substance and the courts is not indicative of such a shift. However, this book questions whether a shift can be judged without viewing its objective outcomes. Arguably, if a shift occurred, it could be detected in the laws produced, explanations given, and judgments issued by the courts. The evidence considered in this book indicates a similarity in all these points before and after implementing the new penal codes.

Hallaq's analysis helps clarify the contradictions posed by the introduction of shari'a statutes and constitutional articles produced under the influence of Islamist groups in the second half of the twentieth century, as Peters points out.[60] Therefore, Hallaq's argument that the creation of a modern Islamic state is "impossible" due to the epistemological shifts that occurred in the legal system holds, if only for the second half of the twentieth century.[61] However, this thesis is not sufficient to describe what took place in the second half of the nineteenth century. Although the modern state's power was growing during this period, the shari'a was conceived of more broadly. Local actors worked outside of *fiqh* to merge colonial influence with Islamic law, searching for the greater principles of the law and aware of the inherent differences between the Islamic and European systems.

In contrast, the calls and steps taken to reapply the shari'a in the second half of the twentieth century were based upon a reaction to the narrative established by the "end of the shari'a" argument described above and a reimagination of what had happened to Islamic law during the period of colonization. These new legal reformers argue that because of colonial interference in the law—primarily through the introduction of new penal codes—the criminal systems of the various regions of the Muslim world became governed by understandings of law that were antithetical to Islamic beliefs. But what if this were not the case? What if, as this book argues, the shari'a continued to form the basis of the criminal law in the codes developed in the middle of the nineteenth century? If this were the case, the narratives of Islamist movements that have dominated Muslim discourse in the twentieth century could be understood as the actual divergence from Islamic legal history. This would also help explain why new legal systems seem to be so divorced from those in force before their implementation. As a legal system, the shari'a, through its interaction with colonialism, was reinterpreted and molded by local actors to fit unique and changing circumstances. Just as had been the case before the colonial period, those working within the shari'a debated, integrated, and sometimes pushed back against external influences. Critical to the development of this understanding is a reenvisioning of the definition of the shari'a. Instead of the shari'a's being a collection of substantive rules constructed by precolonial scholars of *fiqh* and bound by a moral episteme antithetical to the modern state, this book suggests that the shari'a lies at the intersection of multiple forces where state power, *fiqh*, and the application of the law in the courts come together. By seeing the shari'a this way, the question of the role and influence of the modern state can be more clearly interpreted and the state (the leading actor in the new codes) can be integrated into broader discussions of Islamic law. Observers of Islamic law often express apprehension about the state's role (discussed as *siyasa*), particularly in the modern period, and see it as fundamentally separate from the shari'a. This should not be the case, and *siyasa* should be seen as a critical part of the law. Fahmy already suggested this, when he stated that "only a *fiqhi* reality would insist on excising *siyasa* from shari'a and on seeing law and morality as intricately bound together. By contrast . . . a more accurate understanding of shari'a legality must grant *siyasa* a central role in it, both as a legal concept and a historical practice."[62]

As Fahmy has rightly pointed out, the view of the shari'a as bound to morality is central to a reality based upon the writings of *fiqh*.[63] Suppose other elements are incorporated into this definition, such as the roles of the state and the courts. In that case, a different image appears of the shari'a as a legal system, one that is not so drastically different or divergent from its counterparts in the common and civil law traditions. As chapter 3 will show, for example, muftis working in British courts during the first half of the nineteenth century (before the introduction of the Indian Penal Code of 1860) regularly expanded upon *fiqh* rules. They developed categories of punishment never envisioned by the *fiqh* literature. Why they chose to do so—to capitulate to the will of a colonial government exercising its power to change the law, with Muslim actors in the minority—is an important yet not determining factor in this analysis. They could have issued fatwas against the desire of the British and have the judge overrule them. (This sometimes happened upon appeal, with the higher courts often siding with the mufti and overruling the lower judge.) They were primarily concerned with local matters rather than the struggle for political power.

This more comprehensive definition of the shari'a, exemplified by the implementation of the penal codes described in chapters 3–5, is the primary contribution of this book to larger debates within the field of Islamic law. If observers of Islamic law continue to return, as Fahmy has, to the vast body of primary sources available to us and see them as part of the definition and not contingencies or anomalies in a debate of power, they can come to understand the important role the shari'a continues to play in legal systems in the modern Muslim world.[64]

Approaching the Topic: Environment, Actors, and Content

To explore the new penal codes of the nineteenth century and ascertain their relationship to the broader conception of the shari'a, it is first necessary to understand the political and legal environment in which these codes were produced. Therefore, chapter 1 focuses on the writings of Muslim actors in each jurisdiction who believed that the true purpose of Islamic law—that is, the establishment of justice—had been lost by corrupt rulers and resulted in an increase in crime. By using the Islamic legal field of *siyasa*, these actors argued that the state ought to play a more significant role in creating law. In the case of India, this chapter shows how jurists and muftis participated directly in the legal interventions of the British and believed that the colonial powers were continuing in the path of the Mughals who had come before them.

Chapter 2 looks at the people who worked with the codes and the institutions that produced them, focusing on the examples of Nazeer Ahmed of India and Muhammad Qadri Basha of Egypt. As centuries-old institutions of Muslim learning such as al-Azhar became perceived as incapable of meeting society's needs, new educational institutions such as the Egyptian School of Translators and the Indian Delhi College were established. Rather than being mere copies of European institutions, these new colleges were vibrant environments wherein Muslim traditions (including legal ones) fused with those from Europe, producing a new cadre of intellectuals who could straddle the gap between the two worlds. When approaching the new penal codes, each of these scholars took Islamic legal understandings to heart and sought to strike a balance between incorporating new ways of legal thinking and preserving the fundamental objects of Islamic legal tradition.

The following three chapters turn to the content of the new codes, comparing them to understandings developed in the *fiqh* and focusing on the Hanafi school. Each chapter takes up one aspect of homicide law: defining the criminal act, intent, and criminal responsibility. Chapter 3 looks at the classification of homicide and argues that, although the new codes of the nineteenth century modified Hanafi categories of homicide and eliminated the category of semi-intentional homicide (*shibh 'amd*) altogether, the categories developed by the codes remained surprisingly similar to Hanafi understandings, with some even being verbatim copies of examples found in works of Hanafi jurisprudence. This chapter also raises the question of the role of the state in the prosecution of homicide and shows how (with a focus on Egypt) explainers of the new codes justified the expansion of state power within Islamic norms.

Chapter 4 explores the establishment of intent and how the codes attempted to shift the primary method of that establishment from the presence of a weapon to the motive of the accused. While this shift succeeded in the Ottoman Empire and Egypt, in India the presence of an external measure (a deadly weapon) continued to form the basis of criminal intent. Chapter 5 examines criminal responsibility and covers three areas shaped by the codes: juvenile offenders, insanity, and shared criminal responsibility. In each area, European understandings of the law, which were undergoing their own development processes, were combined with Islamic views from Hanafi law to form the content of the new codes and were worked out in cases on the ground.

Finally, chapter 6 connects the "end of the shari'a" thesis to the manifestation of new ideas at the beginning of the twentieth century. It shows that as elites pushed back against European influence, they created the concept of an Islamic civilization with a universal, unchanging shari'a at its core. These developments recast the penal codes of the nineteenth century as foreign imports and shaped legal discourse in the Islamic world for the rest of the century.

1

Establishing Justice through State Law

In the second half of the nineteenth century, the preeminent scholar at the family-run seminary of Farangi Mahal in Lucknow, Muhammad 'Abd al-Hayy (d. 1304/1886), was asked whether it is permissible in Islamic law to seek out the rulings of "contemporary judges" (*'uhda-e qaza*), a veiled reference to British courts. He responded: "Taking [the judgment] of contemporary judges [appointed] by a sultan, whether just or unjust, Muslim or Infidel is religiously permissible. However, if that sultan prohibits the judge from applying what is right (*bi-haqq maman'at sazad*), in this situation, it is forbidden."[1] In support of his ruling, he cited two classical sources of jurisprudence, the *Radd al-muhtar* by the early nineteenth-century Hanafi Syrian scholar Ibn 'Abidin (d. 1252/1836) and the collection of fatwas composed and compiled for the Mughal Emperor Aurangzeb (d. 1118/1707), known as the *al-Fatawa al-'alamgiriya* or *al-Fatawa al-hindiya*. Both sources mention the permissibility of seeking a court judgment from a judge appointed by an unjust ruler (*sultan ja'ir*). However, 'Abd al-Hayy expanded upon this previous opinion to include even judges appointed by non-Muslims, an innovation meant to cover cases adjudicated by the British.[2]

It is difficult to determine precisely when this question was posed to 'Abd al-Hayy, but there is no doubt that he issued this fatwa after the transfer of power in India to the British Crown in 1858 and the application of new laws such as the Indian Penal Code and the reorganization of the court system. From that point until the rise of independence movements in the first half of the twentieth century, no Islamic courts could be found in British territories such as Lucknow. The only places where Muslim rulers and judges could exercise direct control over legal practice were Muslim-ruled princely states, including Bhopal and Hyderabad. In the previous fatwa in the same section, 'Abd al-Hayy was asked about the qualifications of a judge, to which he gave the classical response established in works of *fiqh*:

a judge must be a free Muslim of sound mind, and the capabilities of independent juristic reasoning *(ijtihad)* and proper morals of justice *('adalat)* are primary, if not necessary, conditions *(shart-e awwaliyat)*.[3]

Placing these two fatwas together, we find 'Abd al-Hayy torn between conflicting ideas. On the one hand, he was grounded in his traditional Islamic training, characterized by norms established over many centuries that were based upon the primary assumption that an Islamic system was in place and that Muslim rulers had at least nominal political authority. On the other hand, he faced a new reality on the ground, one that—particularly following the failure of the Uprising of 1857—reflected widening British control in India, sidelined traditionally trained Muslim jurists, and made significant changes to the court system and laws governing Muslims and non-Muslims alike.

Because of this tension, 'Abd al-Hayy sought a middle ground, keeping the *fiqh* interpretations of law while making modifications—namely, allowing judges to be appointed by non-Muslim rulers. Instead of promoting noncooperation with and resistance to the British, an idea that would become mainstream in the Muslim community in the early twentieth century, 'Abd al-Hayy chose a path that did not challenge British authority in the law. With his first fatwa, Muslims who found themselves subject to crimes and disputes could approach British courts without fear of betraying Islamic principles. Additionally, 'Abd al-Hayy seemed to believe that what the British were doing in the courts was not necessarily against Islamic law. There were instances in which it could have constituted a violation of the shari'a, which led to his addition of the requirement that judgments be based on what is right *(haqq)*. However, the core of his ruling still held: accepting the decision of a British-appointed judge was not religiously problematic.

This compromise between traditional understandings and practical realities can be found in many other fatwas of 'Abd al-Hayy. For example, he ruled that it was permissible for Muslims to study English and Western sciences, on the condition that they pursue such study not out of love for *(mahabbat)* or in an attempt to imitate nonbelievers *(mushabahat)*, but rather out of a desire to read and study their works for general knowledge *(itla' bar mazamin-e kalam-e ishan)*.[4]

Although the legal positions of 'Abd al-Hayy might seem uniquely applicable to India, where the non-Muslim British were in complete control of the legal and social system, they resemble the sentiments expressed in areas where Muslim rulers remained in power. In the Gülhane Declaration of 1839, the Ottoman Sultan Abdülmecid I announced his intention to embark on a series of broad legal and social changes that would eventually lead to the Penal Code of 1858. Although his predecessors had laid the groundwork for these reforms, this document is often cited as marking the onset of the *tanzimat* (the reorganization of the empire).[5]

Some historians have argued that the *tanzimat* resulted from Western pressure and relied mainly on Western-leaning Ottoman diplomats posted in the empire's European provinces. For these historians, the Ottoman Empire could have reformed only by adopting European standards of law, citizenship, and rights. Thus, we should classify the *tanzimat* period as an episode in the slow march toward Westernization and secularization.[6] However, other historians have challenged this approach, encouraging observers to see the Gülhane Declaration and the subsequent laws produced in the second half of the nineteenth century as more complex. According to this account, the *tanzimat* resulted from an internal desire to reform an empire that had seen its power and influence wane in the face of wars with Russia and rising nationalist sentiments in the provinces.[7] For example, Butrus Abu-Manneh argued that the contents of the declaration "lend no evidence of ideas or ideals borrowed from Western theory" and were the product of a uniquely internal Ottoman discourse.[8]

There is, of course, a significant power difference between the fatwa of 'Abd al-Hayy, an independent legal scholar working within a system that had come to be entirely dominated by a colonial force, and the Ottoman sultan. However, for the present discussion, we can locate within the text of the Gülhane Declaration an effort to strike a similar balance to that of 'Abd al-Hayy, maintaining traditional Islamic understandings while introducing new concepts to adapt to the needs of the time despite differences in power and influence. The declaration remarked that "Over the last one hundred and fifty years, a series of wars and various other reasons have resulted in the empire conforming neither to the shari'a nor imperial laws. The result is that strength and prosperity have been replaced by weakness and poverty. The situation is that an empire not governed under the rules of the shari'a loses its stability."[9]

To solve this problem and return the empire to its former glory, the sultan sought the help of God and the Prophet "to seek by new institutions to give the provinces composing the Ottoman Empire the benefit of a good administration" through guaranteeing for all subjects "(1) the security of life, honor, and fortune; (2) a regular system for the assessing and levying of taxes; and (3) an equally regular system for the levying of troops and the duration of their service." The language of the Gülhane Declaration, although often viewed in the light of European and Enlightenment values, maintains throughout an attachment to Islamic religious values and, most importantly, the broader goals of the shari'a. The state ensured that, while incorporating new ideas and reforming the empire, the ideological attachment to the shari'a remained intact.[10]

This chapter, therefore, explores the views of local actors regarding the legal changes taking place in the late eighteenth century and throughout the nineteenth in the jurisdictions discussed. It focuses on the state's role in the formation of law, a theme that underlies the scholarly discussions of the time, and looks at the role Muslim thinkers envisioned for the state. In each jurisdiction, local actors believed that there was a growing need to change their criminal law system to respond to the problems of rising crime rates, corruption, and the general failure of the existing system. These changes were seen by those involved as following the shari'a, particularly the concept of state authority (*siyasa*), and as furthering and fulfilling the ultimate goal of Islamic law: the establishment of justice. This viewpoint was by no means monolithic, and there were scholars throughout this period who were wary of the changes taking place. However, in most of the nineteenth century, alternative views remained squarely in the minority: they would only become prominent only at the end of that century.[11] By understanding the state's evolving role in the formation of law, the new criminal laws enacted during the second half of the nineteenth century can be placed in their proper historical and intellectual contexts.

India: Following in Mughal Footsteps
Following the Battle of Plassey, in 1757, the British East India Company took control of the administration of justice in Bengal and—after a brief period of dual government alongside the Mughal representative (*na'ib*)—became solely responsible for the court system and, in particular, the prosecution of criminals. The Company created a multitiered system of courts modeled both in name and structure on that of the Mughals, on whose behalf it was officially ruling.

Additionally, during the latter half of the eighteenth century, several British officers in Bengal were ordered by the governor-general to commission the compilation and translation of classical texts on Islamic law into English or Persian, languages with which many of the British Orientalists were more familiar with than the texts' original Arabic. The best known of these projects was undertaken by the Orientalist Charles Hamilton (d. 1792), involving the translation of the Hanafi *fiqh* text *al-Hidaya*, initially composed by the Central Asian scholar al-Marghinani (d. 593/1197). In the introduction to the original publication of his translation, Hamilton stated that the only way the Bengal government could have reached what he called a "flourishing state" was by continuing with the system that worked best for the local population:

> The permanency of any foreign dominion (and indeed, the justification of holding such a dominion) requires that a strict attention be paid to the ease and advantage, not only of the *governors*, but of the *governed*; and to this great end nothing can so effectually contribute as preserving to the latter their ancient established practices, civil and religious, and protecting them in the exercise of their own institutes; for however defective or absurd these may in many instances appear, still they must be infinitely more acceptable than any which *we* could offer; since they are supported by the accumulated prejudice of ages, and, in the opinion of their followers, derive their origin from the Divinity itself.[12]

While *al-Hidaya* was a general legal text that covered all aspects of the Hanafi school, other projects in this period were specifically created for criminal law. For example, the British judge John Herbert Harrington (d. 1828) commissioned the compilation and translation of works on prescribed *(hudud)* and discretionary *(ta'zir)* punishments from several scholars. These included Salamat 'Ali Khan (alive in 1212/1797), who produced a compilation of criminal law from Hanafi *fiqh* works; Siraj al-Din 'Ali Khan (alive in 1236/1820), who created an independent work on discretionary punishment; and Najm al-Din 'Ali Khan (d. 1229/1814) and his son Muhammad Khalil-al Din Khan, who made Persian translations of the criminal sections of the *al-Fatawa al-'alamgiriya*.

Little information about the first two authors is available, but much more is known about Najm al-Din 'Ali Khan. Described as one of the greatest jurists of the northern Indian town of Kakori, he received his traditional education from his relatives who taught at Farangi Mahal. After a period working as a judge in Lucknow, he was invited by a colleague, Tafazzal Hasan Khan, to join the ranks of the judiciary of the British East

India Company in Calcutta in 1790. It is reported that when Najm al-Din arrived in 1793, Governor-General John Shore (d. 1834) welcomed the scholar warmly, hugging him and appointing him the chief judge *(qazi al-quza)* for all the matters of Muslims in areas controlled by the Company. In addition to his translations in the field of criminal law, Najm al-Din's career of almost twenty-five years included issuing fatwas and judicial rulings applied in "every district from Kabul to the Deccan."[13] When he died in 1814, the Earl of Moira Francis Edward Rawdon-Hastings (d. 1826), who had become governor-general, sent a letter to Najm al-Din's wife expressing the government's gratitude for his service:

> The shock of the death of your husband, the High Judge, has been felt by the Company no less than yourself, given that it has caused the disappearance of such a modest and proficient individual and such an irreplaceable man of learning. Since there is no remedy in the Workshop of Fate except patience and submission, there is no doubt that you will choose toleration in the path of patience. Though your four children are employed in the highest positions, and thus you shall not be burdened by strain during your period of mourning, the government has decided, in recognition of your husband's worth and reputation, to fix Rs. 150 per mensem [month] as your pension for the remainder of your life.[14]

Once published, these translations were to be used in the British courts or referred to by judges to understand how their Muslim counterparts, the law officers or muftis, reached particular conclusions in their fatwas. These were also not obscure texts. Various manuscript copies of each can still be found throughout the major libraries of northern India (such as in the Khuda Bakhsh Library in Patna and the Rampur Raza Library). Additionally, printed copies of these works were produced throughout the nineteenth century and the first half of the twentieth. They can still be accessed in the libraries of Muslim seminaries like Nadwat al-'Ulama' in Lucknow and Dar al-'Ulum Deoband. For example, the most recent publication found for the present study was an Urdu translation of a work by Salamat 'Ali Khan that was originally produced in 1929 at the request of the head advocate of the princely state of Hyderabad, Mir Ahmad Sharif.[15]

The endeavors of colonial powers to produce these translations and compilations could be viewed as attempts to enhance colonial authority and reduce what the powers perceived as the arbitrary nature of rulings provided by Hindu pandits and Muslim muftis to bring more uniformity to the law. For example, the British Orientalist Sir William Jones (d. 1794) stated that "Pure Integrity is hardly to be found among the Pandits and Maulavis, few of whom give opinions without a culpable bias, if the parties can have access to them. I therefore always make them produce original texts and see them in their own books."[16]

However, there are two main features of the legal landscape during the end of the eighteenth century and the first half of the nineteenth that should be considered to show that the exercise of British power was not always meant to sideline the efforts of Muslim scholars, nor did those working with the British necessarily view British colonial intervention as antithetical to their system. First, the legal opinions of Najm al-Din, a Muslim scholar, were not sidelined but were welcomed to a significant degree by the highest levels of the Company administration throughout its Indian holdings, as attested to by the letter from the governor-general quoted above. Second, the British were not referred to as conquerors in these translated texts but were given the same honorific treatment used for fellow Muslim scholars. For example, Salamat 'Ali Khan referred to his patron, Harrington, as "the Aristotle of his time."[17] Likewise, Najm al-Din called Harrington the "protector of the scholars *('ulama)*" and asked God to make his justice and influence spread across the world.[18] The most glowing of such praise was in the introduction to *Jami' al-ta'zirat min kutub al-thiqat* by Siraj al-Din, who stated that he had taken it upon himself to compose the work

> when I took the position as a mufti of the great courts during the reign of two great princes, the heads of the courts and the greatest of the [judges] in honor and pride, the most just in morals and disposition, the most complete in organization and efficiency, the highest in refinement and discipline, the bringers of security and the spreaders of justice and kindness, the shelter of scholars and refuge to the poor and downtrodden, Mr. Henry Corbick and Mr. John Herbert Harrington. May God guide them through their justice and jurisprudence *(fiqh)* to what is good and lasting.[19]

Although this type of honorific language was common in South Asian literature, there is evidence in this statement to indicate that Siraj al-Din was paying more than just lip service to his British patrons. In addition to his positive depiction of two non-Muslim British judges, Siraj al-Din's use of the term "*fiqh*" when referring to their court rulings is particularly striking and is cause for further analysis. Traditionally, the term "*fiqh*" was used to denote the rules produced by Muslim jurists—and, especially following the crystallization of the schools of law around the eleventh or twelfth century, only those rulings by scholars within a particular school.[20] In the case of South Asia, most of these scholars were in the Hanafi school. Comprehensive legal works using the Hanafi method of interpretation continued to be written until the middle of the nineteenth century. However, they mainly came to an end with the death of the Syrian scholar Ibn 'Abidin, whose work was cited by 'Abd al-Hayy above in this chapter. The fact that Siraj al-Din chose to use such a term to refer to the legal opinions of British judges in the eighteenth century indicates that he believed their work was consonant with Islamic law and that their rulings had some form of Islamic legal legitimacy. Unfortunately, little else is known about Siraj al-Din's opinions of the British, so it is impossible to construct a complete analysis of exactly how, on his account, British judges could be considered to produce *fiqh*.

The Law of Infidels and the *Dar al-Harb* Debate

The scholars who accepted wider British involvement in creating and enforcing the law were not without their detractors. For example, some other scholars lamented the fact that foreign powers had come to control parts of the subcontinent. In a manuscript written in 1767, a Delhi-based scholar named Abu Sa'id Zuhur al-Din remarked that although the most just religion of the world was Islam and Muslim scholars had dominated the Indian legal system for centuries, the situation had changed following the Battle of Plassey: "The religion of Muhammad, the best of religions, has been abandoned, and the Muslims have been defeated. Every land of the Guided Path has become the prisoner of the infidels, the oppression of Muslims has been made clear, and the knowledge of non-Muslims has been raised upon high."[21]

For jurists, opposition to British influence in the legal system was discussed through the classical Islamic political methodology that divided the world into two realms: one dominated by Islamic authority (*dar al-Islam*) and another that was openly hostile to Islam (*dar al-harb*). In theory, these two realms were in constant conflict with one another and would remain so until Islam eventually prevailed. Thus, *dar al-harb* was the primary target of offensive wars (jihads), and Muslims had a communal obligation (*fard kifaya*) to participate in these wars if the caliph legitimately declared them. Until the arrival of the British, the Indian subcontinent was considered by most scholars to be part of *dar al-Islam*, as Muslims were able to practice their religion freely. Even in areas governed by Hindus or other non-Muslims, the ruling was the same, as there was little interference in Muslims' daily religious practices.

During the early nineteenth century, however, some scholars began to suggest that the Indian subcontinent had come under the authority of Infidels and should be classified as *dar al-harb*. The best known of these scholars was Shah 'Abd al-'Aziz Dahlawi (d. 1824), son of the famous eighteenth-century reformist Shah Wali Allah Dahlawi (d. 1176/1762). In 1803, the army of the British East India Company, under the leadership of General Gerard Lake, entered Delhi. The Company removed control of the city from the Marathas (who had loosely handled the city's administration since the 1760s) and the Emperor Shah Alam II, then seventy-seven, who retained what remained of Mughal authority. The emperor was left destitute, with one officer who accompanied Lake stating that the emperor was "seated under a small tattered canopy, stripped of authority and reduced to poverty."[22]

Richard Colley Wellesley (Marquess Wellesley), then governor-general of India, made the Mughal emperor a de facto British subject. His family was given an estate on the banks of the Jamuna River, a stipend of 90,000 rupees per month, and legal jurisdiction inside Delhi Fort. In return, "the Emperor would have no territorial jurisdiction, their revenue collection and criminal justice were to be administered by the British Resident."[23] Muslim courts were established in Delhi but were under the British government's direct control, with the emperor retaining only the nominal authority to confirm death sentences.

Shah 'Abd al-'Aziz, who was living in Delhi at the time, must have been shocked by these events. The announcement that the British would have absolute control over the legal system and manage the daily affairs of the Muslims of Delhi and all former Mughal lands meant that the country had taken a severe turn for the worse. Therefore, he composed a fatwa stating that India was now part of *dar al-harb*. The fatwa read in part, "The rule of Muslims [in India] is absolutely not implemented, and the law of Christians are without a doubt the norm, meaning that the foundations of Islamic government, the management of the laity, the collection of taxes, and the conduct of commerce follow their [non-Muslim] rulings. Gangsters, thieves, and other public interactions and punishments are handled by non-Muslim rules. Even though the nonbelievers do not oppose some Islamic traditions like the Friday prayers, Eid celebrations, the call to prayer, and cow slaughter, they are almost without benefit, as they casually destroy mosques."[24] This fatwa has often been cited as the first declaration of jihad against the British, although Shah ʿAbd al-ʿAziz never directly mentioned armed conflict. In fact, he seemed at some level to accept the existence of the colonial government. For example, in other fatwas issued in the same period, he allowed Muslims to take positions within the government if they were not directly oppressing other Muslims.[25]

Therefore, Shah ʿAbd al-ʿAziz might have had a different purpose in mind for his fatwa than a call to arms. In classical Islamic law, the division of the world into *dar al-Islam* and *dar al-harb* had practical legal ramifications. For example, Muslims could live in areas designated as *dar al-harb*, with Hanafi jurists giving them special permission to exempt themselves from legal restrictions because of the hardship inherent in living in a non-Muslim land. Muslims residing in *dar al-harb* could trade using usurious contracts *(riba)*, forgo the obligation to hold congregational Friday prayers, and were not liable for the worldly punishment of crimes like adultery or public drunkenness that would typically require a prescribed punishment *(hudud)*.[26] Therefore, calling India *dar al-harb* might have been advantageous to many members of the local community, facilitating life in an area now under the direct control of non-Muslims.

The connection between Shah ʿAbd al-ʿAziz's fatwa and anticolonial jihad is primarily related to his later involvement in a movement led by Syed Ahmad of Rae Bareli (d. 1831), who launched a military campaign against the Sikh kingdom in Punjab. Although ending abruptly with the death of Syed Ahmad in the Battle of Balakot, this movement became a lightning rod for nationalists in the twentieth century. The idealized image of so-called brave Muslim freedom-fighters seeking to implement the shariʿa has remained prominent in local discourse to the present day.[27]

Few scholars other than Shah ʿAbd al-ʿAziz declared the Indian subcontinent to be *dar al-harb*. Almost all those who did were from Delhi, and many were close relatives of Shah ʿAbd al-ʿAziz.[28] Therefore, little open resistance can be found to British influence on the law during the eighteenth and nineteenth centuries. In his description of the Muslim reception of changing laws and regulations, Francis Robinson spoke of silence from Muslim scholars. In his view, except for the movement of Syed Ahmad and the Faraizis in Bengal, most Muslim scholars were not interested in the British changes to the legal system until the end of the nineteenth century and the beginning of the twentieth, when broader themes of nationalism and religious identity came to fruition.[29]

Robinson's silence could have resulted because, following the Uprising of 1857, the members of the Muslim scholarly class (*'ulama*) removed themselves from centers of power and developed revivalist projects that focused on reforming the individual. For example, at the madrassa of Deoband, scholars "believed that the moral health of the individual [was] inseparable from the social health of the body politic."[30] The later Barelvi Movement, established by Ahmad Reza Khan (d. 1921), was ideologically opposed to trends within Deoband. However, it also emphasized individual adherence to the Prophet Muhammad's example and was "relatively uninterested in participating in the opportunities being opened up by British rule."[31]

As a result, most members of the South Asian *'ulama'* at the very least tolerated—and in some cases cooperated with—the expansion of British authority in the realm of law. As the works mentioned above show, they viewed the British as a continuation of the Mughal legal authority of the past, and they sought appointments in the British judiciary and worked as muftis (in the case of Siraj al-Din and Najm al-Din) and close advisors to their British counterparts. Any opposition to British rule that did materialize in the rest of the nineteenth century remained subdued, addressing legal changes only at the beginning of the twentieth century.

The Ottoman Empire and Egypt: Corruption and the Perception of Crime

While Muslim scholars in India created a space where the non-Muslim British could operate in the legal sphere, thereby granting a degree of Islamic legitimacy to their actions, Muslims in the Ottoman Empire and its Arab provinces focused on something slightly different. Although these geographical areas never faced the problem of non-Muslim rule, at least in name, they and their systems faced the perceived problem of increased crime and the need to control the population.

Fariba Zarinebaf has documented the rise of violent crime in the Ottoman capital, Istanbul. According to her figures, around 10 percent of the convictions in the 1720s were for violent assault and injury. Homicide had grown in the second half of the eighteenth century to the point where "10.4 percent of imperial orders to local officials in Istanbul and its dependencies concerned homicide" alone—that is, excluding other forms of assault and injury.[32] This increase, according to Zarinebaf, was primarily the result of economic downturns after long wars with Russia and the growth in the numbers of single men and unemployed workers who settled in the city during this period. Recognizing this problem, the Ottoman government rapidly expanded its surveillance and policing system during the eighteenth century and paved the way for the creation of a modern police force in the following century.[33]

In Egypt, there is little information regarding the prevalence of crime in the eighteenth century or most of the nineteenth. Regular statistical records regarding the operation of the courts and the police were not kept until after the establishment of the National Courts, and the first figures on homicide, from 1896, cited a relatively high rate of around 0.65 homicides per 10,000 inhabitants.[34] In comparison, in 1900 the homicide rate in England and Wales was 0.096 per 10,000 inhabitants, and in the United States it was 0.1.[35] Despite the high number of homicides, most historians have suggested that during the rule of Muhammad 'Ali (ruled 1805–1848), the Egyptian government's desire to create new criminal laws and become active in the judiciary was not heavily motivated by a perceived rise in the crime rate. Instead, it was due to a shift in the state to one commanded by the central authority, the establishment of a regular army independent of the Ottomans, and the development of the agricultural sector and basic industries (all of which required a regular workforce).[36] As a result, the first criminal legislation created by Muhammad 'Ali, in 1830, focused primarily on punishing offenders who committed crimes against the state, including draft dodgers and people who damaged state property. Many prisoners were sentenced to manual labor or forced into the military as punishment, all in service to the state.[37] This desire for control evolved further during the second half of the nineteenth century, when a new local elite known as the effendis sought to reshape their nation and rural counterparts, reforming the society through the law, education, and culture.[38]

With a rising crime rate and a growing desire to reshape the law to match the needs of the state, observers found the existing criminal punishment system lacking in organization, rife with corruption, and mostly incapable of meeting new challenges. Writing about the environment before the French occupation of Egypt in 1789, the historian 'Abd al-Rahman b. Hasan al-Jabarti (d. 1825) and the Shaykh of al-Azhar Hasan al-'Attar (d. 1835) praised the Ottoman Sultan Selim III for saving their nation from collapse. For al-Jabarti, though the Mamluks in the past had held back Mongol and crusader invasions, they had fallen into the doldrums of corruption and become weak. The Mamluk governors under the Ottoman Empire "stood in the face of time but were not careful of its deceit. They destroyed the front lines and raised palaces. They replaced the heroes of men with the lords of backwardness and brave cavalrymen with beautiful male servants. They race in dirt circles with pride and arrogance to the square of every divergence. They want nothing except the resources of merriment, and they do not care about what harmful reasons they have ignored."[39] According to al-Jabarti, the Mamluks had abanded their military obligations and opened Egypt to foreign invasion. They had also contributed to the disintegration of Egyptian society, the collapse of the economy and the education system, and the ineffectiveness of the courts.

Similar sentiments were echoed more than a century later in *al-Muhama*, a comprehensive study of the judiciary and practice of attorneys written by Ahmad Fathi Zaghlul, an Egyptian legal scholar working in the early twentieth century and brother of the leader of the 1919 Revolution, Sa'd Zaghlul. In terms of criminal law, Ahmad Fathi Zaghlul noted that when officials in the court system were ordered to provide a survey of cases in preparation for launching the new National Courts in 1883, they reported several instances in which criminal proceedings had taken more than a decade to resolve. In the case of a man named Yusuf Dardir, a murder had occurred in 1864, but because of inefficiencies in the court system, over twenty-six years passed before the courts reached a final verdict.[40] In another instance, two defendants were able to take advantage of the court inspectors, most likely through bribery, and were let off without any punishment.[41] According to Zaghlul, these problems were the result of the lack of a formal system to handle cases. Laws were arbitrary, and much was left to the whims of local governors and town administrators (*mashayikh*).

Writing in *al-Kitab al-dhahabi*, a work published in 1933 to commemorate the fiftieth anniversary of the establishment of the National Courts, Muhammad Labib 'Atiya (a scholar and member of the Khedival Law School faculty), stated:

At that time [before the new code], there was no law to clarify rulings, define types of crimes, or name their punishments. No executive authorities had a system responsible for issuing and implementing punishments. People were exposed to a penal system composed of pieces of rulings from the shari'a and regulations issued by governors upon various occasions, without any comprehensive connection to what may be called criminal justice and how to achieve it.

Those who observe these various laws become aware from the first glance that the area defined for crimes expanded and contracted, and punishments lessened and were intensified, according to the whims of administrative rulers.[42]

Khaled Fahmy has warned against seeing the work of Zaghlul and *al-Kitab al-dhahabi* as accurate depictions of the Egyptian legal system. Speaking particularly about Zaghlul, he stated: "All in all, the book [al-Muhamah] is a damning indictment of the entire legal system, which is consistently described as despotic and inherently unjust. While he recounts the story of the establishment of the [judicial] councils by reproducing the original Khedival orders that founded them, Zaghlul failed to uncover the logic that informed their activity, and he could not help but reproduce his modernist thinking of them as failing to live up to Western legal principles."[43]

Fahmy is correct in pointing out Zaghlul's biases in analyzing the court system. Additional studies, such as those by Rudolph Peters and Fahmy himself, have used original court documents to show that the inner workings of the nineteenth-century Egyptian legal system were actually much more complex.[44] However, *al-Muhama* and *al-Kitab al-dhahabi* accurately depicted the view of most Muslim observers at the time: the legal system was corrupt, inefficient, and despotic. This view is a critical factor for understanding the introduction of the new penal codes in the jurisdictions of interest in this book.

Perhaps the most prominent of these observers is the Syrian scholar 'Abd al-Rahman al-Kawakibi (d. 1902). His seminal work presented a call to wipe out what he described as the most significant disease threatening the Muslim world: tyranny. In his introduction to this work, he spoke of a growing desire to find the source *(asl)* of the disease that afflicted peoples "in the East in general and particularly . . . the Muslims": "Some will say that the source of the disease is the neglect of religion . . . while others will say that it is a difference of [political] opinions, [and still] others will claim that the reason is ignorance. . . . I agree with the view that the source of the disease is political tyranny, an opinion I have determined is correct after long contemplation."[45] Al-Kawakibi did not mention any specific governments or officials in his work. Instead, he spoke generally about how tyranny was supported by the religious and educational establishments, permeated every element of society, and hindered development.

Writing at roughly the same time as al-Kawakibi, 'Abd Allah b. Hasan Barakat Zada (d. 1900)[46] spoke more specifically about how in the Ottoman Empire, officials and judges were constantly subject to bribery: "This [bribery] is an old trouble of ours, and it has become more widespread in our time to the point that it has become a great tribulation, how cursed of a calamity it is and the greatness of its woe. It is sorrowful that this vice has become permissible in our country with corrupt interpretations so much that it is now [considered] a respected device [in government]."[47] The result of bribery in the court system, according to Barakat Zada, was that people no longer trusted one another and would file false reports, paying judges and other government officials to issue rulings that favored the unjust and destroyed families and property.[48] During this time, there were similar comments from many other political writers across the empire, as far afield as Iraq and Tunisia.[49]

At the core of these calls to enact legal and administrative change was a growing belief in the need to implement an ideal of justice ('adl). For example, when Muhammad 'Ali of Egypt issued an order to establish new criminal tribunals in 1842, he argued that "if an offender is sentenced to penalties laid down [by law] without the slightest partiality and with justice and equity, then that person will have no further objections."[50] He compared his order to similar legislation in Europe and noted the attention European courts gave to investigations, the clear establishment of fault, and the necessity of punishment. When al-Kawakibi wrote about the cure for tyranny, he cited a robust court system based on the ideal of justice: "Human beings' most significant achievement is their attachment to the foundations of organized government that builds a dam in the face of tyranny, the virus that causes all corruption. This creates a situation in which there is no strength or influence stronger than that of the law, and the law is God's strong rope. They [people] place the power of legislation in the hands of the nation, and the nation can never be led astray. And when they make courts that hold accountable the sultan and the vagrant alike, it emulates the Great Court of God in its justice."[51]

Expanding State Control through *Siyasa*

Amid this environment of a perceived rise in crime, state and judicial corruption, and the desire to expand state control over their populations and establish a greater ideal of justice, legal scholars and governments turned to *siyasa*, the classical Islamic tool of political authority. Long used to justify the involvement of state power within an Islamic legal context, significant advances in the theorization of *siyasa* occurred during the fourteenth century with the Syrian Taqi al-Din Ahmad b. Taymiya (d. 728/1328) and his student Muhammad b. Qayyim al-Jawziya (d. 751/1350).[52] In his introduction to *al-Turuq al-hukmiya fi al-siyasa al-shar'iya*, Ibn Qayyim outlined the definition of *siyasa*: "Indeed, God sent his messengers and brought down his books to establish balance amongst humanity, and this is the justice upon which heaven and earth are placed. If the signs of justice show themselves in any manner, then there is found the law (shari'a) of God and his religion."[53]

Ibn Qayyim believed that in his time, the Islamic legal system had gotten out of balance. On the one hand, stricter opinions, which argued that the interpretation and application of Islamic law in courts were bound by rules of evidence found in Islam's fundamental texts (the Qur'an and the Sunna of the Prophet Muhammad), failed to account for the complexities of reality. On the other hand, political rulers who believed that they could do as they wished outside the bounds of the shari'a ended up "suspending the prescribed punishments *('attalu al-hudud)*, disposing of the rights of individuals *(dayy'au al-huquq)*, emboldening the sinful in corruption *(jarra'u ahl al-fujur 'ala al-fasad)*, and making the shari'a limited [so that it does not] serve the benefits of the people."[54]

His solution to this problem was for political rulers to become more acquainted with two additional types of legal understanding: the general rules of the physical world *(ahkam al-hawadith al-kulliya)* and the lived realities and conditions of the people *(nafs al-waqi' wa ahwal al-nas)*.[55] By combining these understandings with the interpretive methods and rules developed by the schools of Islamic law, a political ruler could better apply God's law, "whose purpose is to establish justice among the believers and create a balance between people."[56]

Ibn Qayyim sought to rein in the unchecked power of local rulers and judges to make law. His effort resulted in granting Islamic legitimacy to rulers' actions within limits, and *siyasa* became one of the pillars of the legal system of the later Ottoman Empire.[57] During the eighteenth and nineteenth centuries, the concept of *siyasa* would be expanded even further and used by scholars to encourage increased state involvement in the law. In India, for example, Siraj al-Din dedicated the final chapter of his work on discretionary punishment *(ta'zir)* to defining the concept of *siyasa*. He encouraged local British leaders to take advantage of *siyasa*, particularly in cases where literal understandings of Islamic legal norms would not suffice:

> Do you not see that if a man strangled another, threw him into a well, or off a cliff, and that death resulted, then he would be given discretionary punishment *(ta'zir)* and not retaliation *(qisas)*, and that if this became a habit and he repeated the crime, then he should be killed using political authority *(siyasatan)*?
>
> The essence of this topic [therefore] is that all serious crimes for which a specific punishment is not outlined, or in cases where the penalty cannot be applied because of the presence of doubt *(shubha)*, and in which there would be a great injustice [in setting the defendant free], the issue is given to the ruler *(imam)* for him to decide. In many instances, which are too numerous even to mention, seeking the ruler's opinion is primary.[58]

When asked about the same issue, 'Abd al-Hayy gave a similar response and widened the scope to include not only the central Islamic ruler *(imam)* but also a local leader *(sultan)* and governor *(hakim)*: "*Siyasa* is a form of discretionary punishment *(ta'zir)* and includes all forms of extreme punishment *('uqubat-e shadida)*, such as execution, life imprisonment, and expulsion from the country. Execution as *siyasa* is not limited to a murderer who has repeatedly choked a victim to death. Instead, it is general and [applicable] in every form of crime according to the public benefit [seen] by the *sultan* or *hakim*."[59]

In India's British courts, Muslim law officers often cited *siyasa* as the reason for allowing British judges to issue rulings when direct evidence was not available. In one case in Bengal in 1853, two defendants (Baij Roy and Suddoo Roy) were charged with the murder of Munshur Aheer and the wounding of Hurkoo Aheer, the prosecutor in the case. During the investigation of, among other things, medical evidence and witness testimony, it became clear that the murder had occurred after a group of people had gotten into a fight over money owed for thatching grass. Under literal interpretations of Hanafi law, the judge could not convict anyone, as no witness could identify one of the two defendants as having committed the murder. Despite this, the Muslim law officer issued a fatwa of guilty for both defendants and, according to the court records, rendered them "liable to *seeasut*." The judge sentenced the defendants to six and five years, respectively, a judgment approved upon review by the appellate court.[60]

In another case in the same records, a man named Sooltan Bhueemya was charged with the murder of his lover's husband, Pauchcowree. The fatwa, based on medical evidence and the testimony of one witness (a person named Roostom, who reached the scene of the crime and saw the defendant running away), "convicts the prisoner of the murder charged, on strong presumption, and declares him liable to the punishment of *Akoobat.*" The sessions judge agreed and issued the death penalty, which was confirmed upon appeal.[61]

In this case, the mufti could not directly convict the prisoner of any of the traditional punishments found in Islamic law. There were no eyewitnesses, and absolute certainty about guilt could not be established. However, the circumstances of the case were clear, and the defendant provided no witnesses in his defense. Therefore, to ensure that the rights of the deceased and his family were preserved and to facilitate the punishment issued by the British judge, he issued a conviction, for which the sessions judge then recommended the severest punishment available.

In addition to the accommodation and justification of expanding state control through the classical legal concept of *siyasa*, scholars also strongly discouraged Muslims from taking the law into their own hands—even when the crime committed was considered a severe breach of etiquette and threatened general harmony. For example, 'Abd al-Hayy refused to apply the prescribed punishment (*hadd*) for adultery (*zina*): "Carrying out a *hadd* punishment without the [approval of] a judge or ruler is not permissible and applying the same punishment if ordered by an informal settlement (*tahkim wasite*) is also not correct."[62]

In the Ottoman Empire, the writings of Barakat Zada, whose statements on corruption and bribery in the judicial system were mentioned above in this chapter, can be used to analyze the role of *siyasa* in the application of the law. Writing with the same tone as Ibn Qayyim, Barakat Zada believed that the Ottoman Empire had lost its balance between two forms of extremism. On the one hand, some people in the empire wrongly thought that *siyasa* was to be used in any situation in which the public good (*maslaha*) necessitated it, causing "the doors of injustice to open, blood to be spilled, and property to be taken in opposition to what the shari'a requires."[63] These views were too close to those of Europeans, calling for the complete translation and application of European laws and court systems. On the other hand, too many other people believed that *siyasa* had no place within the legal system and that the shari'a was limited to only the specific rules of *fiqh* created by previous scholars.

Speaking particularly about criminal law, Barakat Zada's solution to this problem was to expand the realm of evidence within the shari'a, allowing judges to convict with an "overwhelming belief *(al-zann al-ghalib)*" of a prisoner's guilt.[64] The state should rely upon the expertise of the police more readily in an investigation, and judges should confirm the accuracy of witness testimony and confessions with observations of the prior record and reputation of those making statements. The second point is essential in situations of homicide in self-defense. For example, suppose a man came before the court and confessed to murdering another but claimed, before the verdict of retaliation *(qisas)* was issued, that he had done so because the person had attacked him or was attempting to steal his property. In that case, the judge should observe the general nature of the deceased. If that person was known for "disruption, corruption, and theft *(fitna, fasad, wa sariqa)*," the judge should mitigate the punishment; otherwise, the defense of the perpetrator should be disregarded.[65]

On the ground in Egypt, the state employed the power of *siyasa* to expand the rules of evidence and bring more criminals to justice through forensic evidence. As Khaled Fahmy discussed in an article, the Egyptian state during the nineteenth century used types of forensic evidence such as the results of autopsies in criminal procedures to "exercise greater control over society."[66] In one case cited from 1877, a man named Muhammad 'Abd al-Rahman was sentenced to one year in prison for killing his mother-in-law. The case brought by the victim's son had previously been dropped based on statements from witnesses who said that she had died of a stomach illness, but it was reopened when the victim's son became suspicious of the son-in-law and insisted that an autopsy be carried out—which confirmed that she had been murdered.[67]

These new practices were not seen as contradictory to the shari'a, and "none of these medico-legal innovations was couched in a language that would be considered inimical to Islam, something that should not be seen as a polemical trick or a clever ploy resorted to in an attempt to placate the *'ulama*."[68] Instead, during the rest of the century, both traditional scholars and new legal elites alike felt that the use of *siyasa* and forensic medicine complemented and, ultimately, helped uphold the shari'a. For example, when writing about rules of forensic medicine, a doctor named Muhammad al-Shubasi argued that if a student of forensic medicine found a dead body in the street and "says that the victim died as a result of a brain stroke, but death was caused otherwise, then two errors are committed: first the shariʻa-stipulated capital punishment *(qisas)* from his murderer is prevented, and, second, this case would be recorded wrongly in the death registers."[69]

Conclusion

The political and legal environments of the eighteenth and nineteenth centuries in the areas covered in this book share several important themes. In each jurisdiction, there was a growing belief that the society needed reform to cope with a perceived rise in crime. The state exhibited a desire to centralize and control its population, and scholars advocated for a greater sense of justice. Local observers saw a system that suffered from corruption. For example, in Egypt, the application of a crude mixture of traditional Islamic principles modified by imperial orders and overlapping understandings of the law led to confusion and corruption, causing a loss of individual rights and hampering state control. Therefore, a comprehensive suite of reforms was needed to rectify this problem.

The change did not happen immediately. Instead, in each jurisdiction reform occurred in a slow, piecemeal fashion that succeeded in some cases and failed in others. For instance, Egypt implemented several new criminal laws during the nineteenth century before the establishment of the National Courts in the early 1880s and the introduction of the Penal Code of 1883, with the greater Ottoman Empire going through similar iterative transitions both before and after implementation of the Penal Code of 1858. In India, numerous British circulars and criminal legislation slowly brought the legal system to the point of sweeping change. Although the Law Commission composed the final Penal Code in the 1830s, it remained on the shelf until after the transfer of political control to the British Crown following the Uprising of 1857. Still, the motivations for legal reform persisted throughout the nineteenth century and formed the impetus for the final implementation of new penal codes in the second half of that century.

These changes, including the new penal codes, occurred within a context thoroughly defined by traditional understandings of Islamic law—particularly discretionary punishment *(taʻzir)* and political authority *(siyasa)*. In the Ottoman Empire and Egypt, as attested to in the political writings of scholars such as Barakat Zada, the language of earlier scholars such as the fourteenth-century Hanbali scholar Ibn Qayyim was employed to call for the expansion of the rules of evidence and ensure more effective justice. In Egypt, this took the form of introducing forensic evidence that was not seen as an import but as complementing the shari'a and helping achieve its goals. Additionally, in India, Muslim legal scholars worked hand in hand with their British counterparts (both outside and inside the courts) to facilitate these changes and grant them a degree of religious legitimacy. These reformers attempted to reestablish a balance they thought had been lost by their respective governments. They believed that their countries' legal systems should be reformed in light of new realities and with consideration of Islamic legal traditions—a view exhibited in the work of 'Abd al-Hayy, whose fatwas on the state of the judiciary were introduced at the beginning of this chapter.

With this legal and political context in mind, chapter 2 studies the actors who participated in creating the new penal codes of the nineteenth century. It highlights the rise of a new elite whose education had been heavily influenced by European norms. Members of this elite who were tasked with writing, translating, or interpreting the new laws sought to balance Islamic legal norms and external influences.

2

New Elites Shaping the Law

This chapter focuses on the local actors who were critical to the development of the new penal codes during the nineteenth century. The discussion in chapter 1 shed light on how Muslim scholars worked within a changing environment and deployed classical Islamic legal concepts, such as *siyasa*, to create room for increasing state power. However, a new group of Muslim elites rose to prominence during the second half of the nineteenth century and took commanding roles in the creation and application of the new penal codes. These scholars were the products of new educational institutions but existed in the same middle ground as those educated in traditional Islamic institutions, such as Muhammad 'Abd al-Hayy.

Much of the scholarship on these new scholars and institutions has focused on the importance of European influence, noting in particular that the courses in each of these institutions were taught in languages other than that used by the local population, such as French in Egypt and the Ottoman Empire and English in India.[1] Some recent scholars argue that, if people follow a curriculum in a foreign language and study under the influence of European forms of knowledge, the resulting legal outcomes would naturally reflect that foreign influence.

The emphasis on European influence and state power dynamics should be tempered with an understanding of the condition of Muslim education in these jurisdictions during the nineteenth century, as expressed by those who viewed them on the ground. In addition to calling for state intervention in the realm of law seen in chapter 1, Muslim observers advocated educational change because they viewed traditional institutions, such as al-Azhar, to be corrupt, overcrowded, and incapable of serving the needs of a changing society. Some of these problems were caused by the changing state, as Muhammad 'Ali in Egypt restricted the financial resources of al-Azhar and the British in India reduced the role of Muslim institutions. However, an analysis that examines only the role of the state does not produce a complete picture, as demonstrated in the introduction and chapter 1.

According to Robert Hefner, educational reforms of the nineteenth century "took place outside of, rather than in collaboration with, the existing *madrasa* system."[2] Although this might appear to be true, the *madrasa* system had a much more important role to play in shaping modern education than this quote suggests, as this chapter shows. Islamic legal norms continued to dominate the legal discourse within these new institutions and are reflected in the works produced by their graduates. Many of these scholars, such as Muhammad Qadri Basha in Egypt, sought out the *'ulama* in their studies and professional lives. This chapter argues that given their interaction with Islamic discourse and the development of the new codes, these scholars and the institutions that produced them should be seen as a bridge between cultures, responding to both increasing European influence and local needs based on Islamic legal understandings.

This chapter tells the story of these new institutions and how they came to dominate the legal discourse. It then describes the role of Muslim institutions and shows that, particularly in the second half of the nineteenth century, the *'ulama* did not participate in the development of the law. In the case of India, traditional institutions such as the madrassa at Deoband chose to focus instead on the personal development of Muslims and interacted with the British-led legal system only in the areas of personal and family law. This left a void in legal discourse that a new generation of Muslim elites would fill. The chapter then focuses on the lives of two new legal elites who worked with the new codes, Muhammad Qadri Basha of Egypt and Nazeer Ahmed of India. The chapter closes with a look at the importance of institutions and translation, a theme found throughout the development of the new educational institutions.

Educating the New Elite

In India, the most important institution during this period was the Delhi College. Founded in 1792 by Nawab Ghaziu'd-Din II, the school was located in a mosque and a collection of buildings surrounding the tomb of the founder's grandfather, Nawab Ghaziu'd-Din I, and is now known as the Zakir Husain Delhi College, part of Delhi University. Under the British in the 1820s, the college was reorganized as the Anglo Arabic College. Studies at the college were based on the Nizamiya system that had been the standard of Islamic education on the Indian subcontinent since the eighteenth century. The British supplemented the college's Islamic curriculum with studies in English language and literature, as well as in science.

The Nizamiya education system, which remains in use throughout South Asian religious seminaries today, is based on a balance between two sources of Islamic thought. The first, revealed knowledge (*naql*), refers to studies based upon the Qur'an and Prophetic practice as recorded through the *hadith*. This area requires intimate knowledge of Arabic, the language of the Qur'an and the *hadith*. Therefore, the Nizamiya system places a heavy emphasis in its early stages on the mastery of Arabic grammar, morphology, and syntax. The second source of Islamic thought, reason (*'aql*), calls upon students to understand the complexities of Islamic theology and philosophy. Disciplines in other areas of Islamic studies, including jurisprudence and its sources (*fiqh* and *usul al-fiqh*), are derived from a combination of revealed knowledge and reason.

Before the development of the Nizamiya curriculum, Muslim scholars had debated for centuries which of these two sources should take the commanding role in the creation of law. During the classical period, *naql* took precedence. However, during the early years of the eighteenth century, the scholar and de facto founder of the seminary at Farangi Mahal in Lucknow, Mulla Nizam al-Din (d. 1161/1748), established the Nizamiya curriculum, which sought to reaffirm the place of *'aql*. According to Francis Robinson, "the study of advanced books of logic, philosophy, and dialectics sharpened the rational faculties and, ideally, brought to the business of government men with better-trained minds and better-formed judgment."[3] In the eighteenth and nineteenth centuries, many traditional questions of Islamic law were being reviewed and revised, primarily due to calls from reformers such as Shah Wali Allah Dahlawi (d. 1176/1762), who encouraged jurists to reopen legal debates long perceived as settled. Wali Allah and others called for new importance to be placed on independent juristic reasoning (*ijtihad*) in the creation of law, although Wali Allah argued that *ijtihad* could be maintained only within the Hanafi legal tradition.[4] It was in this environment of the revival of legal thought and the pedagogical balance between rational (*'aql*) and revealed (*naql*) knowledge within the Nizamiya curriculum that the Delhi College came to full fruition.

The colonial officers who participated in and supervised the intellectual life of the Delhi College and the city of Delhi in general during the first half of the nineteenth century were usually far from the image of the staunchly Christian officers that would become famous in the latter half of the century.[5] Some of these individuals, termed "white Mughals" by the historian William Dalrymple, lived according to Mughal customs, were well versed in local languages, regularly visited the Mughal court, and often married Indian women.[6] The direction of the school was also international and not directly subject to British power, as the school's three principals—Felix Boutros, Aloys Sprenger, and Gottlieb Wilhelm Leitner—were all non-British and engaged in the development of the college's Islamic curriculum. Most of the teachers at the school were staunch supporters of Wali Allah's school of thought that promoted *ijtihad*, and the local Mughal nobles provided financial support to further the college's goals. For example, in 1829, the prime minister of Awadh, I'timad al-Dawla Nawab Fazl 'Ali Khan, donated 170,000 rupees to the college.[7]

As a result, during the first half of the nineteenth century, the Delhi College became a center of learning, and its students—such as Nazeer Ahmed, whose role in the legal system and the translation of the Indian Penal Code of 1860 is discussed below in this chapter—drove academic debate at a time when successive raids and political division had decimated cities like Delhi.[8] The intellectual climate of the college can be seen in the fact that it was home to several academic journals, including *The Meeting of the Two Planets (Qiran al-Sadayn)*, *For the Benefit of the Observers (Fawa'id al-Nazirin)*, and *The Lover of India (Muhibb-e Hind)*. These journals "made Western innovations in science and technology available to the literate public of north India, but also articulated an ideology of reform that involved openness to knowledge from wherever it issued."[9]

Even as the relationship between the British and Indians began to change in the 1830s, with the promotion of education in English and as Christian missionary activities were increasingly promoted by the colonial regime, Islamic education persisted. In fact, these changes created a lively atmosphere of cross-religious and -cultural debate in which many of the college's students, including Nazeer Ahmed, participated. One crucial figure during this period was Nazeer Ahmed's colleague at the college, Maulawi Zaka Ullah (d. 1910). According to Mushirul Hasan, "Both [Nazeer Ahmed and Maulawi Zaka Ullah] were prized products of Delhi College. Nazir Ahmed studied Urdu and Arabic, whereas 'Master' Ram Chandra, a recent convert to Christianity, 'sowed in Zaka Ullah's mind and heart a seed of another kind, namely a love for mathematics.'"[10] The three would regularly meet at Zaka Ullah's home, debating and discussing their studies well into the night. Such meetings continued until Zaka Ullah's death and were even attended by Anglican priests such as Charles Freer Andrews, Zaka Ullah's biographer.[11]

This environment continued until the Delhi College was abruptly shut down as a result of the Uprising of 1857. Still, throughout the nineteenth and twentieth centuries its mixed culture of Islamic and Western education continued to influence other institutions on the subcontinent—including Aligarh Muslim University, established by Sir Syed Ahmed Khan in 1875. Even more conservative religious establishments, such as Dar al-'Ulum Deoband (established in 1866), were heavily influenced by the environment and organization of the Delhi College, and one of Deoband's founders, Muhammad Qasim Nanotvi (d. 1880), was a graduate of the Delhi College.

In Egypt, two institutions educated people who would work on the new codes: the School of Translators (Madrasat al-Mutarjimin) and the Khedival Law School (Madrasat al-Huquq al-Khidawiya). These would develop into the current 'Ayn Shams University College of Languages (Kuliyat al-Alsun) and the law school at Cairo University, respectively.[12]

Napoleon brought a collection of European academics with his invading army, and during the French occupation (1798–1801) they produced several works on Egyptian geography, language, and culture—compiled and published between 1808 and 1828 in the *Description de l'Égypte*.[13] As a result of the occupation, cooperation between Egyptian and European scholars reached a new high, and Egyptian elites became increasingly interested in the natural sciences. This marked a significant change from the form of interaction with Europe since the Middle Ages, as described by Ibrahim Abu-Lughod: "The French expedition to Egypt in 1798 struck a crushing blow to the complacency of centuries, not just a humiliating one to the Mamluk defenders. Here was a new image of the European; here was an enforced contact of cultures; but here also was a situation more baffling and perplexing than it was illuminating."[14]

For example, Hasan al-'Attar (d. 1835)—a prominent Muslim scholar who would later become the Shaykh of al-Azhar—taught Arabic to some of the French officers and, in return, was given access to French works on the social and physical sciences. He stated: "It is essential for our nation to change and renew its condition with the knowledge and sciences it does not [currently] possess. It is incredible what this nation [France] has achieved in science and expertise, the number of books they have published, and how close they are to being beneficial."[15] With an increased interest in

European knowledge, the government of Muhammad 'Ali began sending groups of students to Europe in the 1820s to broaden their education. This policy would continue officially until the middle of the twentieth century. Once their studies were complete, these individuals would come back to Egypt and work for the state, primarily in education but also in the military and other parts of the government. While the students were in Europe, the government wanted to ensure that they would remain attached to their Islamic roots, so it sent along as a chaperone an imam trained at al-Azhar and selected by al-'Attar: Rifa'a Rafi' al-Tahtawi.

Born in Upper Egypt in 1801, al-Tahtawi had arrived in Cairo in 1817 to study at al-Azhar, where he spent five years as a student and then became a teacher. He was the top student of al-'Attar, who introduced him to geography and math along with the traditional Islamic sciences. As a religious advisor for the students in Europe, he also received permission from the Egyptian government to enroll in studies.

The first months of study in France were difficult for the Egyptians, who found themselves thrown into an unfamiliar culture and intellectual environment. They spent most of their time together and lived in the same home, isolated from the rest of French society. "We would study history in the morning for two hours," recorded al-Tahtawi, "then after noon prayer [there was] drawing, then French grammar, and every Friday three lessons in accounting and engineering."[16] The students spent most of their free time mastering the French language, which would allow them to read the texts they were studying. This environment did not last long. After a few months, and in response to complaints from students and their French observers, the students were separated, distributed among different colleges and specialties.

For al-Tahtawi, who remained in Paris, learning French and translating works into Arabic became his top priority. After spending five years in France, the mission's French supervisory committee gave him a final exam. He presented Arabic translations and compilations of twelve French works in various subjects, including metallurgy, morality, history, Greek mythology, geography, and military arts. Unfortunately, the committee was not convinced that al-Tahtawi had fulfilled the requirements to obtain a degree and asked him to take a further exam, in which he was asked to write out the translation of several shorter texts on the spot. The committee then asked him to orally translate and explain in French some paragraphs from the Egyptian government's newsletter, *al-Waqa'i' al-misriya*. This time the committee was impressed and passed al-Tahtawi, allowing him to return to Egypt in Ramadan 1831.

Back in Cairo, al-Tahtawi worked for two years at the Royal Administrative Academy, but he continued to believe that the greatest need of Egyptian society was to continue the mission of translation. He fought for the creation of an official school, calling on Muhammad 'Ali to "establish a school of languages that the nation could benefit from, and [thereby] dispense with the *alien*."[17] The term "alien" referred to the European advisors brought to Egypt to assist the government in reorganizing and developing the military and administration. Muhammad 'Ali agreed, and the School of Translators was established in 1835, with al-Tahtawi as its head. The first class, whose members graduated in 1839, initially consisted of 80 students and eventually grew to around 150, many personally chosen by al-Tahtawi. Alongside his administrative duties, al-Tahtawi also taught Islamic studies and law and selected which works would be translated and printed at the official government press in Bulaq. During the next fourteen years, the school translated and published hundreds of books in various fields. Graduates of the school took up powerful positions as translators, some (such as Muhammad Qadri Basha) eventually becoming ministers in the Egyptian government.

However, as the power of Muhammad 'Ali began to wane in the 1840s in the face of military failures and increased European pressure, the translation school and the personal influence of al-Tahtawi started to be seen by the government as an internal threat. Two of Muhammad 'Ali's sons, 'Abbas Helmi I and Sa'id, used their influence as heirs to the throne to curb the school's cultural power. They began by canceling Islamic legal studies and dismissing many students and professors. Then they moved the school away from its original building and into a smaller public school. Finally, they ordered the school to be closed in 1849 and sent al-Tahtawi into exile in Sudan, where he became the principal of the Khartoum Primary School. He would eventually return to Cairo in the 1850s, where he would work as an administrator and teacher at the short-lived Royal Military Academy until it too was shut down in 1861, leaving al-Tahtawi unemployed.

It was during the rule of Khedive Isma'il (reigned 1863–1879) when al-Tahtawi's mission of translation would return to prominence, this time with a new focus on the translation and interpretation of the law. At the time, the judicial system of Egypt had multiple overlapping courts. There were the shari'a courts that for centuries had served as the primary administrators of justice. However, these courts and their jurisdiction were being slowly eroded by two other court systems: the consular courts, which adjudicated cases in which a foreigner was involved, and a collection of local councils (*majalis*) that handled most other Egyptian criminal, personal, and civil cases. There were also special councils that handled matters related to the military and religious minorities. The laws of the consular courts were the rules of the host nation, and appeals could take place only in Europe. The local councils were intended to apply the official pronouncements issued by Muhammad 'Ali and his successors, with appeals occurring at the highest council in Cairo—which was presided over by the khedive or his representative. In criminal law, this meant the official pronouncements issued by Muhammad 'Ali in 1829–1830, an amended version of the Ottoman Penal Code of 1850, and several subsequent other statutes and royal proclamations.[18]

Khedive Isma'il, along with many other contemporary and modern observers, believed that this system was unorganized and led to corruption and the failure of justice—as discussed in chapter 1. As a result, the khedive took comprehensive and sweeping steps to change the law beginning in the 1860s. With the support of new elites like Nubar Pasha, an Egyptian diplomat who was deeply concerned about the failure of the consular courts, the result was the creation of the Mixed Courts in 1875.[19] Proceedings in these courts were carried out in French, and the law applied was a compilation of statutes and procedures translated from the French codes as well as judgments of the previous councils published in 1866–1868.[20]

The daily operation of these new courts, the interpretation of their judgments, and the development of the laws that they applied required the training of a new generation of legal scholars who were comfortable in both French and Egyptian contexts. As a result, the khedive turned to al-Tahtawi and his former students 'Abd Allah al-Sayyid, Salih Majdi, Muhammad Laz, 'Abd Allah Abu-l-Sa'ud, and Muhammad Qadri Basha. He tasked them with translating French law into Arabic, working under the new Translation Administration, established within the Education Ministry in 1863. Their project was expanded in 1867, when the old College of Languages was reestablished—with its focus now on legal studies and training judges, with translation taking a secondary position. In the 1880s, this college was split in two. The part of it still called the College of Languages continued to translate and train teachers for public schools, and legal studies became the responsibility of the new Khedival Law School (Madrassat al-Huquq al-Khidawiya).[21]

Headed by French or British principals, the Khedival Law School offered courses in Islamic, Roman, and French law and was the primary center of legal education in Egypt until 1925, when it was integrated into Cairo University as its law school. The school's curriculum was based upon translation, primarily from French, and many of the textbooks used were translations of French texts into Arabic. Graduates of the school worked in the Mixed Courts—which remained active until 1949, when their functions were integrated into the National Courts. According to Leonard Wood, the primary function of the law school during this period was to allow Egyptians to "process the long-term consequences of reform policies set in motion in the early 1880s. They [Egyptians] had now witnessed the deepening impact of Europeanization in Egyptian culture."[22] However, a recent thesis from Cairo University has suggested that the work of this school was significantly more than an effort to "process" European influence: instead, it represented a transformation in the understanding of Islamic law and jump-started an entire movement of comparative legal theory and history. According to the thesis's author, Muhammad Ibrahim: "The men of the Khedival Law School were able to pull the rug from under the scholars of al-Azhar and move Islamic law from the courtyards of the al-Azhar mosque into the halls of Cairo University. The scholars of this institution led the race in many academic, legislative, and judicial fields."[23]

Like the tasks of both the Delhi College in India and the School of Translators in Egypt, the work of these new educational institutions was varied, mainly due to major administrative shifts that were occurring in the country. The Delhi College was shut down due to the Uprising of 1857, and shifting understandings about the purpose and methods of education among both British colonialists and Muslim elites meant that the sort of interaction between European and Islamic knowledge that had occurred at the college would never happen again. British officials retreated into their residencies, while Muslims, shocked by the horror of the massacres during the uprising, turned to an insular focus on the development of the Muslim individual, as I show below.

In Egypt, the School of Translators and the Khedival Law School continue to exist at 'Ayn Shams and Cairo Universities, respectively. Although a revivalist movement at al-Azhar in the early twentieth century meant that Islamic legal concerns would partially be reappropriated by scholars there, the non-Azhar colleges of Egypt have remained the primary source of discourse on and development within Islamic law.

However, the importance of these institutions should not be underestimated. According to the Egyptian historian Jamal al-Din al-Shayyal, in the early to mid-nineteenth century in both Egyptian and Indian education there was "the appearance of extraordinary individuals, pioneers of the social and intellectual reform movement who were qualified with the ability to combine traditional Eastern and Arabic culture with that of modern Western Europe."[24] Through the development of these new institutions, local scholars brought up in traditional Islamic educational environments were exposed to new forms of knowledge—particularly, new understandings of law.

The Fate of Traditional Muslim Institutions

Returning to the words of Ibrahim, who argued that the Khedival Law School "pulled the rug" out from under the scholars of al-Azhar, an important question arises: what exactly happened to traditional institutions of Muslim learning? In the case of Egypt, the great halls of al-Azhar had been at the center of Muslim education and legal debate for a thousand years. However, in the course of nineteenth-century reforms, scholars from these institutions were sidelined in public discourse, particularly related to the creation of law.

Many of these changes can be attributed to the state's expanding and increasingly centralized power. According to Indira Falk Gesink, who studied the development of al-Azhar throughout the nineteenth century, modernist reformers established "a narrative of decline" that saw al-Azhar as the reason for the "backwardness" of the country's education system.[25] As a result, individuals such as Education Minister 'Ali Mubarak (d. 1893), considered one of the leading reformers of Egypt's education system, sought to limit the role of al-Azhar and replace it with a European-inspired collection of schools and institutes.[26] Speaking particularly about al-Azhar, Mubarak remarked that "moral, pedagogical, and philosophical failings" had rendered it "irrelevant to the future of education in Egypt."[27]

However, it is crucial to understand that this narrative of decline was not merely concocted by reformers looking for an excuse to adopt European norms. For most of the nineteenth century, al-Azhar had suffered from several organizational and curricular problems. For example, it had experienced unprecedented growth in its student body, yet the administration did little to adjust its facilities or curriculum in response to the growing number of students. In the early nineteenth century, the university had 1,500–3,000 students: by 1876, that number had increased to 10,780. The number of teachers grew to keep pace in the same period, from around 40–60 to 325.[28] In contrast, in 1882 the College of Languages had only 30 students, and the Khedival Law School had 62.[29] Students were coming to al-Azhar from all over the country and quickly overwhelmed the surrounding student lodges in the old city. Few new housing options were available for students who did not have family members in Cairo, so many simply slept in the mosque's courtyard.

Some of these problems, such as the increased pressure on the charitable endowments (waqfs) established to provide for students, were due to mismanagement by the expanding state. In his attempt to control the administration of the waqfs and increase sources of revenue for the state, Muhammad 'Ali had already brought most of the agricultural endowments under state supervision by 1814, and in 1846 he issued a decree that no new agricultural land could be made into an endowment. As a result, the food rations provided for students through the waqfs were fixed, yet they needed to supply an increasing number of beneficiaries. In one instance in the 1860s, armed police were required to break up a group of students from North Africa who assaulted an elderly professor when their bread rations were interrupted.[30] The crisis of overcrowding at al-Azhar caught the attention of 'Ali Mubarak, who stated: "Most of the time, you can barely pass through al-Azhar as [students] are so packed together, and at times they might push each other around and fight in the middle of class. One can feel the heat in the winter from the number of bodies. . . . The classes are filled with unacceptable smells that distract them [the students] from their ijtihad. Many escape [from this] by studying in other locations."[31] Tied to the problem of overcrowding was the growing failure of the curriculum. Mubarak continued: "The majority of their attention aside from memorization is [given] to understanding phrases, solving grammatical problems, discussing through semantic debates, and that which is directly related to the text. You find many of them are mountains in understanding [what is] in the text, but if you ask about something outside [of the text], you will find few who can answer from their lack of awareness."[32]

This was not the view only of Egyptian state officials: others who visited al-Azhar during the nineteenth century voiced similar opinions. One of the most famous of these was the Indian scholar Shibli Nu'mani (d. 1914), who visited Egypt in 1892 on his way back to India from a trip to

Istanbul. "The method of education [at al-Azhar] is even a greater sorrow," he remarked:

> Here only jurisprudence *(fiqh)* and grammar *(nahw)* are taught as independent and original subjects. . . . Logic, philosophy, math, and other rational sciences are not included. Foundations of jurisprudence *(usul al-fiqh)*, Qur'anic exegesis, *hadith*, literature, and rhetoric are taught, but to . . . a small extent for an institution of such a great size. For [the teaching of] jurisprudence and grammar, there is no attention paid to investigation *(muhaqqiqana)* or interpretation *(mujtahidana)*. They teach and [students] memorize the classical law texts and their explanations, commentaries, and glosses. . . . Many of the students I encountered were busy with completely impractical and unimportant side topics, which saddened me. The impact of this irrelevant method of education is that, for quite some time, al-Azhar has not produced a single valuable scholar or author.[33]

Nu'mani held the same views on the madrassas of Istanbul:

> The most significant complaint [that I have] regarding the old education system is that the standards [of teaching] are deficient. There is no reference at all to literature, while logic and philosophy use the final texts of 'Isaghuji and Shamiya, and the six canonical collections of *hadith* are taught in some schools. Rhetoric and principles of jurisprudence are in the same state. There is a great emphasis placed on jurisprudence *(fiqh)*; however, this teaching as well includes no preparation for interpretation *(mujtahidana)* but rather [teaches at only a] level of the layperson *('amiyana)* and imitation of older opinions *(muqallidana)*. I met a few scholars, and whether speaking on general or specific issues, I was astonished and sorrowed [by their responses].[34]

Conversely, Nu'mani praised the work of new schools in Istanbul such as the Military Academy and the Royal College. In particular, he praised the services they offered to students, such as comfortable housing, uniforms, and the high level of instruction they received in Islamic and Western topics.[35]

At Nu'mani's home in India, the situation was essentially the same. Traditional schools in Delhi had fallen in prominence due to political instability and military invasions during the eighteenth century. Only smaller family-based schools, such as that at Farangi Mahal in Lucknow, continued to function. As noted above, the experiment of the Delhi College in combining Islamic education with European sciences had come to an end by 1857. The events of the uprising, combined with the established British policy to promote English as the primary language of education for the subcontinent, meant that little official attention was paid to traditional madrassas that taught in Arabic, Persian, and Urdu.

In the post-1857 environment, Muslim scholars created new institutions in cities and villages far from the centers of colonial power. The most important of these was the madrassa at Deoband, which was founded in 1867. Established by students of the Delhi College and Professors Mamluk Ali Nanotvi, Rashid Ahmad Gangohi, and Muhammad Qasim Nanotvi, this madrassa grew over the following decades to become one of the most influential models for Islamic education. During the first decades of the twentieth century, students and scholars in the Deobandi tradition participated widely in anticolonial movements such as the Khilafat Movement (1919–24), which sought to give new authority to the embattled Ottoman sultan, and the Non-Cooperation Movement (1920–22), which called for Indians to protest British colonization.

However, during the second half of the nineteenth century, the focus of the seminary at Deoband and most other Muslim movements in South Asia shifted away from interactions with the British colonists. Instead, members of the movements sought to develop what Barbara Metcalf called "a community both observant of detailed religious law and, to the extent possible, committed to a spiritual life as well."[36] This meant disengaging from broader discussions of public law and focusing instead on the personal issues of Muslims. For example, one of the greatest scholars of Deoband, Ashraf 'Ali Thanawi (d. 1943), never discussed questions of civil or criminal law during the British period. The work for which he is best known, *Heavenly Ornaments (Bihishti Zewar)*, was "intended specifically to inculcate the 'proper' understanding of Islamic norms among Muslim women."[37] When he did interact with public law, it was to deal with questions of personal status such as marriage and divorce.[38]

As a result, the role of Muslim religious institutions changed drastically during the second half of the nineteenth century. This was due, in part, to the growing state, as was the case in Egypt. It was also due to changes in the education system forced by colonial powers, as was also the case with the British in India. However, there is ample evidence that madrassas like al-Azhar—which for centuries had been influential in the development of the law—were perceived to have fallen prey to corruption and disorganization. This is consistent with the general narrative of the legal environment of the same period discussed in chapter 1, with advocates for reform seeing the problems of bribery and lack of organization as having permeated the system and thus calling for the creation of new institutions that would offer a new direction for their societies.

With this background in mind, I now turn to two students of these new schools who played a role in creating and implementing the new penal codes of the nineteenth century: Muhammad Qadri Basha of Egypt and Nazeer Ahmed of India.

Muhammad Qadri Basha and the Egyptian Penal Code

Born around 1821 in the Upper Egyptian city of Mallawi, Muhammad Qadri Basha was the son of a Turkish government official named Qadri Agha who had come to Egypt in the early part of the nineteenth century on orders of the Ottoman government and was granted administrative rights over the agricultural land around Mallawi by the regime of Muhammad 'Ali. During his time in Mallawi, Qadri Agha fell in love with and married an Egyptian woman, who gave birth to Muhammad. Muhammad Qadri Basha spent his early years in Mallawi, where he attended the local public school. After he graduated, his father sent him to Cairo to study at the School of Translators, run by al-Tahtawi.

It is unclear which languages Muhammad Qadri Basha studied in Cairo, as the madrassa taught Ottoman Turkish, Persian, French, Italian, and English in a five-year program. His education was probably in Arabic, French, and Ottoman Turkish, as most of his works were directly related to these languages. Following his graduation, he was given a job as an assistant translator, working on the college's numerous translations. He estimated that he worked on around two thousand of them. Both during his studies at the School of Translators and while working as a translator, he became interested in Islamic law and spent much of his free time studying legal texts and attending lessons at al-Azhar.

In 1831, the son of Muhammad 'Ali, Ibrahim Basha, undertook an invasion of Ottoman territories in Syria, and by 1833 he had expanded

Egyptian control into Anatolia. During this time, Muhammad Qadri Basha was hired as a personal secretary to Ibrahim Basha, an impressive feat considering that he could not have been more than fifteen years old. However, the Egyptian occupation of Syria was short-lived, and by 1841 Ottoman forces and a revolt of the local population had forced the Egyptians to leave the area. Muhammad Qadri Basha came back to Cairo and continued to work for the government in numerous positions. He was appointed as an instructor of Arabic and Turkish at the Prince Mustafa Fadil Basha School in Cairo, selected as a private teacher to the future Khedive Tawfiq, and later worked as a translator for the Egyptian Foreign Ministry and as a member of the Alexandria Trade Council.

During the 1860s and 1870s, Muhammad Qadri Basha's focus shifted to the law, as he participated in translating the French penal code into Arabic. Along with his colleague Mustafa Effendi, he was chosen by the Ottoman Sultan Abdülaziz to review and propose changes to the Ottoman constitution. As a result of his efforts, he was appointed a judge in the Egyptian Mixed Courts and eventually became the minister of justice, where he oversaw the creation of the Egyptian Penal Code of 1883. He later retired from government service and lost his sight due to illness. He traveled to Austria to pursue treatment, but to no avail. Despite his declining health, he continued to work as an advisor to the Egyptian government until he died in 1886.[39]

Muhammad Qadri Basha is best known for his *Murshid al-hayran*, a comprehensive code of civil law modeled on the Ottoman Civil Code of 1877 *(Mecelle-i Ahkam-ı Adliye)* that was applied as the civil law of the empire in 1877. *Murshid al-hayran* was not published until 1891, almost five years after his death, and it was never officially established as law in Egypt. However, it is often considered to be one of the most important texts in Egyptian and Islamic civil law. It was made part of the official school curriculum for imperial elementary schools in Egypt and was regularly cited by both scholars and judges alike until the creation of the new civil code in 1949.[40] The writer of that code and perhaps the most significant Arab legal scholar of the twentieth century, 'Abd al-Razzaq al-Sanhuri, consistently cited *Murshid al-hayran* in his work and used it as a basis for the code.[41]

Muhammad Qadri Basha's work in civil law included a direct comparison between European codes and the writings of *fiqh*. In "The Application of What Is Found in the French Civil Code in Agreement with the School of Abu Hanifa *(Tatbiq ma wujida fi al-qanun al-madani—al-faransi—muwafiqan li-madhhab Abi Hanifa*)," he presented an article-by-article discussion of the Civil Code of the French issued by Napoleon in 1804. The analysis sometimes validated articles of the French code. For example, he found no problem with that code's first article, which established the authority of the code across all French territories, with one condition: that it does not contain elements that "contradict the shari'a" (*haythu lam yukhalif al-shar'*).[42] Additionally, he found the following five articles—which limited the code to future cases only, bound judges to the code, and limited the validity of private agreements to those that did not contradict the code—compatible with the Hanafi school (*li-hadha al-band munasaba bi-l-madhhab*). At the end of each article, Muhammad Qadri Basha provided examples from Islamic law (primarily from the work of the nineteenth-century Hanafi jurist Muhammad Amin b. 'Abidin) that justified his ruling. At other times, Muhammad Qadri Basha rejected parts of the code outright: for example, he stated that 7–128, which covered civil rights, "do not comply with the [Hanafi] school" (*la yuwafiq al-madhhab*).[43] Although Muhammad Qadri Basha did not say so specifically, he most likely excluded some of these articles as they dealt with issues that defined the French nation and did not concern Egypt, such as citizenship rules and the status of foreigners residing in France. Other parts of this section stood in sharp contrast to the shari'a: for example, articles 22–33, which stated that a person convicted of certain crimes or who failed to comply with a court summons could be condemned to civil death (Latin: *civiliter mortuus*) and stripped of their fundamental rights. Article 25 would have been particularly troubling for Muhammad Qadri Basha, as it stated that a person condemned to civil death "loses his property in all the goods which he possessed; and the succession is open for the benefit of his heirs, on whom his estate devolves, in the same manner as if he were naturally dead and intestate."[44] This stood in stark contrast to the shari'a, where proportions set out by the Qur'an governed inheritance.[45]

Near the end of his life, Muhammad Qadri Basha composed another work that dealt directly with criminal law and the developing field of Egyptian criminology. Titled *Le bon régime pour diminuer le crime (Ahasin al-ihtiyatat lima yata'allaq bi-taqlil al-jinayat)*, the draft text was presented after the author's death by his son to the Ministry of Justice for approval and publication. Unfortunately, no copy of this work is known to have survived.

When Muhammad Qadri Basha was tasked with creating the 1883 code, he was made part of a team of legal experts from within the government and the existing Mixed Courts. One of the primary foreigners involved was a Frenchman named Gilbert Vacher de Montguyn, who worked as a judge in the Mixed Courts. Also included in the group were several future national political leaders, including the Coptic Christians Butrus Ghali Basha (d. 1910) and Yusuf Wahba Basha (d. 1934), who became prime ministers of Egypt in the early twentieth century. Other lawyers and official translators were also included in the project, such as Amin Fikri Basha, Mustafa Ridwan Bek, and Tadrus Ibrahim Bek.[46]

Therefore, the group assembled to create the code drew most of their experience from the new schools of law and translation formed in the nineteenth century, and except for Muhammad Qadri Basha, no one had extensive experience in premodern Islamic law. To fill this gap, the committee was supported by the mufti of the Ministry of Justice (wizarat al-haqqaniya), 'Abd al-Rahman al-Bahrawi (d. 1904).

Al-Bahrawi hailed from the village of Kafr al-'Is in the delta province of al-Bahayra and came to Cairo as a child to study at al-Azhar. He studied with some of the most important scholars of his age, including the Shafi'i scholar Ibrahim al-Bajuri (d. 1860), and began teaching at al-Azhar in 1847. As a teacher, al-Bahrawi oversaw the editing of the first Egyptian print edition of the al-Fatawa al-'alamgiriya. Mentioned in chapter 1, this Hanafi text was cited by many scholars and relied upon heavily by Mughal and British judges until the middle of the nineteenth century. The successful publication of al-Fatawa al-'alamgiriya earned al-Bahrawi favor with the government, and he was appointed a judge in Alexandria in 1860. He spent the rest of his life oscillating between teaching at al-Azhar and holding government appointments, becoming the head of the Egyptian shari'a court and the mufti of the Ministry of Justice, where he engaged in the project with Muhammad Qadri Basha and his team.[47]

Once the draft code was finished, it was presented to the grand mufti, Muhammad al-'Abbasi al-Mahdi (d. 1897), for approval. He reportedly rejected the draft, saying its rulings were "against the shari'a."[48] This opinion may not have been due to the law's overall approach or even the grand mufti's genuine view. But it was the result of his legal obligation to follow the letter of the law as discussed in Hanafi texts.[49] As later chapters show, a new code that included European influence and synthesized aspects from other schools of law was outside of his purview and required broader examination.

Following the mufti's rejection, the government of Khedive Tawfiq ordered the creation of a committee of Azhari scholars from each of the four Sunni schools of law to review the draft code. In their final report, they stated that "the articles of these laws either match what is found in a text from one of the four schools of law *(madhahib)*, do not oppose them, or are considered as part of the common good *(al-masalih al-mursala)* in which *ijtihad* is permissible, taking into consideration the needs of the population."[50]

The influence of Muhammad Qadri Basha in the development of the Penal Code of 1883, and indeed the other laws that would form the basis for the new National Courts, cannot be understated. For example, when he was given the first draft of the civil code, he reviewed it and "introduced several principles of the shari'a."[51] In the opinion of Yuaqim Mikha'il, a legal historian and assistant public prosecutor, the new laws "considered the shari'a to the greatest degree possible."[52]

Nazeer Ahmed and the Indian Penal Code

Although the Indian Penal Code was implemented in 1860 following the transfer of power from the East India Company to the British Crown, a law committee headed by Lord Thomas Babington Macaulay had initially drafted the code almost thirty years earlier. Once it became law, the British government ordered that its text (the code was written in English) be translated into local languages and published by well-known presses. In northern India, the most important version of this translation was produced in Urdu, the primary language of the literate classes, since Hindi was not yet extensively used in the region.[53] The task was handed to Sir William Muir, secretary to the lieutenant governor of the North-Western Provinces (a region that now is mostly in the state of Uttar Pradesh).[54] At Muir's side was an promising Urdu scholar, Nazeer Ahmed.

Nazeer Ahmed was born just outside of Bijnour in 1831 and received his early education in Arabic and Persian from his father, Sayid Sa'adat 'Ali. He then began studying under other local scholars, but he could not complete his studies as his family moved to Delhi to search for better job opportunities. While in Delhi, he spent most of his time in the local mosque, continuing his education and studying *hadith* under the local imam, Muhammad 'Abd al-Khaliq. During this time, Nazeer Ahmed began to show promise as a student, and the imam was so impressed with his abilities that he offered Nazeer Ahmed his daughter in marriage.

At the same time, Nazeer Ahmed developed an academic relationship with the primary Arabic professor of the Delhi College, Mamluk 'Ali Nanutavi, and expressed a desire to join the institute officially. However, his father forbade it. The professor nevertheless agreed to help Nazeer

Ahmed by allowing the younger man to accompany him to school every day, teaching him while they were on the road. Their unofficial relationship continued until Nazeer Ahmed's father finally relented and allowed him to join the Delhi College and complete his studies of the Nizamiya system. While he was at the college, John Henry Taylor (a British officer who was secretary to the Local Agency of Delhi and a central figure at the Delhi College) frequently met with Ahmed. Taylor encouraged Ahmed to pursue higher studies in English. However, this suggestion met with an even stronger response from Ahmed's father, who said that he would rather face death than have his son learn the language of the British.

Following his graduation, Nazeer Ahmed immediately found work in the British education system. He started as an instructor but was quickly being promoted to the position of deputy inspector for schools in Gujarat (Punjab) under the direction of Sir Richard Temple. During the events of 1857, Ahmed and his family took refuge in a British neighborhood, and he reportedly saved the life of a British woman under attack by rebels. Following the reestablishment of British control over India, the British administration repaid him for his unwavering loyalty by appointing him inspector of schools in Allahabad.

It was there that the paths of Nazeer Ahmed and Sir William Muir crossed. Muir was stationed in Allahabad and had just been tasked with supervising the translation of the new Indian Penal Code into Urdu. Ahmed had just taken it upon himself to study English, and he reportedly mastered the language in a few short months. Two other Indian government employees were also brought in as translators: Karim Bakhsh, the minister of Western education, and 'Azamat Allah, the deputy inspector of schools in Shahjahanpur. The four men devised a system in which the latter two would be responsible for the translation, and every week they would send their results to Ahmed, who would edit their work and meet with Muir to discuss the translation's accuracy.

Nazeer Ahmed's biographer, Muhammad Mahdi, recorded an interesting moment during the translation process. One week the mail was delayed, and the translation of Bakhsh and Allah had not arrived. Afraid that he would have nothing to show to his supervisor, Nazeer Ahmed worked through the night and ended up translating far more than the typical weekly amount. Surprised that so much work had been done in a single week, Muir asked Ahmed who had done it. Ahmed answered that he had undertaken the translation on his own due to the mail delay. Muir was impressed at such an achievement and encouraged Ahmed to continue working directly on the translation in cooperation with Bakhsh and Allah, rather than simply acting as an editor.

Following his work on the translation of the Indian Penal Code, the British government rewarded Nazeer Ahmed by granting him high-ranking positions in the tax collection service—notably high ranks for an Indian subject in the post-1857 environment. Ahmed was called upon to help translate the Income Tax Act of 1860 and the Stamp Act of 1899, along with working on the translations of works written by British officials, such as the Resident of Kashmir. His translation work also caught the attention of other governments on the subcontinent, and he was offered a position in the government of Hyderabad under the rule of Salar Jung I. During this period, he advised the government on the reform of the education system and dedicated his free time to memorizing the Qur'an, a task that he had not been able to complete in his childhood. After Salar Jung I's death in 1883, his son and successor, Salar Jang II, fought with Ahmed and dismissed him from his post, forcing Ahmed to return to his family home in Delhi. He spent the rest of his life there, writing and advocating for the development of the Indian Muslim community. He supported Sir Syed Ahmed Khan's Aligarh Muslim University and founded charitable endowments to establish schools like the Islamiya High School in Etawah. Ahmed regularly taught and delivered lectures until he died in 1912.[55]

The resulting language of the Urdu translation of the Indian Penal Code was a reflection of Nazeer Ahmed's dual identities, English and Islamic: he took the English code and rendered it in an ideological and terminological form that was understandable to and applicable by Indian attorneys, defendants, and judges—many of whom were Muslim or had inherited the norms of an Islamic penal system applied during the Mughals and the early years of British occupation.

Beginning with the Urdu title, *Majmu'-e qawanin-e ta'zirat-e Hind*, Nazeer Ahmed attempted to place the new code within the classical Islamic legal concept of discretionary punishment *(ta'zir)*. He saw himself as continuing the tradition of integrating state law into the Islamic system. In an explanation of Ahmed's translation of the Penal Code, published in 1885, Babu Kunj Bihari Lal and Munshi Muhammad Nazir, both attorneys in the British court system, quoted Ahmed's definition of the term *"ta'zirat"* as "to make laws based on political authority *(siyasat karna)* or the issuance of rulings *(hukm)* upon the entire ruled population *(ra'aya)*."[56] The definition of *siyasa* given by Nazeer Ahmed is almost identical those presented in chapter 1 of this book, but it left out the eighteenth-century restrictions regarding the repetition of crime and followed more closely the general definition of Indian scholars of the later nineteenth century, such as 'Abd al-Hayy. Nazeer Ahmed employed a more expansive definition of *siyasa* in which the political authority, Muslim or not, was empowered to develop law within an Islamic context, thereby situating the Penal Code within the Islamic definition of discretionary punishment. In so doing, Ahmed was at the very least attempting to keep the code within the fold of Islamic law and did not view the British influence as antithetical or alien to the Indian context.

Where there was no local counterpart, Ahmed chose to translate English terms directly. This is most clearly noted in his transliteration of the word "India." Before the British presence in the subcontinent and until the transfer of authority to the British Crown in 1858, there was no concept of a united India, as the subcontinent was ruled by several different and periodically warring political entities. It was only in the second half of the nineteenth century and with the lead-up to the independence movements of the twentieth century that the idea of a united India began to appear.

The path Ahmed navigated between the code and Islamic legal norms can also be seen in the section regarding homicide—specifically in the classification of the crime. Ahmed translated the two English categories of murder and culpable homicide into *qatl-e 'amd* and *qatl-e insan mustalzim-e saza*. The first corresponded most closely to the nineteenth-century Hanafi legal understanding of intentional murder, so it was given a direct translation from classical Islamic sources in Arabic. In contrast, the second did not have an obvious counterpart in nineteenth-century Islamic legal texts. Therefore, Ahmed used the closest Urdu rendering of the English category, directly translated as "the killing of a person which necessitates punishment."

The content and meaning of the categorization mentioned and its relationship to Islamic law are set aside for a detailed discussion in chapter 3. However, it is essential to note here that Nazeer Ahmed was not interested in creating a code that simply moved English terms into Urdu. Instead of *ta'zir*, for example, he could just as easily have used *saza, 'uqubat, or jaza'*— all terms that denoted punishment in a more general sense. These terms were used by the other codes I surveyed, with the Egyptians using *'uqubat* while the Ottomans used *jaza'*. The difference is that the Egyptians and Ottomans were not dealing with the immediate crisis of Islamic authority or the question of whether law produced by a non-Muslim commission could have any relevance to Islamic law. The presence of these tensions made translating the Indian Penal Code unique. This point was not lost on the observers of Nazeer Ahmed's life and work. Mahdi noted in his biography that Nazeer Ahmed "created several legal terms that at the time had no equivalents in Urdu and [this achievement] was well received by contemporary specialists and laymen alike, including "criminal betrayal" *(khiyanat mujrimana)*, "from the methods of local custom" *(az ala haythiyat 'urfi)*, "attempted crime" *(iqdam-e jurm)*, "commission of a crime" *(irtikab-e jurm)*, "forced exploitation" *(istihsal bi-l-jabr)*, "intentional murder" *(qatl-e 'amd)*, [and] "unrestricted confinement" *(habs beja)*, among many others. All of these are examples of Nazeer Ahmed's intelligence and nature."[57]

Through the development and application of these terms that traced their Urdu versions to Persian, Arabic, or broader Islamic tradition, it can be seen that Nazeer Ahmed viewed the code he was charged with translating as within the Indian and Islamic legal traditions. His work was meant to create a sense of understanding among the Urdu-literate classes of India at the time, many of whom were Muslim or familiar with the Islamic criminal system that had been used in their territories for centuries. Therefore, although he did not have as much direct impact on the content of the law as Muhammad Qadri Basha did in Egypt, Nazeer Ahmed's translation of the Penal Code nevertheless expressed the exact desires of convergence and compatibility with Islamic norms.

Conclusion

The purpose of this chapter was to look at the lives of the people who worked on the penal codes implemented in the second half of the nineteenth century and the new institutions that educated them. From this analysis, two crucial theoretical points emerge: the relevance of institutional change and the role of translation.

Whether in the legal environment in Egypt, India, or even the broader Ottoman Empire, the institutions that created the scholars who developed the new penal codes were very different from those that had dominated legal culture in previous centuries. New degree programs, courses, and textbooks that were not part of the older Islamic curriculum were introduced. Many of the scholars who taught in places such as al-Azhar in Egypt were not directly involved in the education of the new legal class. However, the new educational institutions were not as divorced from their traditional counterparts as might be argued. For example, the Khedival Law School in Egypt evolved from the translation school founded by al-Tahtawi—who, although he completed his education in France, was grounded in the work of al-Azhar. Muhammad Qadri Basha's path was similar: before joining the School of Translators, he received his primary education at local schools that used the traditional curriculum. He never lost interest in studying traditional Islamic subjects throughout his education and professional life, regularly attending lectures at al-Azhar. And when he was tasked with creating the 1883 Penal Code, he enlisted the help of an Azhar-trained scholar, al-Bahrawi. In India, Nazeer Ahmed's completion of the Nizamiya curriculum, the standard approach to Islamic studies on the subcontinent, was facilitated by scholars at the Delhi College such as Mamluk 'Ali Nanutavi.

However, despite the presence of connections with prior educational systems, did the apparent differences between the traditional and new centers of education created in the nineteenth century mean that their graduates could still be considered to work within the context of the shari'a? This question strikes at the core of the definition of the shari'a. If the shari'a is understood only as that which is created or sanctioned by classically trained jurists (*fuqaha'*)—one of the elements of the "end of the shari'a" thesis outlined in the introduction to this book—then all those educated outside of the institutions that produce *fuqaha'* must be working in some realm other than that of Islamic law. The product of their endeavors, therefore, was secular or, as chapter 6 shows, man-made law (*qanun wad'i*).

However, few of the elites working on the new penal codes in the jurisdictions covered understood what they were doing as being outside the realm of the shari'a. This was not unique to Egypt and India. In the Ottoman Empire, one of the most often cited examples of the divide between Islamic and non-Islamic (or religious and secular) legal institutions in the nineteenth century is the Ottoman creation of State (*Nizamiye*) Courts in 1864. Many historians have seen this development as a move into "uncharted territory where incompatible legal systems, Islamic on the one hand, and secular, on the other, would exist and compete, generating confusion and conflict until the issue could eventually be resolved in favor of one or the other."[58] However, Avi Rubin has suggested that "litigants, state employees, and lawyers did not perceive their legal realities in terms of a dichotomy: secularity or religiosity."[59] Describing a similar situation in Egypt, Khaled Fahmy has expanded upon this thesis, showing that the use of state power, whether in the form of institutions or laws, was perceived by actors on the ground as necessary "not only to defend and protect the interests of the state but also to uphold and complement shari'a."[60]

Following the views of Rubin, Fahmy, and others, this book suggests that the shari'a should not be subject to institutional limitations, and that there is not necessarily a venue (educational or judicial) that is inherently *shar'i* while all others are not, by default. Instead, the shari'a is a process of engagement with the fundamental texts of Islam, the rules developed by the *fuqaha'*, and the circumstances of the time. That process can be executed—and the shari'a reached—regardless of where it occurs or who is doing it.

When it comes to the issue of translation, postcolonial studies have drawn attention to the fact that moving a text from one language to another involves much more than simply selecting terms. Rather, the translation of the texts discussed in this book arguably brought European knowledge and authority into the minds of local audiences and cemented ideas of Western superiority.[61] As seen in the lives of both Muhammad Qadri Basha and Nazeer Ahmed, the translation of European texts did have a significant influence on both their education and their resulting works. Still, there is no evidence that either of these two individuals were unaware of their local Islamic legal context or of what the adaptation of European influence meant for their own legal systems. Each noticed points of contention between Islamic and European understandings of the law. Categorizing their work as the product of an unconscious process of Westernization deprives them of agency, fails to recognize the intentions of their efforts, and effectively reduces the complex dynamics at play to the categories of colonizer and colonized.

Ultimately, the importance of the institutions in the nineteenth century and the scholars that they produced lay in the fact that they were able to comfortably navigate a changing legal landscape. By studying at new institutions, being exposed to different traditions, and working within a multicultural and multilingual environment, scholars such as Muhammad Qadri Basha and Nazeer Ahmed sought to balance Islamic and European legal understandings. They neither rejected the long-present rules of *fiqh* nor blindly accepted European norms. Instead, their efforts acted as a bridge, carefully negotiating increasing European influence and local needs based on Islamic legal understandings. They both saw points of agreement and disagreement with the European legal tradition and synthesized them with their Islamic tradition by adapting terminology and concepts (Nazeer Ahmed) and a point-by-point engagement with the law (Muhammad Qadri

Basha). In doing so, they attempted to solve the perceived problems of the existing system and enhance the implementation of justice, while at the same time reflecting a continuity of the process of the shari'a through new educational and legal institutions.

This concludes the first part of this book, which has discussed the social environment in which the new penal codes were formed and the lives and methodologies of those who created them. The next part of the book looks at the new penal codes themselves. Focusing on the topic of homicide, the following three chapters look at the content of the codes and their relationship to the Hanafi tradition, the dominant premodern school from which the codes sprung. The development of Hanafi law is presented chronologically, tracing the prevailing theory within the school through the centuries and placing the new codes at the end of that development—thereby arguing that the new codes should be interpreted as a continuation of a more extended history of legal development. The discussion begins with the classification of homicide and the role of the victim's family in prosecution (perhaps one of the most significant changes in the nineteenth century took place in that role). It then moves to the establishment of intent. Finally, it closes with subjects related to the status of the perpetrator that would mitigate the severity of punishment because that person was either underage, mentally insane, or acted in concert with others.

3

The Classification of Homicide

This chapter looks at the changes to the classification of homicide in the penal codes produced in the nineteenth century. In precolonial Islamic systems, criminal theory was based on a growing tension between opposing ideas. On the one hand, jurists, based on the fear that executing a criminal without the absolute certainty of their guilt would result in a tremendous religious injustice, created an increasingly complex system of classification that attempted to avoid the most extreme punishment of execution and favored the payment of blood money *(diya)*. On the other hand, political authorities sought and needed extra leeway in punishment because they felt that harsher penalties fulfilled the law's true objective: to deter potential offenders *(rad')*.

This conflict resulted in a compromise at the end of the classical period wherein the political authorities were able to administer harsher punishments through the concept of *siyasa* and *ta'zir*, with legal scholars acting as a balance to limit the reach of political authority. This compromise took a different turn in the nineteenth century, as state power increased and both the legal and judicial systems were changed. When these changes occurred, many jurists either condoned or participated in them. As this chapter shows, even Muslim law officers in India worked in British courts to find ways for colonial judges to punish convicted murderers outside of the juristic classification system.

When it came to constructing the new penal codes in the second half of the century, scholars preferred simplified classifications of crime. Armed with the belief that crime reduction could be achieved only through clear and evenly applied laws, they created the possibility for a significant increase in the number of murderers punished by execution. They also sometimes sought solutions from outside the dominant legal schools of their region (the Hanafi tradition in the Ottoman Empire and Egypt) and incorporated alternative approaches (such as those of the Malikis) to construct laws that better suited their new circumstances. This is most clear in the Egyptian context, where scholars working in an otherwise Hanafi-dominated environment adopted Maliki understandings.

The most significant change to homicide law during the nineteenth century, and the largest point of contention for Muslim scholars and observers of the law, is that prosecution was placed in the hands of the state. In *fiqh*, homicide was almost always constructed as a crime of personal retaliation *(qisas)*. In contrast, the new codes removed the power of the victim's family to bring forth the perpetrator and placed the burden of prosecuting criminals on the state instead. Although this appears to be a significant divergence from traditional juristic norms, those working on the codes were aware of this change and worked to justify it through the deployment of a classical principle of criminal theory: the state needed to intervene to prevent blood feuds and endless cycles of retaliation. This understanding was not new to the Islamic world: it was found in the exegeses of Qur'anic verses on *qisas*. However, its application to justify the right of the state to prosecute homicide represented the climax of a conflict between the state and traditional Muslim scholars.

To analyze the content of the codes, it is necessary to provide an overview of how the dominant Islamic school of law (the Hanafi school) in each of these jurisdictions approached the issue of classification of homicide before the nineteenth century. This also requires a description of the reasons for punishment and the tension within juristic discourse between a desire to reduce punishment in cases of doubt and allowing the state to implement harsher penalties in the name of protecting society. This is illustrated below through the specific example of muftis in the courts of British India in the first half of the nineteenth century. The chapter then turns to the codes and how the categories of punishment compared to those constructed in the Hanafi school. It begins with the Indian Penal Code (IPC) and then moves to the Ottoman and Egyptian codes. The chapter concludes with a discussion of the shift in the new codes from understanding *qisas* as a crime against the victim's family to seeing it as a crime against society (represented by the state) and how the explainers of the codes justified that shift.

Developing Hanafi Doctrine

In Hanafi *fiqh* works, homicide was considered as part of a general category of crimes termed *jinayat*, meaning an assault of one person on another by taking their life or limb. This category included personal injury and homicide.

In the early centuries of Hanafi legal theory, there were three different ways that a person could kill another: intentionally *('amd)*, semi-intentionally *(shibh 'amd)*, and wrongfully *(khata')*. According to the tenth-century Egyptian scholar Ahmad b. Muhammad al-Tahawi (d. 321/935), *'amd* occurred when one individual intentionally attacked another with a weapon designed to kill (like a sword or a spear), with death as the ultimate result. For a crime to be considered *'amd*, death did not have to occur immediately. Even if the victim died from their injuries within a few days, the crime was still deemed to be intentional. The punishment for *'amd* was the execution of the perpetrator, unless the victim's relatives accepted the payment of blood money *(diya)*, defined as one hundred camels (or their equivalent monetary value) divided into four categories of twenty-five, each of varying quality. Alternatively, the perpetrator could negotiate with the victim's family to settle on a lower amount of blood money or even seek forgiveness *('afu)* that would mitigate the penalty entirely.

At the opposite end of the spectrum, *khata'* included instances in which one person was killed, but the perpetrator intended to kill someone else. This category involved only a financial payment given to the victim's family, defined as the monetary equivalent of a hundred female camels, divided into five separate categories of twenty, each having a varying value. Again, a negotiation could occur between the victim's family and the perpetrator to mitigate the sentence. An example of such a crime would be if a person threw a spear at someone, mistaking them for an enemy soldier or an apostate.

The intermediate category, *shibh 'amd*, covered instances in which a person was intentionally attacked and killed, but the act was carried out with a weapon that was not designed to kill or would not typically be used for an act of homicide. Al-Tahawi gave examples of a switch, a wooden stick, or a slap of the hand. He added as an exception cases in which a weapon could be repeatedly used to the point that it might be conceived *(mawhum)* to cause death: in such cases, the crime would be raised to the category of *'amd*. The punishment for *shibh 'amd* was paying a larger amount of blood money *(diya mughallaza)*, the monetary value of a hundred female camels from the most expensive category.[1]

The first two categories of homicide, intentional and wrongful, find their textual backing in the Qur'an, in Surat al-Nisa':

Never should a believer kill a believer, but (if it so happens) by mistake *(khata'an)*, (compensation is due): If one (so) kills a believer, it is ordained that he should free a believing slave, and pay compensation to the deceased's family, unless they remit it freely.

If a man kills a believer intentionally *(muta'ammidan)*, his recompense is hell, to abide therein (forever): and the wrath and curse of Allah are upon him, and a dreadful penalty is prepared for him.[2]

The worldly punishment for intentional homicide came from a *hadith* in which the Prophet is reported to have said, "Intentional homicide [necessitates] execution *(al-'amd qawad)*." This *hadith* is found in two collections: the *Musannaf* of 'Abd Allah b. Muhammad b. Abi Shayba (d. 235/849) and the *Sunan* of 'Ali b. 'Umar al-Darqutni (d. 385/995).[3]

Hanafi jurists used a court judgment made by the Prophet to develop the third category of semi-intentional homicide. In this case, two women from the Hudhayl tribe were fighting with one another, and one woman picked up a rock and threw it at the other, killing her and her unborn child. The victim's family then approached the Prophet with the situation, and he ruled that the death would require enhanced blood money to be paid by the perpetrator's family to the family of the victim.[4] The Prophet did not suggest the death penalty from the outset, although it was clear that such a punishment was warranted as all of the criteria—intent, act, and correct target—had been fulfilled. The only element that differed here was the weapon: a single rock is typically unlikely to cause death, particularly of both a woman and her unborn child.

During the time of al-Tahawi, the early period of legal development, Hanafi law left out other situations in which death occurs and punishment is usually warranted, including deaths that occurred from secondary actions in which no specific intent to kill existed—for example, when a person died because of another's unrelated legitimate or illegitimate acts. This and other categories were developed slightly later, beginning with the Central Asian scholar Abu Bakr b. Mas'ud al-Kasani (d. 587/1191). He defined three different categories of homicide, two of which—*'amd* and *shibh 'amd*—were similar to those proposed by al-Tahawi. However, in the third category of wrongful homicide, *khata'*, al-Kasani broke from al-Tahawi's concept and identified two subcategories: "Wrongful homicide could occur in the act itself or the mind of the perpetrator. The first is in situations in which a person intends to strike a game but injures a man or that he intends to hit a particular person but injures someone else. The second is when a person attacks another with the belief that he is an enemy combatant or apostate, but [in fact] he is a Muslim."[5]

Both of these categories required the payment of blood money, though the payment could be forgiven by the victim's family. Al-Kasani therefore expanded the realm of homicide to include a broader range of instances in which death occurred.

However, there remained cases in which no intention to kill existed. Two other scholars filled in this gap: the Iraqi Ahmad b. Muhammad al-Quduri (d. 428/1036) and the Central Asian jurist 'Ali b. Abi Bakr al-Marghinani (d. 593 /1197). Their works, which would spark numerous commentaries and become primary texts taught in the later Ottoman and South Asian education systems,[6] added two additional categories: crimes that met the same criteria as wrongful killing *(ma ujriya majra al-khata')* and killing as a secondary outcome of an action *(al-qatl bi-sabab)*. The first category included instances of death in which intent to kill was not present but in which death occurred as an immediate result of a person's action, with the classical example being a person rolling over onto and killing another in their sleep. The second covered instances of death occurring as the secondary result of an action carried out by an individual: for example, when a person had dug a hole in a public street and someone else fell in and died.

In summary, the Hanafi school developed a total of five categories of homicide: (1) intentional, (2) semi-intentional, (3) wrongful, (4) that which meets the same criteria as wrongful, and (5) killing as the secondary outcome of an action. These categories would remain largely fixed for the remainder of Hanafi legal history, and jurists made only minor adjustments to their definitions and boundaries. For example, the last prominent writer in the Hanafi school, the late eighteenth- and early nineteenth-century scholar Muhammad Amin b. 'Abidin (d. 1252/1836) confirmed these categories yet stated that there were other instances of death that they did not include. However, he held that these other instances do not belong in a discussion of *jinayat* because they do not warrant the punishments of execution or the payment of blood money, nor do they include the same secondary legal and spiritual repercussions as those discussed in this section.[7]

Thus, the history of categorization of homicide within the Hanafi school began with a simplified system that covered only types of death in which intent was present. This slowly developed into a system that included most instances in which death occurred. While the spectrum of punishable offenses widened throughout Hanafi legal history, the area of the law that required the highest penalty of execution remained limited to cases in which a deadly weapon was used. The use of the weapon in establishing intent will be set aside for the moment, as it is the focus of chapter 4. This chapter will proceed with a discussion of the underlying methodology behind this categorization of crime and the desire to lessen the application of the most extreme punishments.

Avoiding Punishment and the Doubt Canon

The apparent question throughout the previous section is: why did Hanafi scholars create a system in which only the most certain cases of intentional homicide would be punished by execution? Al-Kasani answered that by stating: "The fourth condition [for applying retaliation] is that the death must have been carried out with a clear intention, without the *doubt (shubha)* that intent was not present, as the Prophet's statement 'intentional murder [necessitates] execution' carries the condition that it be completely free from all other elements. Such completeness cannot exist with doubt of intent because doubt in this area of the law carries with it the assumption of fact."[8]

In al-Kasani's statement, he referred to the concept of *shubha*, or the idea that a punishment mandated by religious law cannot be carried out unless it is free of all forms of doubt. As described by Intisar Rabb in her study of fixed criminal punishments *(hudud)* as the "doubt canon," Islamic legal scholars internalized the idea that the harshest penalties were to be avoided in as many cases as possible. Regarding execution for murder, Rabb cited the origins of this principle in an early case she termed "the Case of the Falsely Accused Butcher." During the rule of the fourth Rightly Guided Caliph 'Ali (d. 40/661), a man was found standing over a murdered body holding a bloody knife. The man was arrested and immediately confessed, after which he was brought in front of the caliph. Before the sentence was carried out, another man rushed forward and claimed that he had committed the crime. In the face of contradictory confessions, 'Ali chose to avoid punishment, letting both men go free.[9]

Although critical to understanding the underlying methodology and principles that drove *fiqh* discourse, Rabb's analysis raises two issues. The first is that, while the development and application of the doubt canon in Islamic legal history are well documented in *hudud*, they are more difficult to trace in the realm of homicide and personal injury *(qisas)*. Aside from the falsely accused butcher, Rabb's table of twenty-four early cases in which punishment was avoided mentions only instances of *hudud* crimes and not crimes of personal injury or homicide.[10]

The second issue is that Rabb relied almost entirely on *fiqh* works for her historical narrative after the doubt canon was adopted, in the first centuries of Islam. The role of the political authority, court cases, and other works are notably absent from her discussion. Therefore, the image of Islamic law from the point of view of jurists is well established. However, the question remains: what happened on the ground? The lenity offered by the doubt constructions of jurists, vital as it is for offenders, must therefore be analyzed together with other state concerns.

During the nineteenth century, clear instances of the application of the doubt canon can be found in the courts. In one case from the Egyptian city of Damanhur in 1861, a man named Abu Iltija' Abi Zayd was charged with severely beating his wife, who died from her injuries three days later. During the court proceedings, the defendant confirmed that his wife had died. However, he claimed that he had never laid a hand on her, and that she had fallen ill six days before dying: a natural illness placed upon her by God had caused her death. The court then asked for further investigation, and witnesses were brought forward who testified that they had seen the deceased's body. It appeared to them that she had been severely beaten with either a staff or a whip. The court found this evidence sufficient to convict and, as there was no specific intent to cause death from the beating, ordered that the defendant pay a reduced amount of blood money.[11] The presence of the marks on the wife's body matched the initial charges brought against the husband, and the presence of multiple witnesses fulfilled all the requirements necessary to either execute him or allow the victim's family to ask for an aggravated amount of blood money. However, the court chose not to follow this path and instead used the doubt about the exact cause of death to mitigate the sentence.

Ibn 'Abidin, writing about the conditions for applying *qisas*, stated that the general legal maxim regarding avoiding punishment—"avoid criminal punishments in cases of doubt" *(idra'u al-hudud bi-l-shubuhat)*—was used in the area of homicide. However, it was qualified with seven exceptions. Three of these are significant for the present discussion: (1) a judge may rule for punishment based on circumstantial evidence where in *hudud* he may not; (2) there is no statute of limitations for witnesses in cases of *qisas*; and (3) written testimony and the indication of mutes is acceptable in cases of *qisas* while in *hudud* it is not.[12] With these exceptions, Ibn 'Abidin expanded the applicability of punishment for homicide and personal injury beyond the more stringent evidentiary requirements of the *hudud*—which, in theory, would allow convictions only with the presence of at least two male witnesses or the confession of the accused.

Ibn 'Abidin may have chosen this method because while the *hudud* crimes such as fornication, public drunkenness, and theft deal mainly with personal violations of morality, the crime of murder created a more general and immediate threat to public security. When investigating the reasons behind the implementation of the rules of *qisas*, jurists often spoke about the pre-Islamic tendency toward blood feuds. If one person from a particular tribe was murdered, it often led to back-and-forth revenge killings that would throw the entire society into disarray. The Qur'anic verse cited as justification is "In the Law of Equality there is (saving of) life to you, O ye men of understanding; that ye may restrain yourselves."[13] One of the early explanations of this verse by Muhammad b. Jarir al-Tabari (d. 310/923) mentioned that it was revealed by God "to prevent you from killing one another, as a strike [to restrain] you against [harming] one another, and with this, you are brought to life, as My ruling between you is life."[14] In a much later explanation by the early twentieth-century scholar Muhammad al-Tahir b. 'Ashur (d. 1973), the rulings of *qisas* "ensure that those on both sides [of the conflict] accept the ruling . . . as in [the verse] is a deterrent against killing . . . and if the issue were left to blood feuds as in pre-Islamic Arabia [people] would become extreme and start a chain of killing."[15] This sentiment was also echoed in the *hadith*, with the Prophet reported to have said, "Do not return after my [death] to disbelief, striking the necks of one another."[16]

Stemming from this desire to protect and control society, both judges and political authorities regularly expanded their reach beyond the restrictions of *fiqh* and issued additional punishments to murderers. For example, Christian Lange has documented how the military governors and their police force *(shihna)* in the Seljuq period regularly investigated and prosecuted murderers outside of the court system, sending many of them to be hanged in a public display.[17] In the Ottoman Empire, the sultan and his governors did the same. Armed with the legal authority of local custom *('urf)*, political authority *(siyasa)*, and discretionary punishment *(ta'zir)*, the empire executed individuals (including those convicted of homicide) based on the notion of protecting the society and the political regime.[18] During the first half of the nineteenth century in India, Muslim law officers in British courts would continue this tradition of stretching the classical rules of punishment to allow British judges to give murderers sentences of execution or impose other penalties.

Muftis in India: Adapting to Accommodate Punishment

During the first half of the nineteenth century in the courts of British India, the British sessions judge would often sit with a local counterpart, such as a Muslim mufti, who would issue a ruling on each case according to custom. The fatwa of a mufti was not always necessary, and British judges increasingly relied upon juries made up of around three high-ranking community members. However, the judge frequently agreed with the fatwa when a mufti was called upon. And in cases when the sessions judge and mufti disagreed—a matter that would necessitate an appeal to the higher court, known as the Nizamut Adawlut—the appellate judges would usually side with the mufti and follow his recommendation for punishment, overturning the ruling of the initial British judge.

For example, in one case adjudicated in Bengal in 1854, five defendants were charged with the willful murder of a person named Manik Bangal in a fight following the discovery of an affair between one of the defendants (Upoorbokisto Mundul) and a widow in the victim's family. The mufti acquitted all of the defendants, stating that the eyewitnesses' testimony was questionable because they had all taken part in covering up the affair. However, the sessions judge disagreed and sentenced one defendant to life in prison and three others to seven years in prison. Upon review, the appellate judges (A. Dick and B. J. Colvin) remarked that the mufti was correct in his suspicion of the witnesses' testimony and overruled the conviction, acquitting all of the defendants and ordering their immediate release.[19]

There is some evidence that the British were concerned about the competence of muftis and whether they could view the circumstances of a case without prejudice. For example, in one case from Bengal in 1854, two defendants, Gowhur Ally and Choolahee Singh Rajpoot, were accused of carrying out the murder of a former police officer named Dhoomun Khan. The crime occurred in a bazaar in broad daylight, and the defendants were a well-known group of bandits, resulting in the prosecution presenting numerous eyewitnesses. The mufti believed that the charges were trumped up and acquitted both prisoners. However, according to the sessions judge, the mufti "labors very incorrectly and in a very strained manner . . . to discredit the evidence for the prosecution, which, he is of opinion, is got up." The judge then implied that this was because the gang of bandits could have intimidated the mufti—something they apparently did to the eyewitnesses, torturing them to change their testimony. In this case, the appellate judges sided with the sessions judge, sentencing both defendants to fourteen years in prison.[20]

Aside from these limited examples, the cases surveyed for this book show that the relationship between the muftis and the British judges in India was primarily one of cooperation, which can be seen in the classification of punishments for homicide issued in their fatwas. Muftis issued punishments within five different categories. The first three were standard applications of Islamic legal theory and fit within the classification of homicide discussed above: (1) kisas (Arabic *qisas*), the death penalty; (2) diyyut (Arabic *diya*), the payment of blood money; and (3) seasut (Arabic *siyasa*), discretionary punishment defined by the state.

For example, in a case from Bengal in 1854, four defendants were charged with the murder of a woman named Mussumat Gungea and with stealing jewelry that she had bought for her son. During the investigation, it was clear that only one defendant (Sobow) had borrowed a sword and committed the murder, while the other three defendants had only gone to the woman's house later upon Sobow's command and taken the jewelry. Sobow confessed in front of the police magistrate but recanted when brought in front of the lower court. Two female eyewitnesses were brought forward, and based upon their evidence and Sowbow's earlier confession, the mufti issued a fatwa of willful murder that "makes him liable to capital punishment by *kisas*." Another defendant (Bissessur) was convicted of the robbery and held "liable by '*tazeer*.'" The mufti acquitted the other two defendants of any wrongdoing. The sessions judge approved the conviction and sentenced Sowbow to capital punishment and Bissessur to five years imprisonment. Upon review, however, the appellate court disagreed with both the mufti and the sessions judge, citing the medical report indicating that Mussumat Gungea had not died as a direct result of the injuries caused to her by Sobow, and ultimately reduced his sentence to life in prison.[21]

In another case from Bengal in 1853, a defendant (Kirtinarain Shaha) was charged with the murder of his niece, after which he attempted suicide. The fatwa convicted him and called for discretionary punishment *(seasut)*, and the sessions judge agreed. In his final review, the appellate judge (J. Dunbar) considered the fact that the defendant had been repeatedly committed to an insane asylum and acquitted him of the charge, while ordering him to stay in a mental hospital until the doctors were assured of his treatment and recovery.[22] In this particular situation, all of the evidentiary requirements of

Hanafi *fiqh* had been met: the defendant had confessed on multiple occasions to the crime with which he was charged. Under Hanafi law, if the question of insanity were raised, it would be negated as the defendant had freely admitted his guilt and did not appear insane at the time of the case. However, the mufti was clearly concerned about the defendant's repeated commitment for insanity and deferred the final details of the ruling to the state.[23]

The final two categories of punishment used by the muftis in their fatwas are not found within standard works of Hanafi law: (1) *'uqubat* (punishment); and (2) *uqubat-e-shadid* (severe punishment). For example, in Bengal in 1853, a man (Sooltan Bhueemya) was charged with the murder of his lover's husband, Pauchcowree. The fatwa, based on medical evidence and the testimony of another person (Roostom) who had reached the scene of the crime and seen the defendant running away, "convicts the prisoner of the murder charged, on strong presumption, and declares him liable to the punishment of *'uqubat*." The sessions judge agreed and ordered the death penalty, which the appellate court confirmed upon appeal.[24]

In this case, the mufti could not directly convict the prisoner of any of the traditional punishments found in Islamic law. No eyewitness evidence had been provided, and absolute certainty could not be established. In addition, most standardized fatwa collections did not punish a defendant who murdered his wife and/or her lover if he caught them having unlawful intercourse.[25] However, the circumstances of the case were clear, and the defendant provided no witnesses in his defense. To ensure that the rights of the deceased and his family were preserved and to facilitate the punishment sought by the British, the mufti issued a conviction, and the sessions judge then recommended the severest punishment available in law. In another instance, the same fatwa was issued to convict accomplices to a murder, a case in which the sessions judge issued and the appellate court confirmed a sentence of life in prison.[26]

Each of these cases shows that during the first half of the nineteenth century, the muftis who worked in British courts regularly adapted categories of punishment created by Hanafi jurists to allow punishment to be carried out by the state. In so doing, the muftis ensured that rulings issued by the British judges were well within the Islamic guidelines and retained legal legitimacy. Even when the categories established by Hanafi jurists conflicted with the circumstances of the case at hand, the mufti issued recommendations that supported the British understandings of law. For example, in the 1854 case of *Government v. Nusseeruddeen*, a man was arrested for the murder of his son. Based on his confession, the fatwa "declare[d] him liable to discretionary punishment extending to death by *akoobat*." The appellate court confirmed the verdict, and the man was sentenced to death.[27] In classical Islamic legal theory, punishment would not be imposed for such a crime, and only *diya* would be required from the father.[28] However, the mufti had no problem with calling for the death penalty and left it to the British judges to make the final decision.

In an 1853 case from Delhi, a woman named Mussumat Oodee was charged with the willful murder of her five-week-old child, Kishna, who had been found suffocated to death and wrapped up on a bench outside her home. The investigation turned up no direct evidence that Mussumat Oodee had committed the crime, but it was discovered from questioning her family and other community members that Kishna was the product of a relationship between her and a man named Goomanee, and that she had run away from her husband. Her husband had then gotten the court to order her to return home. She had threatened to get back at her husband by framing him and other members of his family for the murder of the child, and it was upon this circumstantial evidence that the mufti issued a verdict of guilty and declared her liable for severe punishment (*'uqubat-e shadid*). The sessions judge agreed and requested the death penalty, which the appellate court approved.[29] In this case, a child found dead from exposure to the elements would not have required a punishment under Islamic law unless someone was accused of placing them outside,[30] and no direct evidence was available that Mussumat Oodee had committed the murder. Regardless, the mufti decided to issue his fatwa to support the British judge's desire to execute her.

With the implementation of the IPC and the judicial reforms that followed, the position of mufti was removed, and only a British judge, usually supported by a jury, was responsible for deciding cases. For many observers, removing the position of mufti meant an end to the role of Islamic law and the system of Anglo-Muhammadan law.[31] However, as argued below, the IPC incorporated many concepts of Hanafi law, and the influence of Islam continued even without the facilitation of muftis.

Categorization in the Indian Penal Code

The IPC placed all instances of bodily harm in chapter 16, titled "Of Offences Affecting the Human Body," which included not only homicide but also offenses involving physical harm. It excluded instances in which homicide was either accidental, "where death is caused by accident or misfortune without any criminal intention or knowledge by one who does a lawful act in a lawful manner and with proper care and caution,"[32] or justified, "where the taking away of life is justified because it is taken by a judicial act, or in pursuance of a judicial sentence pronounced by some Court or Judge, or because it is taken in the exercise of a power given, or supposed in good faith to be given, by law."[33]

This categorization mirrored that of the Hanafi school, which combined rulings dealing with homicide and other forms of bodily harm in a single chapter. According to Ibn 'Abidin, *jinayat* were legally defined as "forbidden actions that impact assets or the person. Legal scholars have [created] special categories of usurpation *(ghasb)* and theft *(sariqa)* for those that impact assets, and *jinaya* for those that impact the person or [his] extremities." Excluded was "killing that is legally permissible *(al-ma'dhun bihi shar'an)* such as [legally sanctioned] retaliation *(qisas)* or stoning."[34] However, this differs from the IPC, as Ibn 'Abidin included in this chapter acts that would be considered accidental in the category discussed above as those that met the same criteria as wrongful homicide *(ma ujriya majra al-khata')*. The IPC continued by creating a general category of culpable homicide in article 299, which stated, "Whoever causes death by doing an act with the intention of causing death, or with the intention of causing such bodily injury as is likely to cause death, or with the knowledge that he is likely by such act to cause death, commits the offence of culpable homicide." The code provided examples of this category:

1. A lays sticks and turf over a pit, with the intention of thereby causing death, or with the knowledge that death is likely to be thereby caused. Z, believing the ground to be firm, treads on it, falls in, and is killed. A has committed the offence of culpable homicide.
2. A knows Z to be behind a bush. B does not know it. A, intending to cause, or knowing it to be likely to cause Z's death, induces B to fire at the bush. B fires and kills Z. Here B may be guilty of no offence; but A has committed the offence of culpable homicide.
3. A, by shooting at a fowl with intent to kill and steal it, kills B, who is behind a bush, A not knowing that he was there. Here, although A was doing an unlawful act, he is not guilty of culpable homicide, as he did not intend to kill B, or cause death by doing an act that he knew was likely to cause death.[35]

The first example can be found in Hanafi *fiqh*, but there it is sometimes as a tort and not personal injury *(qisas)*. If only injury occurred, it would be prosecuted as a tort, with the digger required to pay compensation *(daman)* for the physical damage to the victim. Alternatively, the outcome of death would classify it in the later Hanafi category of killing as the secondary outcome of an action *(al-qatl bi-sabab)*, subjecting the digger to the payment of blood money or discretionary punishment. However, Muslim jurists would have made a critical distinction between a pit dug on the digger's property, one dug on a regularly traveled path, and one dug in the middle of the wilderness. They would also have distinguished between a pit dug with the permission of the political authority (the imam) and one dug without that permission. A person who digs a pit is criminally liable only if it was dug outside of his property, on a path used by others *(tariq)*, and without the permission of the political authority.[36] In other situations, the Hanafis would rule the death as not criminal. This seems to fit with the IPC, particularly as pits dug without permission on a public path would have been done "with the knowledge that death is likely to be thereby caused."[37] Those dug on an individual's private property, in the wilderness, and/or with the permission of the political authority would not fulfill this condition of the code. Therefore, the main difference is that the IPC definition has clearly moved this type of activity out of the category of tort and into that of homicide. In contrast, Hanafi *fiqh*, although accepting a degree of criminal liability for the digger had the conditions been met, kept this type of activity within the realm of financial compensation. In the second example, the IPC and Hanafi *fiqh* match, as Hanafi scholars would hold "A" criminally responsible for the death but not for intentional killing because he committed the act through his agent.[38] "B" would not be held criminally responsible for the death at all, as he did not know that "Z" was there.

The third example is particularly important as it separated out death that occurred during the commission of another criminal act. This was a common element in nineteenth-century European criminal law, particularly in Britain—where it was known as the "felony-murder rule" and remained an element in British criminal law until that was altered in 1957.[39] However, the concept still exists in a lesser category known as constructive manslaughter.[40] It is essential to note here that the IPC took an approach opposite to that dominant in Britain and chose to follow more closely the understanding established within the Hanafi school—seeing constructive manslaughter as only wrongful *(khata')*. According to article 300, culpable homicide could be aggravated to the crime of murder:

> If the act by which the death is caused is done with the intention of causing death, or
>
> Secondly, if it is done with the intention of causing such bodily injury as the offender knows to be likely to cause the death of the person to whom the harm is caused, or
>
> Thirdly, if it is done with the intention of causing bodily injury to any person and the bodily injury intended to be inflicted is sufficient in the ordinary course of nature to cause death, or
>
> Fourthly, if the person committing the act knows that it is so imminently dangerous that it must in all probability cause death or such bodily injury as is likely to cause death, and commits such act without any excuse for incurring the risk of causing death or such injury as aforesaid.[41]

The code gave the following examples:

1. A shoots Z with the intention of killing him. Z dies in consequence. A commits murder.
2. A, knowing that Z is laboring under such a disease that a blow is likely to cause death, strikes him with the intention of causing bodily injury. Z dies in consequence of the blow. A is guilty of murder, although the blow might not have been sufficient in the ordinary course of nature to cause the death of a person in a sound state of health. But if A, not knowing that Z is laboring under any disease, gives him such a blow as would not in the ordinary course of nature kill a person in a sound state of health, here A, although he may intend to cause bodily injury, is not guilty of murder, if he did not intend to cause death, or such bodily injury as in the ordinary course of nature would cause death.
3. A intentionally gives Z a sword-cut or club-wound sufficient to cause the death of a man in the ordinary course of nature. Z dies in consequence. Here A is guilty of murder, although he may not have intended to cause Z's death.
4. A, without any excuse, fires a loaded cannon into a crowd of persons and kills one of them. A is guilty of murder, although he may not have had a premeditated design to kill any particular individual.[42]

Therefore, according to the IPC, there were two differences between culpable homicide and murder: the gravity of the act (examples 1–4) and the direct intent of the perpetrator to cause death (examples 1–3). As in the category of culpable homicide, the illustrations for murder closely followed examples found in the Hanafi school. The first example would fall in the category of intentional ('amd), with the identity of the weapon being the deciding factor. The issue of the weapon and its place in establishing intent is left for chapter 4, as it necessitates a much longer discussion. It is sufficient here to note that by the nineteenth century, particularly according to Ibn 'Abidin, example one would have fallen in the category of intentional homicide, as a gun was in the category of weapons that separate body parts (tafriq al-ajza').[43]

The second example reflects a slight differentiation, as there is little evidence that the Hanafis considered the perpetrator's prior knowledge of the victim's condition. In one question regarding the extent of shared responsibility—in which one person struck a victim across the stomach, spilling his intestines, and another came later and slit his throat—the penalty would be applied to the person who slit his throat based on his intention (if he intended to cause death it would be 'amd and if not khata'), while the person who struck the stomach would be sentenced to pay one-third of the blood money. However, if it were clear that the victim would not have survived the initial strike to the stomach (judged by whether the victim would have lived for a day or so afterward), then the full penalty would be applied to the person who struck the stomach. The perpetrator of second strike would receive discretionary punishment.[44] In this situation, the victim's condition was considered, but there is no mention of whether the perpetrator's knowledge of the victim's change of surviving would have affected the punishment.

The third example is found in fatwa collections. According to the al-Fatawa al-'alamgiriya, "Whomsoever injures a man, and he remains in bed [from the injury] until he dies, then he must be executed."[45] Finally, the fourth example would also fall under intentional murder ('amd), as the killer was known and fired into the crowd intentionally to cause death. It would not be necessary to establish that a particular victim was intended. This would change only if the crowd killed an individual or the murderer was unknown. In the first case, it would necessitate a series of oaths made by each community member that they did not know who killed the victim (qasama). In the second case, the blood money for the victim would be paid by the state.[46]

Articles 302 and 304 of the IPC named the punishments for the crimes established. Murder was to be punished "with death, or transportation for life, and shall also be liable to fine," while culpable homicide

> shall be punished with transportation for life, or imprisonment of either description for a term which may extend to ten years, and shall also be liable to fine, if the act by which the death is caused is done with the intention of causing death or of causing such bodily injury as is likely to cause death; or with imprisonment of either description for a term which may extend to ten years, or with a fine, or with both, if the act is done with the knowledge that it is likely to cause death, but without any intention to cause death or to cause such bodily injury as is likely to cause death.[47]

It is in punishments where the IPC differed significantly from the Hanafi school. As mentioned above, in a case of intentional murder, the culprit would be executed, required to pay blood money, or forgiven. In contrast, the perpetrator of wrongful homicide would either be required to pay blood money or be forgiven by the victim's family. The IPC added the elements of fines and the punishment of prison. Punishment by fine could be understood as linked to the payment of blood money because it monetizes the value of human life, as was done within the Hanafi school. However, the fine would be paid to the state rather than the victim's family in this case. Paying a fine to the state is not entirely without precedent in Islamic legal history, as the Ottoman Empire regularly imposed financial penalties for crimes, including murder.[48] In some instances, these fines were meant to replace blood money. For example, the Ottoman criminal code produced by Sultan Suleyman I in the sixteenth century stated that if retaliation (qisas) in the form of execution or blood money was applied, "the shari'a will [thereby] have been executed; nothing else shall be claimed, and no fine is collected."[49] Otherwise, a series of fines would be payed to the state, determined by the perpetrator's financial status.

Imprisonment was also a regular feature of discretionary punishment (ta'zir) in fiqh discourse. Beginning with a case where the Prophet commanded the arrest of a group of people involved in a fight that resulted in a homicide, the concept of punitive detention was expanded to include accessories to manslaughter, highway robbery not involving homicide, and repeat offenders of hudud crimes.[50] As has been seen above in the work of muftis in nineteenth-century India, British courts regularly sentenced murderers to long prison terms, even life in prison, with the Islamic backing of the mufti's fatwa.

Therefore, the similarities between the IPC and the Hanafi school in the categorization of homicide represent a continuation of the content of Islamic law in the new code. Some of the examples presented in the code have almost verbatim counterparts in Hanafi fatwa collections, while others closely mirrored and were developed upon Hanafi understandings of law. This means that the IPC dealt directly with Hanafi law, at least concerning the categorization of homicide. For example, in the situation of the felony-murder rule, the code ignored the established law in Britain and chose an interpretation closer to the local context, dominated by Islamic understandings.

Recent analyses of the IPC have remarked that the committee responsible for constructing the code, led by Lord Thomas Babington Macaulay, had "radically reconstituted the existing English law."[51] One observer even states that Macaulay's classification of homicide was "an impressive model of progressive thinking and clear formulation quite outclassing the English Commissioner's contemporary efforts."[52] However, none of the authors of these studies was aware of the premodern Hanafi tradition or has attempted to find mentions of Macaulay's work in the discussions of other English jurists of the time. The analysis of the classification of homicide here shows a direct connection to Hanafi law as envisioned by jurists and practiced in Indian courts during the nineteenth century, although Macaulay never acknowledged local influences in his work.

There were also apparent differences and departures from the Hanafi tradition, most notably in the types of punishment and the removal of the rights of the victim's family. These can be connected directly to the changing nature of the state, which was one of the fundamental changes during the nineteenth century. The nature of this change, the evolution of the state's role in homicide, and the reaction from scholars working on the codes are discussed below.

Here, however, the chapter turns to how the Ottoman and Egyptian penal codes dealt with the classification of homicide and whether those codes contain the same similarities can be found with traditional understandings of *fiqh* present in the IPC.

The Ottoman and Egyptian Codes

The Ottoman Penal Code of 1858 defined four categories of homicide: intentional *('amd)*, unintentional *(ghayr mut'ammad)*, wrongful *(khata')*, and death that occurred as the result of an injury. Intentional homicide, punishable by execution or a prison sentence of twenty-five years to life, required that the perpetrator "constructed [the act] in his mind and settled upon it in his heart," a description of premeditation.[53] Unintentional homicide, in contrast, covered acts in which a perpetrator "killed a person out of intensity or an outburst of anger without premeditation."[54] The punishment for this category was fifteen years in prison. However, if the death occurred before, during, after, or in order to commit another crime, the punishment was execution. Wrongful *(khata')* homicide covered instances in which a person died due to another's actions or failure to follow the law. Explanations of the code provided the example of a man carrying a loaded gun in the street. If the gun went off accidentally and a person died as a result, the death would fall in this category, as carrying a loaded gun in the street was illegal. Crimes in this category were to be punished with a prison sentence ranging from six months to two years.[55] Finally, if a person died as the result of an injury inflicted by the perpetrator, and there was no intent to kill, the punishment would be imprisonment for no less than five years.[56]

The Egyptian Code of 1883 followed similar lines, with article 208 establishing intentional homicide *('amd)* as requiring the presence of premeditation *(sabq israr wa tarassud)* and necessitating execution. Article 213 mentioned that if premeditation did not exist, the punishment would be limited to fifteen years in prison. However, if the homicide took place during the commission of another crime, the penalty would be automatically raised to execution.[57] The category of wrongful homicide *(khata')* entailed death that occurred without intent or as a result of stupidity *(ru'una)*, a lack of precaution *(ihtiyat)* or care *(taharruz)*, or as the result of negligence *(ihmal)*.[58] Finally, death resulting from a grave bodily injury *(afda ila al-mawt)* was punished with 3–5 years in prison. If that injury was premeditated, the sentence was increased to 5–10 years in prison.[59]

Like the IPC, the Ottoman and Egyptian penal codes eliminated the Hanafi category of semi-intentional homicide *(shibh 'amd)*. Crimes that would have fit into that category were either moved up into intentional or down into wrongful killing. For example, the Prophetic case mentioned above in this chapter that was used to establish the category of semi-intentional homicide (a tribal fight in which a woman was killed by a rock thrown by the other party) would have fallen into the wrongful *(khata')* category in both the Ottoman and Egyptian penal codes as it occurred as the result of a fight and there was no clear intent to kill. Alternatively, choking a person to death, an act that would have typically been judged as semi-intentional by the Hanafis, would be considered intentional in the new codes. The new codes also consolidated the Hanafi category of wrongful killing *(khata')*, removing the distinctions created by later Hanafi scholars and returning to the more general classification found in the work of al-Tahawi.

Another substantial departure from the Hanafi school had to do with the factor of time. Both the Ottoman and Egyptian codes required that to be considered intentional *('amd)*, death had to occur at the moment of the attack. Conversely, the Hanafi school and the IPC allowed death to occur several days later and still fall within the realm of intentional. To cover this area, the Ottoman and Egyptian codes created a special category in which crimes that caused injuries leading to a later death would be separated from the other types of homicide.

In terms of punishment, the Ottoman and Egyptian codes exhibited two new elements. First, like the IPC, they widened the realm of execution. This is particularly the case in which the homicide took place as the result of another crime. In the explanation of the Ottoman code, the example of this was given when a man attempted to rape a woman who fought back or called for help. If in the attempt to continue the commission of the rape, the perpetrator killed the victim or those trying to stop him, the punishment was automatically increased to execution.[60] Second, unlike the IPC, the codes limited the payment of money paid to the state as fines and replaced them with terms in prison.

As a result, the Ottoman and Egyptian penal codes appear to have significantly more divergences from the Hanafi classification of homicide and its punishments than the IPC did. Scholars who support the "end of Shari'a" thesis have attributed this to the influence of French law, with evidence suggesting that these divergences reflect a direct application of the Napoleonic Code of 1810. For example, the Ottoman and Egyptian articles defining non-premeditated, premeditated, and wrongful homicide mirror the French Code's articles 295, 296, and 319, respectively.[61]

While there is no doubt that French influence was important in the development of these codes, it is also true that in the late eighteenth and early nineteenth centuries, the French participated in the study of Islamic law (particularly in the Maliki tradition) through their colonial holdings in North Africa. Muslim scholars working within the developing legal system, particularly in Egypt, were fully aware of these influences and produced works to emphasize the similarities between the French and Islamic legal traditions. In their view, the connection between the Maliki and French legal traditions meant that the resulting laws were still in line with Islamic understandings.

French Influence through Maliki Rulings

Looking deeper into the Maliki school can help explain many of the departures from the Hanafi tradition found in the Ottoman and Egyptian penal codes and show how comparative legal work ensured that Islamic law remained at the core of the new codes. For example, the Malikis never developed a category of semi-intentional murder (shibh 'amd), and jurists of this school treated all forms of murder as either intentional ('amd) or wrongful (khata'). The school's founder, Malik b. Anas (d. 179/795), was reported to have said, "I don't know what semi-intentional homicide is. Homicide is either intentional or wrongful."[62] As chapter 4 shows, the influence of the Malikis did not stop with classification. Their discussions on establishing intent and premeditation were also critical to creating the new penal codes in the Ottoman Empire and Egypt.

This notion appears to be a clear divergence from the past, since the law in both Egypt and the Ottoman Empire before the introduction of the new codes is usually seen as a product of Hanafi jurisprudence. The empire declared the Hanafis its official school and applied Hanafi jurisprudence to its provinces, such as Egypt. Reem Meshal has discussed this notion in detail, showing that through the empire's attempts to regulate law and procedure in the sixteenth century, the state created "a new social orthodoxy fundamentally at odds with the pluralism of Islamic law, its multiple schools, and their standing conventions on local custom."[63] This set the stage for the centralizing changes of the nineteenth century. The influence of the opinions of other schools is also key to understanding these historical developments, and Ahmed Fekry Ibrahim has argued that judges in the seventeenth and eighteenth centuries often resorted to a form of "pragmatic eclecticism," choosing to apply rulings from different schools if they met the needs of the case at hand.[64] For example, although an individual might have approached a Hanafi court, the judge might resort to a Maliki, Shafi'i, or Hanbali ruling. According to Ibrahim, this process was not unique to the Ottoman courts, and Islamic legal scholars regularly allowed the different positions of schools to be adopted if a case required it—albeit only by specialists.[65]

In the nineteenth century, the method of choice for many of the reformers in the Ottoman Empire and Egypt would be modifying their Hanafi background with Maliki understandings, and the work of French Orientalists heavily influenced that choice. In his work on the development of what he referred to as the "Franco-Egyptian" legal system, Leonard Wood placed the beginning of this process in French Algeria, with the intellectual movement that would culminate in the founding of the Algiers Law School (École de Droit d'Alger) in 1879.[66] During this period, which stretched back to the 1830s, the French colonial government "produced translations, critical editions of classical texts, historical studies, analytical studies, field manuals, and new codifications, both official and unofficial."[67] Many of the chosen texts, such as the *Mukhtasar* of Khalil b. Ishaq al-Jundi (d. 767/1374) and the *Tuhfat al-hukkam* of Muhammad b. 'Asim al-Andalusi (d. 869/1464), were standard manuals of the Maliki school. Wood argued that even Muhammad Qadri Basha's seminal work on civil law, the *Murshid al-hayran*, was directly influenced by a French work produced two years earlier by Édouard Sautayra and Eugène Cherbonneau.[68]

Egyptian scholars were therefore keenly aware of the French-Maliki connection, and other works that took this comparative approach appeared during the latter half of the nineteenth century. Aside from the work of Muhammad Qadri Basha discussed in chapter 2, the work of Muhammad Hasanayn b. Muhammad Makhluf al-'Adawi, known popularly as Makhluf al-Minyawi (d. 1878), stands out. Makhluf al-Minyawi was a judge by profession and had worked most of his life in the shari'a courts of Upper Egypt. In the 1860s, around the same time that Rifa'a Rafi' al-Tahtawi was tasked with translating the French codes, Khedive Isma'il ordered Makhluf al-Minyawi to produce a work comparing the Napoleonic Civil Code of 1804 with the rules of the Maliki school. The result closely followed the organization of Muhammad Qadri Basha's work on the same subject.[69] This tradition of comparing Islamic (read: Maliki) *fiqh* to French law would continue well into the twentieth century. Another author, 'Abd Allah 'Ali Husayn, would produce a work in the 1940s titled *Legislative Comparisons between Manmade Civil Law and Islamic Legislation*.[70] The changes to classifications show that the Ottoman and Egyptian penal codes reflect a substantial French and Maliki influence. That influence was filtered through the French colonial interaction with the Maliki tradition of North Africa, specifically in Algeria, and the use of Maliki rulings worked to temper French influence and ensured that it would comply with Islamic understandings.

From Personal to State Crime

As can be seen in each of these codes, the primary departure from the Islamic understanding was in the role of the state, as the family of the victim was removed from the equation and the prosecution of the crime of homicide was placed in the hands of the political authority. Typically, contemporary observers of Islamic law have viewed this difference as one of the most significant substantive changes in criminal law in the Muslim world. According to Rudolph Peters, "The most salient aspect of the Islamic law of homicide and bodily harm is the principle of private prosecution. The claims of the victim or of his next of kin are regarded as claims of men and not as claims of God. This means that the plaintiff is the *dominus litis* and that the prosecution, the continuation of the trial and the execution of the sentence are conditional upon his will."[71]

With the new codes, the punishment of homicide, once classified as being in the personal category of retaliation (*qisas*), had become a crime committed against society. However, this should be seen not as a radical divergence from Islam but rather as a gradual shift to a new position within Islamic legal practice that came to full fruition in the nineteenth century. Although rarely discussed in *fiqh* works, Muslim political authorities have regularly involved themselves in law since the inception of Islam, using the power of discretionary punishment to punish murderers—sometimes despite the wishes of the victim's family. For example, Radika Singha has noted that in nineteenth-century India, in cases of personal injury, the family of the victim would sign (sometimes under pressure from the state) a "deed of agreement" (*razinama*) with the offender, which would in most circumstances mitigate capital punishment.[72] This put significantly more power in the hands of the state and allowed it to punish murderers according to its will, since the family's rights had been put aside. As this chapter has argued, during the first half of the nineteenth century, muftis working with the British invented new categories of punishment that allowed the colonial officers to issue sentences according to their desire.

The Ottoman and Egyptian codes provided a more explicit example of this shift, with the Ottoman law codifying the balance between the rights of the state and those of the victim's family. Article 171 stated that the punishment issued by the state court (execution or imprisonment) "does not invalidate personal rights" of the victim's family and that if the victim had living heirs, the case must first be referred to the shari'a court, where the family could seek either execution or the payment of blood money.[73] Additionally, article 182, which defined the category of wrongful killing (*khata'*), required that the state punishment of imprisonment be applied only "after the shari'a rights of the victim's family" have been met.[74] In the case of a conflict between the state court and the shari'a judge, "the shari'a court ruling is preferred after the issuing of the royal order," and the more severe punishment should be applied.[75] For example, if the state court called for execution and the shari'a court called for only the payment of blood money, the execution would be carried out and the blood money taken from the murderer's inheritance. Alternatively, if the state court ruled for imprisonment and the shari'a court ordered execution, the execution would be carried out "fulfilling the retaliation (*qisas*)."[76]

The explanation of the articles outlined above suggests that following the wishes of the victim's family, sought through the shari'a court, remained the primary way that the punishment for homicide was determined. However, there is evidence from the courts that shows this was not always the case. In one case from Istanbul in 1880, a man named Muhammad b. 'Uthman was charged with the murder of two individuals, a Muslim called Rajab and a Spanish national named Jalabon. The court convicted him and sentenced him to death, but Rajab's surviving son made a shari'a claim against the perpetrator. The court paused to review the claim, eventually overruling Rajab's son and insisting that the execution be carried out. It cited the supremacy of the state (*Nizamiye*) court ruling and that it was carried out "according to the shari'a (*ber nehc-i şer'*)."[77]

In Egypt, the Lebanese Christian attorney Amin Afram al-Bustani's explanation of the 1883 penal code provided a detailed justification of the role of state power, particularly in cases of personal injury and homicide (*qisas*). In an introductory section titled "In the Assignment of Punishment to Government (*fi ikhtisas al-hukuma bi-l-mu'aqaba*)," he began by stating that individuals are incapable of achieving justice alone, as: "People are the furthest from balance, the most displaced from justice, and the most removed from the truth if they possess the [ability to] discharge their affairs by their own hands. [Therefore] it is necessary to return to government alone to institute punishment legislated by the framers of the law."[78] As a result: "If, for example, a man kills his neighbor's son, it is not permissible for the victim's father to kill him for it. If he does, he will be executed because the perpetrator has become with his crime in the grasp of the law and the property of its justice. According to the conditions of the crime, the law then has the option to apply retaliation (qisas) or abstain."[79] This is nothing new, and: "The framers of our penal code have not innovated in assigning punishment to the government, as is stated in Article 1, as it is an ancient assignment in every legal system. There is no meaning to adjudication, no authority for the government, and no protection for societal welfare if it is not present."[80]

Al-Bustani then cited article 1 of the Ottoman Penal Code of 1858, which used more Islamic language. He translated the article to state that "the shari'a guarantees the right of the political authority (uli al-amr) to specify the categories of discretionary punishment (ta'zir) and its punishments."[81] He then stated that Egyptian law had followed this precedent, something never mentioned in French law, without any contradiction to traditional Islamic legal discourse.

According to al-Bustani, when murder is discussed as a crime against the person, the victim's family can waive its right to retaliation and forgo punishment—an idea against the fundamental understandings of justice, which is a more fundamental objective of Islamic law. Therefore, "the issue of applying retaliation (qisas) for homicide is removed from the realm of personal rights that accept [the idea] of waiver and enters the field of general rights that never accept a waiver under any circumstances."[82]

Al-Bustani then cited an 1889 case of murder against a person named Fairuz Agha in which the defendant's attorney argued that it was not the right of the public prosecutor to seek punishment. In the attorney's view, according to the Egyptian Penal Code, "the rules of the shari'a apply, and the right of asking for retaliation is only for the family of the victim."[83] In its verdict, the court of first instance refused the attorney's argument and explained that the rights of the shari'a "carry [only] the intended meaning of blood money (diya)." Therefore, "it is the right of the heirs [of the victim] to only claim the payment of blood money, which is the demanding of compensation calculated according to the Holy shari'a." The attorney appealed, but the lower court's decision was confirmed, and the defendant was sentenced to death.[84]

As evidenced by this case and al-Bustani's preceding explanation of the new code, the Egyptian legal system created a division between the individual's rights and those of the state. Only the political authority (in this case, the state) can physically punish a murderer through execution or imprisonment: the victim's family can only make a civil claim for the payment of blood money. This division is somewhat similar to an idea from traditional Islamic discussions, according to which individuals were never allowed to take the law into their own hands and execute murderers. Those who did were categorized as criminals themselves and subject to the prescribed punishment for waging war against society *(hiraba)* and spreading disorder in the land *(fasad fi al-ard)*.[85] Al-Bustani was keenly aware of the Islamic rules of vigilantism and the danger posed to society when individuals took the law into their own hands, stating throughout his introduction that it was always the prerogative of the political authority to punish. The innovation of the Egyptian Penal Code lies in its enshrining this principle within the law while not ignoring the discussions of traditional scholars.

This legal innovation of establishing the state as the primary claimant in a case of homicide has its origins in case law from earlier in the nineteenth century. Before implementing the new code in 1883, the state was allowed to make a claim for execution—defined through retaliation *(qisas)*—but only in cases where no descendants of the victim could be found. In such cases, the state was considered to be the "family" of the deceased. For example, in one case from the Sudanese region of Kurdafan in 1861, a man named Muhammad walad Sahib al-Sam'awi was charged with stabbing his wife to death. His case was brought to the court by a state representative named Ibrahim Effendi, who called for the defendant's execution. The defendant confessed, and the court passed the execution sentence that was later confirmed by the grand mufti, with the justification that the victim "had no descendant except for the state treasury *(bayt al-mal)*."[86]

Many of the cases that fell within this category referred to the necessity of the state to intervene in cases in which there was no descendant to make a claim for punishment because of the presence of "public harm *(darar li-l-'amma)*." According to the *fiqh* of Ibn 'Abidin, "the judge is like the father in cases like [those in which] a person was killed without a descendant. It is therefore for the ruler to execute the defendant or come to an agreement [for the payment of blood money], and not to forgive because of the public harm."[87] In light of this precedent in the shari'a courts, it is not surprising to see the laws implemented in the latter part of the nineteenth century expanding the role of the state and the courts to act as the "father" or protector of all victims of homicide and to be responsible for the prosecution of crime—a change explained by those such as al-Bustani in discussions of the new code.

This point would be explicitly made by a later scholar of Egyptian criminal law, Ridwan Shafi'i al-Muta'afi, a shari'a court employee and graduate of the Islamic college of Dar al-'Ulum. Writing in 1930, he began his argument on retaliation (*qisas*) by stating that there are three categories of individuals that can claim retaliation: the family of the victim, the owner of the victim (if they were a slave), and the ruler (*al-saltana aw al-mamlaka*). The second category was irrelevant, as slavery had been outlawed. The third category, according to al-Muta'afi, was available only in cases where there were no surviving family members.[88]

However, it is in the first category where al-Muta'afi made his contribution. He began by stating that traditionally, all of the inheriting family members of the victim must be consulted. The absence of even one member could be grounds for dismissal of a case because that person might not wish to proceed with the prosecution. However, the family members could have agents act on their behalf. These agents could volunteer their services or be appointed by the court, and they could include parents of children who did not have the legal capacity to make a criminal claim. Al-Muta'afi took the concept of agency as his point of departure from the *fiqh* understanding, arguing that the public prosecutor "represents every individual in cases of public claims (*al-da'awi al-'umumiya*), among which are cases of homicide. The representation [of the prosecutor] is therefore general for every individual equally, and the meaning of [the office of] the prosecutor is equal to the meaning of agency. A member of the public prosecutor is [therefore] a public agent."[89]

When investigating and bringing offenders to justice, al-Muta'afi compared the public prosecutor to the *fiqh* concept of the market inspector (*muhtasib*). Before the colonial period, the inspector took on the responsibility of seeking out illegal or immoral activity (*al-munkarat*) in addition to checking prices and preventing cheating in weights and measures. Al-Muta'afi argued that, like the *muhtasib*, the public prosecutor and his employees (among other things):

1. Carry out their position for the public good (*al-maslaha al-'amma*), and individual religious requirement (*fard 'ayn*),
2. Are the only individuals who can carry out such a role in society,

3. Are sought out by those who see immoral activity in front of them and fulfill their religious obligation to report it,
4. Are required to investigate any claim until they reach the truth and, if necessary, present criminals to the leader or his representatives (*imam aw na'ibihi*) for punishment,
5. Can seek the cooperation of other enforcement agencies (for example, police) in their mission,
6. Can receive a state salary, and
7. Can use their own interpretation of the law (*yajtahid ra'yahu*) during investigation and apprehension, leaving the case's final outcome to the courts.[90]

As a result, for al-Mut'afi, like his predecessor al-Bustani, viewing the state apparatus (embodied by the public prosecutor) as the primary agent that investigates, apprehends, and prosecutes offenders of crime was not contradictory to the earlier understanding of the market inspector. While not dismissing the role of the victim's family entirely, al-Mut'afi argued that the prosecutor acted as the representative not only for the family but also for the entire society. Therefore, the prosecutor and his agents fulfilled the fundamental religious requirement of stopping immoral or illegal activity (*al-nahi 'an al-munkar*).

Conclusion

The classification of homicide found in the penal codes constructed in the second half of the nineteenth century was largely in line with broad understandings of Islamic law. The IPC was most similar to Hanafi norms, with many of the examples provided by the code exactly following theoretical situations discussed in both works of Hanafi *fiqh* and *fatwa* collections. The Ottomans and Egyptians took a slightly different path, adapting rulings found within the Maliki school brought to them through French interaction with Islamic law in North Africa. Rather than seeing these French adaptations as foreign, Egyptian scholars adopted a comparative approach and found that the French laws complied with the understandings of the Malikis, an approach that would continue until the middle of the twentieth century.

In the most drastic change made by the new codes—the shift of the prosecution of homicide from the victim's family to the state—explainers of the codes such as al-Bustani placed the change within the broader principles of Islamic law. They justified the state's new role as working toward the more general goal of protecting society as a whole by preventing revenge killings and blood feuds, an idea found in the explanation of the Qur'anic verses establishing the category of *qisas*.

The shifting classifications of homicide in the new penal codes—and, most important, the removal of the secondary Hanafi category of semi-intentional murder—were enacted primarily by adapting the definition of intent. While the Hanafis theoretically established intent by observing the method of killing and the weapon used, the new codes called for a search into the perpetrator's motives. Other essential points of contention in nineteenth-century criminal law were how these motives were established and the role of intent in classifying homicide, points discussed in chapter 4.

4

Establishing Criminal Intent

C hapter 3 discussed categorization to establish the types of criminal acts that would be legally understood as homicide and how they were to be punished. The present chapter takes up the second element in defining a crime: the establishment of criminal intent, or mens rea. How a legal system proposes to establish criminal intent is critical to a complete understanding of the definition of a crime.

This chapter addresses establishing intent with a deadly weapon in cases of homicide. It explores the differences of opinions that developed within the Hanafi school before the nineteenth century and how those differences influenced the development of the law. It argues that although the new penal codes of the nineteenth century introduced new methods of establishing intent, the discussion of the weapon continued to dominate the discourse in each jurisdiction and remained the primary way that a specific intent to kill was established and through which the most extreme punishment (execution) was justified. By examining the place of the deadly weapon and particularly its presence in the courts, the chapter elaborates on the main point of the previous chapters—namely, that Islamic understandings continued to dominate in each of the jurisdictions of interest, even after the implementation of new penal codes.

The chapter begins with a general presentation of the concept of the deadly weapon in the Hanafi school and shows how the school developed an increasingly material approach to defining such weapons. It then turns to nineteenth-century British India, where—in an attempt to expand the realm of punishment and move away from Islamic understandings of the law that were seen as too lenient—colonial authorities encouraged courts to look at the perpetrator's motive for committing the crime. However, a description of the weapon used in a crime continued to figure prominently in court rulings. With the introduction of the IPC, the presence of a deadly weapon would once again serve as the primary way of determining intent, a divergence from the practice in Britain at the time. The chapter concludes with a discussion of the establishment of intent in the Ottoman and Egyptian codes.

The new codes of the nineteenth century made significant changes and additions to the Hanafi doctrine of the deadly weapon. For example, the codes expanded what could be considered a weapon by using minority opinions within the Hanafi school. Choking or beating a victim to death, which would not fall within the standard Hanafi definition of using a weapon and thus would not result in the homicide's being treated as intentional ('amd), would now be considered a use of deadly force. Additionally, the Ottoman and Egyptian codes used the concept of premeditation from the Maliki school and developed it, considering premeditation as sufficient evidence to establish murderous intent and subject the perpetrator to execution. These changes were made within the context of the tension between the Islamic legal tendency to reduce the application of the harshest punishment in cases of doubt (described in chapter 3) and the state, which sought to expand the realm of punishment. This tension and the ultimate triumph of the state were present throughout Islamic and Hanafi legal history, and the changes to the law were mainly justified within the framework of precolonial Islamic law. They were not seen as a divergence from Islamic law or a blind adoption of European understandings.

From a general Islamic point of view, intent is critical to evaluating an individual's actions. This is based on a *hadith* of the Prophet that states, "Actions are defined by their intent, and to every person what he intends."[1] As a result, every act of worship ('ibada) or worldly transaction (mu'amala) in Islamic law includes a discussion of the intent required to render that act valid. In the realm of criminal law, jurists focused on a perpetrator's external actions to determine intent. Paul Powers showed how this contrasts with the approach to intent in other areas of the law: "Rather than give legal weight to intentions per se, as they theoretically do to some extent in ritual, contract, and family law, jurists consistently rely on indirect, objective evidence when assessing subjective states in penal situations. Further, jurists recognize limitations in their ability to know and evaluate human intentions, and some explicitly acknowledge that, because of this, they can achieve no more than a provisional form of justice."[2]

In homicide and personal injury (qisas), intent was established according to the presence or absence of a deadly weapon. Homicides committed with a deadly weapon fell within the Hanafi category of intentional murder (*'amd*) and necessitated execution. In contrast, the use of all other types of weapons fell into the semi-intentional (*shibh 'amd*) category. According to the nineteenth-century jurist Muhammad 'Abd al-Hayy: "Things in the category of a weapon are a condition [for intentional murder] because murder is by definition a deliberate act done by the heart and therefore cannot be definitively established. The use of a deadly weapon takes the place of intent to facilitate [its establishment], in the same way that travel is used in [establishing] hardship [for the shortening of prayer]."[3] Therefore, the question of what constituted a deadly weapon formed the core of Islamic scholarly debates well into the nineteenth century. Interestingly, the presence of a deadly weapon was also crucial in common law for establishing a connection to the perpetrator's state of mind. Beginning with cases involving the British clergy in the sixteenth century, this slowly came to be known as the "deadly weapon doctrine," which is "a vehicle from the deadliness of instrumentality to the state of mind. It constitutes a specific (perhaps the original) application of what has come to be a generally accepted principle: that one is 'presumed' to intend the natural and probable consequences of his acts."[4] In common law, just like in the definition provided by 'Abd al-Hayy, the presence of a deadly weapon linked the external actions of an individual to their internal intent, located in "the mind" in common law and in "the heart" in Islamic law.

Deadly Weapons: The Hanafi Approach

In the work of Muhammad al-Shaybani (d. 749/750), a student of the Hanafi school's founder, Abu Hanifa, the term used to describe items used in the commission of a crime is a general word for a weapon (*silah*). Although this was not specified or elaborated on by al-Shaybani, at the time, the Arabic term *silah* typically referred to a weapon of war, such as a sword or spear.[5] This was clear in al-Shaybani's definition of semi-intentional murder as one carried out with nonconventional weapons such as "a switch, a rock, or a hardened piece of mud."[6] Through the slightly later work of Ahmad b. Muhammad al-Tahawi (d. 321/935), two general opinions were presented and attributed to the first generations of the school. Abu Hanifa reportedly stated that the weapon must be one capable of wounding (*jarh*). His two primary students, Abu Yusuf (d. 182/798) and al-Shaybani (d. 189/805), disagreed, believing that "all [weapons] which kill, whether they wound (*yajrah*) or not, if they are intentionally applied to take a life, then the murder is intentional *('amd)* and requires execution by the sword."[7] Al-Tahawi took the report of Abu Hanifa's students as his basis for discussion and built upon it to include the use of nondeadly weapons that cause death, such as in cases of "a strike with a switch or a club, or with a slap of the hand."[8] Although these weapons would not have fallen under the theoretical concept of *jarh*, their repeated use reaches that effect and therefore falls in the category used by Abu Yusuf and al-Shaybani.

By the time of Ahmad b. Muhammad al-Quduri (d. 428/1036), the difference between the school's earlier jurists had been modified, with new details added. According to al-Quduri, intentional murder occurred with "a weapon *(silah)*, or that which is similar to a weapon *(ma ujriya majra al-silah)*." He defined the second type of weapon as an item that "separates body parts *(tafriq al-ajza')*," such as weapons made of wood smelted with iron *(muhaddad min al-khashab)*, rocks *(hajar)*, or fire *(nar)*. According to this definition, al-Quduri argued that Abu Hanifa would place every act committed with anything outside of these two types of weapons in the category of semi-intentional murder. Al-Quduri then reinterpreted the opinions of Abu Yusuf and al-Shaybani to read, "If he strikes [someone] with a great rock, or a large piece of wood, then it is intentional. Semi-intentional is if he intends to strike with *what does not generally kill (ma la yaqtul ghaliban)*."[9]

Al-Quduri's contribution to the definition of a deadly weapon indicates two crucial developments. The first is the modification of the meaning of wounding *(jarh)* to include only wounds caused by weapons that physically separate body parts. The second, which further modifies the definition of *jarh*, is the addition of the idea of weapons that generally kill *(ma yaqtul ghaliban)*. Although unknown to the Hanafi school in its formative period, this is the primary definition of a deadly weapon described in the early Shafi'i school, which has now been adopted by the Hanafi tradition and attributed to Abu Yusuf and al-Shaybani.[10] The importance of these two contributions is that they have created general types beyond the specific examples of rocks, slaps, and switches provided by the early scholars and opened the door for additional types of weapons to be considered and placed in their respective types.

Roughly a century later, Abu Bakr b. Mas'ud al-Kasani (d. 587/1191) further developed the concept of the deadly weapon, this time focusing on the material from which the weapon is constructed. A murder weapon, in his view, is made "of iron *(hadid)* with a point and [has the ability to] stab *(ta'n)* like a sword, knife, spear, awl, needle and what is similar to it." Therefore, the point of consideration for the weapon was whether it was "iron itself, whether it wounds *(jaraha)* or not."[11] In this definition, al-Kasani abandoned modifications made by al-Quduri and returned to al-Tahawi's understanding of *jarh*. Al-Kasani placed the material from which the weapon was fashioned as the primary point of consideration, and as a result, he included other items that are made from iron but not normally considered weapons in the category of intentional murder, such as "[iron] bars, scales, the backs of axes, metallic rocks, and things like these."[12] He also created an analogy to weapons made from other metals, including copper, brass, lead, gold, and silver, saying that "their ruling is that of iron."[13]

This shift in focus to the material from which the weapon is made is one of the most important changes in the Hanafi school's understanding of a deadly weapon. Later attempts to integrate the concept of *jarh* with the weapon's material continued to prioritize the material as the determining factor. For example, the *al-Fatawa al-tatarkhaniya* dismissed the idea of weapons that generally kill and stated that the "consideration in this section [of the law] is [whether the weapon is made of] metal."[14] If the weapon was made of a material other than metal, then the rule of separating body parts *(tafriq al-ajza')* was applied. If the weapon was made of metal, no additional consideration was necessary. The same opinion is found in the *al-Fatawa al-anqarawiya* and the work of Muhammad Amin b. 'Abidin.[15] The only slight deviation from this opinion is in the *al-Fatawa al-'alamgiriya*, which attempted to return to the rule of *tafriq al-ajza'* in all cases—although the collection dismissed the minority opinion accepting weapons that generally kill.[16]

Another attempt to augment the material approach in the classical period came from the incorporation of an additional element from the Shafi'i school. This idea, first introduced by the Persian scholar Muhammad b. Ahmad al-Sarakhsi (d. 490/1096), stated that if a person were stabbed by a small weapon, such as a pin, and died as a result, it would not be considered intentional murder. However, if the stabbing occurred in a vulnerable area of the body and so was likely to cause death *(maqtal)*, it would be regarded as intentional.[17] This idea was largely ignored by Hanafi scholars of the time and is not found in the discussions of al-Kasani. However, this opinion was mentioned in the *al-Fatawa al-tatarkhaniya* and the *al-Fatawa al-'alamgiriya*, as well as the work of Ibn 'Abidin.[18] After a brief mention, each of these texts claimed that the discussion of an attack on a vulnerable area of the body was irrelevant in the face of the rules regarding the material. Pins would automatically be considered deadly weapons regardless of where they were used, as they are made from metal. This point shows that, even when attempting to introduce non-Hanafi approaches to a deadly weapon to move away from adescription of the material, the standard approach of the school held firm.

Thus, the initial periods of development of the Hanafi school attempted to widen the definition of a deadly weapon to include general categories of separating body parts *(tafriq al-ajza')* and incorporated understandings from the Shafi'i school, such as weapons that generally kill *(yaqtul ghaliban)*. However, by the end of the twelfth century, the Hanafi school became firmly committed to judging a deadly weapon by its material.

The development of the material standard according to which a weapon was categorized reflected another instance of the "doubt canon," as discussed by Intisar Rabb. According to Rabb, when searching for an individual's intent, judges were concerned about reaching a high level of certainty in their rulings. By examining only the internal indicators of the motive to kill, the judge could "never reach evidentiary *certainty* about guilt" and apply the strictest punishment.[19] The presence of a weapon that did not fall into the defined category of metal objects allowed judges to forgo the most extreme penalty of the law. Instead, they could opt for more lenient punishments, such as the payment of blood money or a discretionary punishment, because they could not establish absolute certainty of the perpetrator's intent.

There is one point within Hanafi law where the concept of a deadly weapon ran into trouble: cases in which no weapon was present, exemplified in the *fiqh* discourse on strangulation. In this case, the overwhelming majority of jurists agreed that a person who choked someone to death would not be subject to the death penalty but could be executed through discretionary punishment if the perpetrator was in the habit of choking his victims. The *al-Fatawa al-tatarkhaniya* and *al-Fatawa al-anqarawiya* presented a slight alternative. Citing the opinions of Abu Yusuf and al-Shaybani, these fatwa works stated that if a person continued to choke another to the extent that "a person would most likely die *(ma yamut al-insan minhu ghaliban)*" then it was intentional, "because he meant *(qasada)* to kill him." If the perpetrator choked a person for a moment, then stopped, and the victim died later due to the attack, the question that must be asked was whether that amount of choking fit the definition of generally killing *(ghaliban)*. Here we see a return to the Shafi'i principle introduced above regarding a weapon, now applied to strangulation. Like the previous applications, however, this opinion was rarely cited and found only in the *al-Fatawa al-tatarkhaniya* and the *al-Fatawa al-anqarawiya*, meaning that it was a minority opinion within the Hanafi school. The same difference of opinion was found in cases of drowning or throwing a person off a cliff or building.[20]

As the juristic tendency to use doubt and limit the types of weapons considered deadly came into conflict with the desire of states in the nineteenth century to expand the realm of punishment, states looked to dismiss this understanding of the deadly weapon altogether and attempt to redirect judges toward viewing the perpetrator's motive. The rest of this chapter covers this tension, how the weapon was discussed, and how the presence of a weapon continued to establish intent in the jurisdictions studied.

Deadly Weapon versus Motive in British India

In British India, colonial officers quickly took note of the Hanafi approach to the weapon and sought to amend it, seeing it as a barrier to applying punishment. The governor-general, Earl of Moira Francis Edward Rawdon-Hastings (aka Lord Hastings), suggested, "If the intention of murder be clearly proved, no distinction should be made with respect to the weapon by which the crime was perpetrated."[21] For the British, this method of establishing intent resulted in the passing of much lighter sentences and the dismissal of some cases altogether. "Since the present Raja's ascension," remarked the colonial official Jonathan Duncan when referring to the ruler of Bengal, "he has not ventured, nor will of himself venture, to punish with Death, the most notorious offenders."[22] In 1790, the then governor-general Charles Cornwallis, First Marquess Cornwallis (Lord Cornwallis) issued regulations ordering that crimes were to be judged by their motive and not the weapon used. This was because, in his view, the Islamic provision of barring capital punishment was "of barbarous construction and contrary to the first principles of civil society by which the state acquires an interest in every member."[23]

Appellate judges throughout British India regularly cited this regulation, emphasizing the importance of distinguishing the understanding of the law to be applied in British courts from that of Islamic law. For example, in one case adjudicated in Bengal in 1853, three individuals were charged with the murder of Button Mooshur. There were no eyewitnesses to the case, and as a result, the fatwa of the law officer classified the charge as culpable homicide and ordered the payment of blood money *(diya)*. The sessions judge apparently agreed with this classification and imposed prison sentences of five years on two of the defendants and seven years on the third. Although there seemed to be no conflict between the understanding of the law officer and the sessions judge regarding the guilt of the prisoners, the appellate judge, J. R. Colvin, took serious issue with the initial law reports created by the Muslim officers that classified the crime as culpable homicide. He stated that the British had "set aside the distinctions of the Mahomedan law schools as to the particular instrument by which the death is caused" and confirmed the sentence of the sessions judge and the ruling of the mufti.[24]

However, the importance of a deadly weapon in the establishment of intent did not disappear so easily, and the precise nature of the weapon used continued to serve as one of the primary ways through which courts established intent. In a case from Bengal in 1853, a man named Nokory Bagdee was charged with the murder of Roopchand, the younger brother of the prosecutor Gorachand Singh. The perpetrator had purchased food from Gorachand's sister, refused to pay, and run off. When Roopchand confronted him, the perpetrator stabbed and murdered him. The sessions judge convicted the perpetrator of willful murder and asked for the death penalty, but the mufti disagreed and found the perpetrator "guilty of culpable homicide, and declares him liable to discretionary punishment by *deyut*." Upon appeal, one of the appellate judges (H. T. Raikes) pointed to the medical report, which stated that death was caused by "a penetrating wound between the fourth and fifth rib on the left side of the chest, extending deeply into the lungs. It was 1.5 inches in length and 7 inches in depth." In the opinion of Raikes, "The deadly weapon used by the prisoner, the part struck, and the wound inflicted, seven inches and a half in depth evince a determination to take life, which makes the prisoner's crime willful murder, and he is therefore liable to suffer death." However, the other judges disagreed and cited the circumstances of the case (a death caused amid an altercation) in sentencing the perpetrator to the mitigated punishment of life in prison. Although the judges eventually sided with the mufti in imposing a lighter punishment and not the sessions judge, who had ruled for execution, the presence of a deadly weapon—that is, one capable of stabbing, just as in the definition of the Hanafi school—gave them a ground to convict the perpetrator of willful murder, even though the circumstances ultimately led them to a mitigated punishment.[25]

In a case from the Northwestern Provinces in 1854, a woman named Mussumat Mohuree was charged with the willful murder of her husband, Chootkaie. Either the mufti was absent during the proceedings or his opinion was not recorded. The sessions judge ruled for capital punishment, mainly based on the prisoner's confession. The appellate judges disagreed, eventually convicting her of willful murder but only sentencing her to life in prison. The entire rationale for this lighter punishment rested upon the nature of the weapon used, a large rock, "in consequence of which blow he died, without her designing to kill him." In this case, even when a mufti was not present and the regulations regarding the treatment of the deadly weapon in Islamic law were not considered, it was still the material nature of the weapon and not the perpetrator's motive that determined the prisoner's level of guilt and dictated the punishment.[26]

The framers and explainers of the IPC brought the discussion of the deadly weapon back to prominence. They replaced the regulations that had been in use since the end of the eighteenth century. In an explanation of the code, the section on culpable homicide noted: "The existence of a particular evil motive, such as hatred, avarice, jealousy, etc., is not necessary. It is no part of the definition of Culpable Homicide that the act which causes death should be a malicious act. Malice is not made a necessary ingredient. Whatever may be the motive which incites the action, and whether or not any motive whatsoever be discoverable, the question for investigation is this: did the accused person intend to cause death, or a bodily injury likely to end in death; or did he know that death was a probable result of his act?"[27] The explanation continued: "How can the existence of the requisite intention or knowledge be proved, seeing that these are *internal* and *invisible* acts of the mind? They can be ascertained only from *external* and *visible* acts."[28] One of the leading external indicators of such intention was the presence of a deadly weapon. An example of this application would be in cases of provocation in which a person was insulted or encouraged to attack by the actions of another. Typically, the presence of provocation would be considered as a mitigating factor for punishment. However, "if a person strikes another with a deadly weapon, or assaults him with blows causing great bodily pain or bloodshed, or if he in a serious personal conflict assails him, having a great superiority of personal strength or skill, the provocation would seem sufficiently grave to extenuate."[29]

Thus in promoting the definition of intent established through the act committed, the IPC remained close to the Hanafi school, which took as its primary consideration the nature of the weapon used. While the regulations passed by colonial officers in the eighteenth century sought to move away from using the weapon as the primary way to establish intent, cases of homicide throughout the first half of the nineteenth century with or without a mufti regularly rested on the nature of the weapon used in the attack. With the introduction of the new code, the regulations regarding motive were sidelined, and the external act that caused death was placed at the core of the definition of homicide, so the use of a weapon became the defining aspect of homicide. This appeared to contradict the common-law understanding of the time, with the Offenses against the Person Act of 1861 explicitly rejecting the idea of the method and considering only the malice present: "It shall not be necessary to set forth the Manner in which or the Means by which the Death of the Deceased was caused, but it shall be sufficient in any indictment for Murder to charge that the Defendant did feloniously, willfully, and of his Malice aforethought kill and murder the Deceased; and it shall be sufficient in any Indictment for Manslaughter to charge that the Defendant did feloniously kill and slay the Deceased."[30] However, the problem with the act was how to judge an external act as having the requisite intent. In the IPC, local understandings, which were influenced by Hanafi law, dictated that the presence of a weapon would adequately meet this requirement. Examples of this can be found in cases brought to the Indian appellate courts following the code's implementation.

For example, in a case brought to the High Court of Allahabad in 1874, a police officer had gone to the home of his superior and struck him over the head with "a heavy bamboo club." The victim did not die from the attack, and therefore the officer was convicted of attempted murder and sentenced by the lower court to seven years in prison. Upon appeal, the attorney for the officer argued that his client had not intended to cause the death of his superior and meant only to fight with him to cause injury. "Had his intent been murderous," the attorney argued, "he might have armed himself with a weapon more certain of lethal effect than a club." The appellate judge, Justice Turner, agreed:

> The weapon with which he attacked him is described by the witnesses in the Magistrate's Court as a heavy bamboo *lathee* or stick: it was produced in Court, and if the Judge had considered the description of it incorrect, it must be presumed he would have stated so in his judgment. Moreover, from the tenor of his judgment, it is evident the Judge regarded the weapon as such as could produce death, and the committing officer, to whom also the weapon was produced, describes it as a *heavy bamboo club*. Looking at the

appellant's act, and *the nature of the weapon* with which it was perpetrated, I come to the conclusion that he intended and attempted at the least to inflict grievous hurt.[31]

The appellate judge dismissed the initial ruling of the lower judge and instead sentenced the officer to three and a half years in prison for the crime of "attempting voluntarily to cause grievous hurt," following articles 325 and 511 of the IPC.[32] Had this case been one of homicide, the use of a club, according to the Hanafi school, would have automatically categorized the crime as semi-intentional *(shibh 'amd)*. In this case, the judge extended the deadly weapon rule to personal injury and established that using a bamboo club did not constitute a deadly weapon and lessened the sentence.

Outside of British jurisdictions, the issue of the weapon used remained controversial. In the late 1880s, in Muslim-ruled Hyderabad, a government employee named Jay Singh shot his brother-in-law Behna Singh, who died of his injuries the following day. Jay Singh was brought to court and charged with murder, and the question immediately arose if the weapon used—a gun whose bullets were made of lead—could fall under the category of a deadly weapon. The opinion of the city's most prominent scholar of the time, Mufti Lutfullah, was sought. He ruled that the homicide was to be treated as semi-intentional and that the death penalty could not be applied. He cited as his justification the condition of "separating body parts *(tafriq al-ajza')*," stating that a bullet creates only a minor wound and cannot cut off limbs like a sword.

This ruling presented a unique problem. Typically, and as the first section of this chapter showed, *tafriq al-ajza'* was meant to extend the definition of a deadly weapon and move beyond its material nature. However, Lutfullah used the same logic to limit the scope to create doubt and remove the possibility of applying the death penalty. This ruling threw the city-state's judiciary into disarray that lasted for several months. Their confusion was resolved only by an official announcement from the government's High Judicial Council (Majlis-e 'Aliya-e 'Adalat) declaring once and for all that deaths that occur as a result of the use of guns and bullets were to be officially classified as intentional murder *('amd)*, overruling Lutfullah.

In their decision, the council's members took turns challenging the approach of Lutfullah, particularly the criteria of *tafriq al-ajza'*. The main question posed was what was more important to the definition of a deadly weapon: its material or its ability to wound *(jarh)*?

The head of the council, Mawlavi Khuda Baksh Khan, supported the latter view by pointing out the case of fire, which is considered intentional (*'amd*) even though it does necessarily separate body parts (*tafriq al-ajza'*). If fire is considered a deadly weapon, bullets fired by a gun could surely fall into the same category. Another council member, Mawlawi Syed Afzal Husayn, analyzed three other opinions that Lutfullah had given on the same issue. He suggested that Lutfullah had shifted his position following the events of 1857 to accept bullets as deadly by using the opinions of al-Tahawi (and expanding the definition of *jarh* through *tafriq al-ajza'*). Therefore, his most recent statement must stand. Finally, the report cited another fatwa collection—namely, the *al-Fatawa al-anqarawiya*—to state that the presence of metal was not a requirement and that bullets fired from a gun should be considered deadly. Finally, the report cited nine other legal scholars working in the Hyderabad courts who ruled that bullets were deadly and argued that, as this is the common practice within the courts, it can override the opinion of an individual scholar regardless of his rank.[33]

Through this ruling, the expanded definition of a deadly weapon became the standard in both British and Muslim jurisdictions on the subcontinent, following the understanding of the IPC and the Hanafi school. Therefore, considerations of motive, which dominated colonial discussions of law from the late eighteenth century through the first half of the nineteenth, were sidelined, and local understandings triumphed.

Weapons and Premeditation in the Ottoman and Egyptian Codes

During the first half of the nineteenth century, the Ottoman and Egyptian criminal systems widened the definition of the deadly weapon. For example, in Egypt in 1858, the appellate court (Majlis al-Ahkam) ruled that bamboo sticks (*nabbut*) were to be considered as deadly weapons and instructed judges to use the broader Hanafi definition of weapons that generally kill (*ma yaqtul ghaliban*).[34] This ruling was mentioned in several instances in the courts, and it appears that the wider meaning of the deadly weapon was respected. For example, in one case from 1860, one man was charged with murdering another by striking him with a wooden stick. In his ruling, the mufti cited the definition of the deadly weapon given by the two students of Abu Hanifa—that is, a weapon that generally kills (*bi-ma yaqtul ghaliban*).[35]

However, like the courts of British India, the Ottoman and Egyptian courts sometimes considered motive or broader discussions of the perpetrator's intent. For example, in one case from 1860, al-Shaykh Muhammad al-Habishi was charged with the murder of 'Ali Hijazi. The two men had been on opposite sides of the courtroom on an unrelated business matter, and while in the courtroom, Muhammad beat 'Ali with a switch. After leaving the court, Muhammad kicked 'Ali four times, and 'Ali died from his injuries eight days later. During the court proceedings, Muhammad argued that he had only meant "to scare" 'Ali and had no intention of killing him. The court and mufti agreed, ruling that Muhammad should be required only to pay blood money in compensation for the death.[36]

In a case from in 1880, a woman named Sofia was walking down the street with three of her daughters when they were attacked by a group of men armed with a knife. Sofia and one of her daughters, Tuti, were injured in the attack, and Sofia died of her injuries the following day. After an investigation and interviews with witnesses from the neighborhood, two men (Amin Rafiq and Hasan) were arrested and charged with the murder. They categorically denied the charges. After further investigation (including an autopsy of the victim) and interrogation, it was determined that Amin was the primary actor and Hasan was merely an accomplice. Amin was sentenced to fifteen years of hard labor for wrongful homicide, while Hasan was sentenced to five years for participating in the crime.[37]

In both cases, the punishment would have been harsher if the court had viewed only the nature of the weapon, which might have necessitated the death penalty. The crime in the first case was carried out with extreme bodily force, taken as a deadly weapon under the minority opinion within the Hanafi school. In contrast, the crime in the second case was carried out with a knife made of metal, a deadly weapon according to majority opinion. However, the court chose to look at the motive and the other circumstances of the case, finding that the first happened due to a connected court disagreement and that the second was a street fight, and decided to lessen the punishment to that for wrongful homicide (khata').

One explanation of the Ottoman Penal Code of 1858 detailed two criteria for establishing intentional murder: "The first is that the death must be proceeded by a purpose (qasd), intent (niya), and conception (tasawwur). The second is that the instrument (al-ala) or the means (al-wasita) used be valid [to produce] death." Most important was the "investigation of the instrument used in the killing [and asking] whether it is amongst those which are valid for killing or not."[38] With regard to the nature of the weapon, the explanation continued: "Intentional murder must include that the instrument used for its commission [be] a weapon *(silah)* or what is like it *(ma yajri majrahu)* like a piece of metal that obtains as an effect [of its use] the general taking of life *(zuhuq al-nafs ghaliban)*, or it [intentional murder] is done by drowning in water or burning with fire or strangulation in its different forms."[39] This definition reflected a direct application of the concept of a deadly weapon within the Hanafi school. Using this definition to its widest possible extent, the Ottoman code not only included the material definition of the weapon as metal that dominated later Hanafi discussions but also expanded the definition to include minority opinions regarding all types of strangulation and cases that would be considered as semi-intentional, such as drowning, within the larger idea of a deadly weapon.

Focusing exclusively on the weapon with this definition could create a problem for judges. For example, what would happen if a person picked up a sword or other deadly weapon that just happened to be lying around during a fight and used it in an attack to kill someone? The circumstances of the homicide would render it not intentional. However, following the letter of the Hanafi school and looking at the weapon alone would require a ruling of intentional murder. The Ottoman and Egyptian codes solved this problem by introducing the concept of premeditation. According to an explanation of the Ottoman code,

> Preceding intentional murder includes conceptualization [of the crime] in the killer's mind and resolution [to carry it out] in his heart. It is a legal condition for murder to be considered intentional that he previously visualized [the crime], determined to commit the act, and realized with certainty the concept of destroying *(itlaf)* the person he intended to murder. He has prepared and made ready the instruments of death and its tools, then approached him, removed his soul, and took away his life. For example, if a person not prone to rage or in a fit of anger purposefully desired to kill or lay in wait for him to pass and with purpose took him unknowingly. Actions of this type are considered intentional murder.[40]

Premeditation also covered instances in which no weapon was used, as in a case where a person "stalks the one he wants to kill without a weapon, taking advantage of an opportunity throw him into a pit that he would not have normally fallen into, or [waiting for him to] sit on the edge of a river, coming behind him and pushing him in."[41]

The Egyptian code codified the idea of premeditation and, as the previous chapter mentioned, used it as the element in distinguishing between the highest degree of murder and other categories. In the earliest explanations of the code, written by Muhammad Yasin in 1886, the presence of a weapon was explicitly discarded: "There is no difference between the types of intentional murder whether the killing occurred with a sharp weapon such as a sword, knife, or dagger, or if it was [done] with a firearm such as a pistol or a shotgun, or whether [the weapon] was neither sharp nor a firearm such as killing with a club or a rock, or even if it was carried out with no weapon at all, such as a person throwing another in an ocean or river intending to drown them."[42]

To establish premeditation according to the Egyptian code, one or both of the following two elements (taken almost verbatim from the French Code of 1810) had to be present: (1) the murderer intended to kill before committing the act (al-israr);[43] and/or (2) the murderer lay in wait for the victim (al-tarassud).[44] In the first instance, evidence must be presented that the murderer planned to commit his act before its commission, typically in the form of statements made to others regarding the intent to murder. These statements could have been made at any time before the crime, be it months or even minutes. In the second instance, evidence must be provided that the murderer had waited and prepared for the act, taking at least some time (even if only a few minutes) to pause and consider the homicide. The murderer could have been waiting on the same path their victim took home or picked a place they knew would be quiet enough and out of sight of onlookers and witnesses. According to the code, either of these elements could be proven with either a confession from the defendant or the presence of two witnesses—an interesting connection to the standard practice in *fiqh*.[45]

Thus, the Egyptian code took the most significant step away from using the presence of a deadly weapon to establish intent and instead focused on the concept of premeditation. Unlike the Ottoman code, which clung to the importance of the weapon, the Egyptian code denied the relevance of the weapon used and instead instructed courts to focus on the circumstances surrounding the crime, particularly premeditation.

Using premeditation in the Ottoman and Egyptian codes—an element drawn from French influence and, as we will see, also found within the Maliki school—gave judges a way out of the complex problem of discovering the internal intent of the perpetrator. It also helped the law move away from the problematic Hanafi focus on the material from which the murder weapon was made. However, even in the more straightforward case of Egypt, premeditation did not solve all of the law's problems. The deadliness of the weapon remained a factor, as shown in the explanation of the code by Yasin. He wrote that for an individual to be convicted of intentional murder (*'amd*), "the act must be done in a way that *ends life normally (i'dam al-haya 'adatan)*, such as striking a person with a knife, sword, or dagger, a stab to the stomach, or with a bullet to the head or the middle of the chest, etc."[46]

This approach was also applied in rulings of the courts and fatwas from the muftis. In one case from 1888, for example, a man named Sayyid 'Abd al-Muta'al was charged with the murder of his former wife, Zanuba bt. Muhammad. He confessed to the murder to other family members, stating that he had choked her to death. The question arose during the proceedings whether this constituted intentional or semi-intentional murder, since the categorization of choking was a point of contention within the Hanafi school. The judge ruled that the court should continue to follow the standard Egyptian practice and consider choking as sufficient for a verdict of intentional murder, so the defendant was sentenced to death.[47] Although the Egyptian Penal Code had been in place for roughly five years, the question of the weapon remained important to the courts in establishing intent, and previous government rulings regarding the broader definition of the deadly weapon continued to remain influential.

As stated above, the adaptation of premeditation from French law developed in the Egyptian and Ottoman codes was new to Hanafi legal theory and can be explained in two ways. First, an earlier concept of premeditation existed within the Maliki school. Understood as an aggravated category of homicide known as *al-qatl ghila*, this entailed the perpetrator's "either murdering secretively *(khifyatan)* or tricking the victim *(khid'atan)*, luring him to a location and killing him [there] to take his property. [This even applies] if the murder took place in public, in a situation where [the victim] could not call for help."[48] As discussed in chapter 3, the Maliki school was used by the Egyptians in the development of the legal system to justify changes made under French influence, with Egyptians arguing that the French understandings of the law were compatible with Maliki interpretations and, therefore, in line with Islamic law.

Second, and more critical for the integration of premeditation into the Ottoman and Egyptian codes, is that the use of premeditation reflected the outcome of the tension between the Islamic legal desire to avoid punishment and the state's desire to expand its application. That tension was most clearly expressed in an explanation of the Ottoman Penal Code: "A group of theorists in the field of criminal punishment indeed believes that it is necessary to limit the penalty of a murderer to what he might benefit from, [seeking to] reform him without exterminating him as retaliation for intentionally destroying the creation of God, in that he has killed a person unjustly and without right. However, it is necessary to enact this [punishment, such as execution] as when a murderer receives [retaliation], it closes the door of wrongdoing and prevents its expansion, disposes of enmity, and eradicates the remnants of distrust and friction from the hearts of people."[49]

The desires of the state to expand the realm of punishment were justified as complying with the ultimate purpose of *qisas* as established in the Qur'an: preventing blood feuds and revenge killings. However, the expansion of the state's role needed to be checked to ensure that only the most deserving criminals would receive the extreme punishment of execution. The Egyptian code provided the justification: "The premeditated murderer *(al-qatil bi-israr aw tarassud)* is the greater sinner and the more extreme violator of the law than one who kills in the state of passion because of the circumstances. The state of passion places a person in a state of partial insanity as opposed to premeditated murder, as a person in this state is neither passionate nor deficient in reason."[50]

The presence of premeditation helped establish the perpetrator's state of mind and, as discussed in the explanation of the Ottoman code, indicated that the perpetrator had "conceptualized" the crime and had the "resolution in his heart" to carry it out. Premeditation, therefore, can be understood as a contemporary adaptation of the doubt canon, allowing jurists to reach a higher level of certainty by removing any doubt that the perpetrator had not fully intended his actions and should not be subject to execution. In the specific case of the Ottoman code, the concept of premeditation acted in concert with the expanded concept of the deadly weapon. Given that the Ottoman code now used the broadest possible definition for such weapons, the requirement of premeditation for the severest punishment served as a check against punishing with execution those who had no prior intent to kill their victim.

Therefore, although the Ottoman and Egyptian penal codes embodied new demands of the state to expand the punishment for homicide, this was tempered by the introduction of premeditation. Just as the previous system had balanced the political authority's power to enact punishment *(siyasa* and *ta'zir)* by subjecting it to strict rules and developing the doubt canon, the new codes in the Ottoman Empire and Egypt attempted to do the same. The codes balanced an expanded definition of the deadly weapon (in the case of the Ottomans) or removal of the means (in the case of the Egyptians) by adding the new requirement of premeditation, which would ensure that only those who acted in a way that showed they fully intended the results of their crime would receive the most extreme punishment.

Conclusion

By analyzing the deadly weapon doctrine and the establishment of intent, this chapter has shown that although the new codes brought several significant theoretical shifts, they were still based on understandings found in Islamic law. For the British in India, the change in intent came full circle from focusing on the weapon to emphasizing the motive and eventually returning to the external nature of the act committed, where the weapon was critical in establishing intent. In the first half of the nineteenth century, regulations were put in place to remove consideration of the weapon described in the Hanafi school. Still, as time progressed, the weapon continued to figure prominently in the rulings of British judges, with or without the help of a mufti. With the introduction of the IPC in 1860, the weapon returned to prominence, acting as the most accurate and demonstrative link between the external act committed and the internal will of a perpetrator. Using the presence of a deadly weapon and defining the external nature of the act committed, the code was in direct opposition to the Offenses against the Persons Act of 1861, which required that only the internal motive be used to establish intent. Writing in the second half of the century, the Hanafi jurist 'Abd al-Hayy felt the same way and believed that the presence of a deadly weapon was the best indicator of what action a person desired to commit in his heart. The same approach was taken in the Ottoman code, with the nature of the weapon used considered to be the most important investigation required by the judge to pass a verdict of murder.

What changed from the traditional Hanafi approach to establishing intent was the definition of the weapon. Starting in the classical period, the Hanafi school became embroiled in discussing the material from which the weapon was produced. Driven by the doubt canon to mitigate situations in which the death penalty would be applied to inflict less severe punishments, the school's jurists severely limited the understanding of the deadly weapon to those made from metal, making only limited exceptions (such as in the case of fire). With the state's increasing desire to deter more murderers, the nineteenth century saw a move away from the majority opinion of the school and toward a broader definition of the deadly weapon to expand the realm of capital punishment. When looking for a way to expand the definition of the deadly weapon, the new codes did not have to search far, as the Hanafi school already contained minority opinions attributed to the two primary students of the school's founder: Abu Yusuf and al-Shaybani. The British in India made the first move to direct judges toward the minority opinion, and the Egyptians soon followed, with the Ottomans incorporating this expanded definition in their penal code of 1858.

The Ottomans and the Egyptians, influenced more directly than the British by French understandings, made the greatest shift in their codes, using the new element of premeditation to help regulate their acceptance of new forms of deadly weapons. The Egyptians went the furthest in downplaying the role of the weapon used. The concept of premeditation in the Ottoman and Egyptian codes, although not present in Hanafi legal discussions, became a new form of the doubt canon, serving as a check on the new expanded concept of the deadly weapon and limiting the most extreme punishment to instances in which the perpetrator had planned the attack—thus ensuring the establishment of intent.

Chapters 3 and 4 were concerned with establishing the composite elements of the crime of homicide: the categorization and characteristics of the act committed and the intent required for a crime to fit in that category. However, areas remain in which an individual's degree of criminal responsibility is altered and the person is considered not responsible for the acts committed, even if the main elements of the crime are established. This is particularly important when the perpetrator committed the act as a child, was insane, or had the participation of others. Chapter 5 turns to the concept of criminal responsibility in cases of homicide within Hanafi law and the approaches of the new penal codes.

5

Criminal Responsibility

For a crime to be categorized as murder (see chapter 3), the intent to be fully established (see chapter 4), and punishment to be carried out, the perpetrator of the act must have full legal capacity—that is, the ability to be held responsible for their actions. In works of Islamic jurisprudence, individuals who were sane *('aqil)* and adult *(baligh)* at the time of the crime's commission had that capacity, but children and the insane were not considered fully responsible for their crimes. In the Hanafi tradition, these rules were first established by Abu Hanifa, and had their first complete iteration in the work of Ahmad b. Muhammad al-Tahawi. According to al-Tahawi, "If a child who has not reached puberty or a person in a state of insanity attacks a man and kills him, then the blood money is upon his (the perpetrator's) family, as there is no [consideration of] intentional killing *('amd)* for them. Similar [to this] are all injuries committed by [them] to the hands, eyes, or what is similar to them, as the blood money is upon his family."[1] This status of full responsibility is referred to as an assignment from God *(taklif)*. It applies not only to criminal law but also to acts of worship *('ibadat)* such as prayer, fasting, pilgrimage, and charity. *Taklif* is often constructed in Islamic thought as a burden that carries a reward for fulfillment and punishment for neglect. There are numerous instances in the law of worship when that burden is lifted. For example, Muslims are exempted from fully performing their prayers when sick or traveling, and women are not expected to pray on time or fast while menstruating.[2] In the realm of criminal law, children and the mentally insane, legally believed to be unaware of the actions that they are committing, are also exempted from the burden of punishment.

There are two other general elements of *taklif* within Islamic law that should be mentioned: the gradual development of *taklif* over a person's life and the difference between spiritual and worldly responsibility for actions. While still in the womb, children obtain their first *taklif*: they are held responsible for the mandatory charity to be paid by every Muslim at the end of Ramadan fasting *(zakat al-ʿid)*. Although the responsibility for paying this amount is temporarily placed upon the child's parent or guardian, the burden moves to the child when they become an adult if they realize that it was not paid. At around the age of seven, known as the age of discernment *(sinn al-tamyiz)*, the next step in the development of *taklif* occurs. Children at this age are believed to have a basic understanding of right and wrong and can, for example, carry out basic commercial contracts and act as temporary agents. In family law, the Shafiʿi school held that a child who had reached the age of discernment could choose which parent they felt would act as a better custodian and decide to live with that parent in a custody dispute.

A child becomes an adult and subject to complete *taklif* once they have undergone the natural process of puberty—that is, becoming physically capable of bearing children. They carry the full responsibility of taking care of others and, thus, bearing the consequences of crimes committed. The precise point at which this occurs is debated within *fiqh* works, and its relationship to criminal responsibility is discussed below in this chapter.

There are instances outside the category of *taklif* in which criminal responsibility is modified. For example, if there was more than one participant in a crime, the punishment would be shared by those involved. Potentially, responsibility would be divided among the participants according to the relative degree of severity of their participation.

Although criminal responsibility is a relatively minor point in the new codes of the nineteenth century, an exploration of it is critical to understanding how the codes were developed and upon what sources they relied. Rather than directly importing European norms, the codes regularly incorporated elements from Hanafi law and followed local precedent. In the case of juvenile offenders, for example, the IPC fixed the age of adulthood at twelve but gave significant leeway to judges to ascertain the mental state of the perpetrator. If the perpetrator was determined to be able to fully comprehend the consequences of their actions, the judge could issue a more substantial punishment. This reflected a development in the law that balanced a desire, expressed in both Hanafi and European traditions, to determine a fixed age of responsibility but be able to see each case in its own circumstances. Alternatively, in his explanation of the Egyptian code, Amin Afram al-Bustani held that the definition of a child in the code conformed with that in European traditions that had their source in Roman law. While this was true, the content of the code was still an adaptation of Hanafi understandings—even more so than the mixed approach adopted in British India.

The realm of criminal responsibility was also where Islamic and European definitions grappled with their own problems. This can be seen most clearly in the discussion of insanity. Both European and Hanafi law had struggled to develop a comprehensive legal definition of insanity. Through court practice, in 1843 common law created a test known as the M'Naughten rules, while Muslim jurists placed the responsibility of defining insanity on the shoulders of medical experts. These problems continued to appear in the new codes, with the IPC sticking more closely to the M'Naughten rules and the Ottoman and Egyptian codes continuing to rely on psychiatrists.

Comparing the definitions of criminal responsibility in Hanafi law and the new codes offers a nuanced view of what happened with the implementation of the new codes. In dealing with complex problems such as defining a child, insanity, and shared criminal responsibility, the framers of the codes chose solutions that were in line with changing European and Islamic understandings, creating new solutions that would suit their unique circumstances. For example, in the case of shared criminal responsibility, the Hanafi requirement of cooperation between perpetrators remained the standard rule in judging responsibility in the IPC, while allowing room for judges to evaluate each participant's action on its own merits. In contrast, the Ottoman and Egyptian codes chose to adopt the French view of equal punishment for all perpetrators as the basis of the law, but in practice, judges often chose to follow the Hanafi (and general *fiqh* view) of dividing punishment according to the degree of participation.

This chapter compares the understandings of criminal responsibility in Hanafi *fiqh* and the new penal codes of the nineteenth century. It begins by looking at juvenile offenders and insanity and then moves to the idea of shared responsibility. Each section presents an overview of the general Hanafi and common law understandings and then explores how those ideas were applied in British India before implementation of the IPC. The sections next explain the definitions established in the IPC and how they were implemented in the courts and close by examining the approaches of the Ottoman and Egyptian codes.

Juvenile Offenders

As mentioned above in this chapter, for all the schools of *fiqh*, children were not held to be criminally responsible for their acts—with a child being defined as an individual who had not exhibited the physical signs of puberty. Those signs were typically considered the first ejaculation for a man and the first menstruation for a woman. They could appear at different ages according to local conditions, and jurists set both minimum ages (the point at which a claim of adulthood could not be made) and maximum ages (the point at which the absence of puberty could not be claimed to dismiss legal responsibility). According to Muhammad Amin b. 'Abidin, the minimum age was twelve for boys and nine for girls. Additionally, a boy or girl could be assumed to have reached puberty if they had reached the age of fifteen, regardless of whether or not they had exhibited the physical signs—a condition that Ibn 'Abidin referred to as "puberty by age *(al-bulugh bi-l-sinn)*."[3] Only the Malikis differed from this definition, placing the maximum age at eighteen.[4] In cases of homicide, children's acts were always to be considered wrongful *(khata')*, and the punishment was always be reduced to the payment of blood money to be paid by the child's guardian.

In contrast, in English common law until the middle of the nineteenth century, there was no specific age at which a person was determined to be capable of being held responsible for a crime, and children were regularly subjected to the harshest punishments. In one case from 1829, a boy named T. King was convicted of being part of a gang of thieves and confessed to what the local press described as "several murders and robberies." He was publicly hanged at the age of twelve, and the press remarked, "We hope the dreadful example of this wretched youth may produce a lasting warning to the world at large."[5] The method of dealing with children would change with the passing of the Juvenile Offenders Act of 1847, which declared that children under the age of fourteen (the age was raised to sixteen in 1850) were to be tried before two magistrates in a special court separate from that used for adults. And in 1854, the Youthful Offenders Act called for the establishment of special schools where children under the age of sixteen who had been convicted of crimes were sent for varying periods in an attempt to reform them. However, children were still regularly sent to adult prisons until the early twentieth century, when the practice was significantly reduced.

British India

During the first half of the nineteenth century in British India, children were sometimes tried for homicide. However, they typically received reduced sentences in light of their age. For example, in one case from

Bareilly in 1853, two individuals named Roopun and Khooshalee were charged with the willful murder of a five-year-old child in an attempt to steal his silver jewelry. Based on their confession in the presence of witnesses, the sessions judge sentenced them both to execution. However, the appellate judges took note of the age of Khooshalee, which was stated to be sixteen, and reduced his sentence to life in prison while confirming the death sentence for Roopun.[6]

In a case from Bengal in 1853, a ten-year-old child, Mathur Bewa, was charged with the murder of her much older husband, Shaik Ameen. According to her confession, her husband had ordered her to prepare some tobacco and she had refused, at which time he had hit her twice with a bamboo stick. In revenge, she took a knife from their home and murdered her husband in his sleep, stabbing him in the head and severing one of his fingers. Based on her confession, the magistrate and lower judge convicted her of willful murder and suggested a sentence of life in prison. The appeals judges debated the punishment, with particular attention paid to her age, and cited three additional cases in which boys aged nine and twelve were either sentenced to life in prison or released. The judges repeatedly quoted the precedent in English law, according to which "between the age of seven and fourteen years an infant shall be deemed *prima facie* to be *doli incapax*, yet so that the presumption weakens as the prisoner's age approaches puberty." The judges also remarked that women of the perpetrator's region were "still lower in the scale of civilization, and a child, under the circumstances in which the prisoner stands, must be dealt with accordingly." As a result, the appeals judges agreed that the most appropriate sentence would be ten years in prison.[7]

In both cases, the lower sessions judge believed that the defendant deserved a much harsher punishment than what was imposed by the appellate judges. In their analysis, the appellate judges considered English law, which stated that children below the age of seven would automatically be regarded as not culpable for their actions. Such consideration dissipated as the defendant reached the age of fourteen or when the law considered puberty to occur. The judges also mentioned local customs, referred to as the "civilization" of a cultural group. This ultimately resulted in almost all defendants under the age of fourteen being considered as children, an idea that was not far removed from the Hanafi designation of puberty by age, placed at fifteen years, or (as in the general *fiqh* understanding) the attainment of natural puberty.

The Indian Penal Code

According to article 82 of the IPC, children under seven were not responsible for their actions. Article 83 stated that between the ages of seven and twelve, a child was to be assessed by the judge to determine whether they had "attained sufficient maturity of understanding to judge of the nature and consequences of his conduct on that occasion."[8] Children older than twelve were considered adults unless the judge determined that they could not understand their actions.

This put the line between children and adults at a much younger age than that found in common law and lower than the precedent cited in cases from the first half of the nineteenth century. The definition was closer to the Islamic understanding of the age of discernment, discussed above in this chapter, which held that children older than the age of seven could understand the consequences of their actions. The code eliminated the Hanafi description of puberty by age, placed at fifteen years, and gave significantly more discretion to the judge than Islamic and common law typically allowed. Therefore, the focus for the IPC was much more closely connected to the observance of a child's state of mind—discussed in Islamic thought as the presence of reason *('aql)*—rather than their achievement of puberty.

The definition of a child in the IPC represented a point where shared legal concerns were brought together. On the one hand, both the Hanafi school and common law desired to establish fixed ages for assuming adulthood. On the other hand, both systems continued to claim that the assessment of the perpetrator's awareness of their acts and their consequences was more important. By setting fixed ages and allowing for judicial discretion, the IPC satisfied the requirements of the Hanafi school and common law, allowing each case to be judged individually.

Ottoman and Egyptian Codes

The Ottoman code followed the rules of the Hanafi school, creating three successive categories of criminal responsibility where an individual became gradually more responsible for their actions. According to articles 985–986, a child was considered an adult once they exhibited the physical signs of puberty—defined as the first ejaculation for a man and the first menstruation for a woman. The earliest age when a child could express these signs was twelve for a boy and nine for a girl. However, if the physical signs could not be ascertained, all children were assumed to have reached puberty by age fifteen. Before puberty, if a child could discern *(yumayyiz)* the difference between right and wrong or understand, for example, that buying and selling means the absolute transfer of ownership from one person to another, then that child should be classified as an adolescent *(murahiq)*.[9]

According to article 40 of the Ottoman code, each category required different degrees of punishment. People older than fifteen or who could be proven to have exhibited the signs of puberty would be subject to the fullest extent of responsibility for their crimes. However, children who had not reached puberty or could not understand the gravity of their actions were to be released to their parents or placed in prison until they were determined to have been reformed. There was also a third category for people who had reached the age of discernment but were not yet adults—the adolescent *(murahiq)*. If the standard punishment for an adult was death or life imprisonment, the adolescent would be subject to a prison sentence of 5–10 years. In any other type of crime where the punishment for an adult was less than life, the adolescent would be subject to between a fourth and a third of the standard sentence.[10]

Article 57 of the Egyptian code established seven years as the lowest age at which a person could be held responsible for their actions. The explanation of the code written by al-Bustani stated that in this determination of the age of responsibility, the Egyptians "followed the path of the English legislators which also complies with Roman law." Al-Bustani continued by stating that this was because below the age of seven, "he is still an immature child, not able to differentiate between what is good and evil, nor to discern *(yumayyiz)* between what is preferred and what is abhorrent."[11] The emphasis on discernment is important to note here, as this was how jurists within the Hanafi school chose to explain the same point. Al-Bustani also cited Austrian and German law, which set entirely different ages (ten and fourteen years, respectively), and stated that, despite their differences, they all followed Roman law. The remainder of article 57 and article 58 set the upper limit:

> Article 57: If the age of the accused is more than seven years but has not yet reached 15 years, then the judgment is based upon the principles established in the following section,
>
> Article 58: If it is proven that the accused acted without *discernment*, then there will be no punishment issued upon him. Instead, the court will order his release to his family or to honorable and respectable people who would take care of him, or pursue agriculture,

manufacturing, or education, whether public or private, until he reaches ten years.[12]

Articles 59 and 60 limited the punishments of children below the age of fifteen, stating that if the sentence would typically be execution, life imprisonment, or exile, then the court could sentence the child to prison for 5–10 years, or either a fourth or a third of the punishment if the code typically required a temporary prison sentence.[13]

Although the Egyptian code and its explanation cited English, Austrian, and German law, while confirming their connection to Roman law, the content of the code mirrored Islamic law—specifically, the Hanafi opinions as expressed by Ibn 'Abidin. Children under the age of seven were considered to be not responsible for their actions because they failed to discern the nature of their acts, the same concept in *fiqh* as the age of discernment *(sinn al-tamiz)*. And the upper range of responsibility was set at age fifteen, at which point a person was automatically considered to be an adult—precisely where Ibn 'Abidin placed his "puberty by age."

The Egyptian code added a final point, indicating that reform of a child could take place by forcing them to work in either manufacturing or agriculture. This is not a surprising development, as most of the major public works projects conducted in the nineteenth century—the most prominent example of which was the Suez Canal—were carried out through a sweeping system of forced labor.[14] Such projects did not exist at the same scale in the wider Ottoman Empire, and thus the creators of the Ottoman Penal Code did not include such a provision. Instead, the framers of the code stuck to the option found in the French Code of imprisonment under supervision.

In the Ottoman and Egyptian codes, the definition of a child represented yet another example of the convergence of multiple forces in the formation of law. In both codes, the Islamic definition of puberty and classification of childhood were maintained, although they were expressed more explicitly in the Ottoman code. This was slightly different from the French Code, the source of inspiration for the Ottoman and Egyptian codes. In articles 66 and 67 of the French Code, the same three categories of child, adolescent, and adult were defined, but no reference was made to puberty, and the age of adulthood was set at sixteen.[15] The French Code punished adolescents with 10–20 years of imprisonment if the typical punishment was life, or between a third and a half of the standard sentence in other situations. This is slightly harsher than the penalties in the Ottoman and Egyptian codes, both of which limited the punishment to 5–10 years for life sentences and between a fourth and a half of the standard penalty for other cases.

With the Egyptian code's addition of forced labor, the law reflected the needs of the growing state. As previous chapters have argued, the needs of the state became increasingly prominent in the nineteenth century, and reformers called on the state to take a more prominent role to protect society and fulfill the greater purpose of the law: the implementation of justice. Article 58 of the code did just that, placing the responsibility for the lives of children who committed criminal acts squarely on the shoulders of the state. The children's reform into productive members of society and not their exoneration from punishment would further the course of justice, and the Muslim creators of the law worked to meet those needs.

Insanity

In common law, the development of the legal definition of insanity began with the writings of Sir Matthew Hale (d. 1676). Hale divided insanity into two categories: partial and total. Individuals who were totally insane were "destitute of the use of reason" and could never be held responsible for their criminal acts. Those who were partially insane, "such as a person as laboring under melancholy distempers hath yet ordinarily as great understanding, as ordinarily a child of fourteen years," could be found guilty of a felony such as murder or treason.[16] Several important cases from the eighteenth and nineteenth centuries furthered this understanding. In *R. v. Arnold* (1724), the defendant murdered a man, Lord Onslow, believing that he was the cause of all the country's problems. The judge instructed the jury to determine whether the defendant was "totally deprived of his understanding and memory, and doth not know what he is doing; no more than an infant, than a brute, or a wild beast."[17] The defendant was convicted and sentenced to death, but the Crown reduced his sentence to life in prison. In the case of *R. v. Hadfield* (1800), the defendant believed that he could bring about the second coming of Christ through his own execution and had therefore attempted to assassinate King George III. The defendant's attorney, Thomas Erskine, challenged the definition of "total deprivation" established with *Arnold* and argued that in this case "reason is not driven from her seat, but distraction sits down upon it with her, holds her, trembling upon it and frightens her from her propriety." Hadfield's plea of insanity was accepted, and according to the newly adopted Criminal Lunatics Act of 1800, he was placed in an insane asylum for the rest of his life.[18]

The next advance in the definition of insanity, leading to the rule that continues to be applied in most common-law jurisdictions today with only slight changes, came in the 1843 case of M'Naughten. The defendant was charged with the murder of Edward Drummond, a government official, thinking that he was Prime Minister Robert Peel. The defense successfully proved that M'Naughten was insane, and as a result he was found not guilty. Members of Parliament called several judges to discuss the matter and, as a result, issued a set of rules that created the standard legal definition of insanity. To be considered legally insane, a person must:

1. Labor under a defect of reason, and
2. That the crime was caused by a disease of the mind, so that either
3. He did not know the nature and quality of his acts or did not know what he was doing was wrong.[19]

In contrast, in the works of *fiqh*, jurists did not provide a specific legal test for insanity.[20] The Arabic word for an insane person *(majnun)* refers to someone who lacks the full capacity of reason *('aql)*, defined as the "knowledge of necessary perceptions, either by the senses or the soul."[21] Therefore, a person incapable of discerning the physical world around them or distinguishing between right and wrong would be considered insane, similar to a child who had not reached the age of discernment. Works of *fiqh* stated that insanity could be either a permanent affliction placed upon the individual by God *(mutbaq)* or a temporary illness that could be treated medically *(ghayr mutbaq)* and could come and go at different times in a person's life.

Regardless of the insanity's permanence, individuals determined to be insane when committing a criminal act were not entirely responsible for their actions. For example, in the specific case of homicide, an insane person would not be subject to execution but would be accountable for paying blood money *(diya)* to the victim's family as compensation for the crime. Hanafi *fiqh* also forbid execution when a criminal had become insane after committing a crime and reduced the punishment to the payment of blood money.

The common-law and Islamic definitions of insanity shared a number of themes. Both definitions tied insanity to a loss of reason and the inability of a person to comprehend the world around them and the consequences of their actions. They also recognized temporal differences in insanity and believed it could be either a temporary or a permanent affliction. Additionally, both the common-law and Islamic approaches to insanity accepted the idea that every human being was born with basic reason. In Europe, this idea is often understood as an invention of modernity and the Enlightenment. According to the twentieth-century German philosopher Ernst Cassirer, for example, "The eighteenth century is imbued with a belief in the unity and immutability of reason. Reason is the same for all thinking subjects, all nations, all epochs, and all cultures."[22] Muslim jurists spoke of reason in similar terms and saw insanity (junun) as an affliction from an external source. The word junun comes from the Arabic root j-n-n, which means "to cover (satara),"[23] indicating that a person's natural state of sanity ('aql) was covered or removed by an external affliction. This distinction is important because the legal presumption in courts would be that an individual is sane, and insanity (rather than sanity) would have to be proven.

However, the Islamic and common-law understandings of insanity differed in their connection to medical science. Islamic law and the Ottoman and Egyptian penal codes relied on expert advice to determine whether or not a person was insane. However, the common-law system developed a legal definition of insanity separate from the medical definition.

British India
In the first half of the nineteenth century in India, insanity was used as a defense to mitigate punishment. In a case from Bengal in 1853, a man named Kunhai Chung was charged with the murder of Ramsoonder, the wounding of Ramsoonder's sun, and setting the house of their neighbor on fire. The case was summarized as follows:

> It appears that the prisoner went out of his mind five or six days prior to the commission of the act now laid to his charge. His madness showed itself by his wandering frequently into the jungle and there concealing himself, and from his never speaking to any one who addressed him.
>
> The mufti issued a fatwa barring punishment, as the crime was committed while the perpetrator was insane. The British judge agreed, acquitting him of all charges. The appellate court concurred but ordered that the prisoner be kept in custody until the court was satisfied that he was no longer a danger to others.[24]

Determining whether or not a person was insane was frequently a challenge for the courts and involved seeking the opinions of medical specialists and multiple judges. In another case from Bengal in 1853, a man named Abool Hossein was charged with the murder of his wife, Murrium, by striking her multiple times with a pole while she was asleep in their home in 1851. In front of the magistrate, the defendant fully confessed to the crime but claimed insanity, saying:

> I did kill my wife with this weapon. I don't know the date, but it was in Cheyt [Chaitra, the first month in the Hindu lunar calendar]. My wife and I were asleep in the house with the door facing the north. I was going out early in the morning when my wife Murrium said, you must not leave your home. Hearing this, I became like a mad man, and with this weapon, which was below a table in the same room, I gave my wife several blows and killed her. I then ran out and was going towards Attaullah, the policeman's house, when Buddon Seel seized me. For 8 or 10 days before this, my heart was in a very unsettled state, and I committed the deed when I was out of my mind. It was 11 days before the murder that my wife told me I must not go outside my house.[25]

An interrogation by the magistrate was also recorded, during which the defendant claimed that a man from a different caste, Maun Sheekdar, wished to marry his wife forcibly. When the defendant learned of this plot, it caused him to become insane. When a medical officer was brought in to observe the defendant, he deposed on two occasions that he believed the defendant was faking insanity. The magistrate felt it unwise to proceed and placed Abool Hossein in a mental hospital for treatment. He was brought before the sessions judge for a further trial and final ruling when he was discharged from the hospital. Multiple witnesses from the community were brought in to attest to his insanity, and they claimed that at times he "abused people and chased them, and at others, he would do dirty tricks." At this point, Abool Hossein changed his confession and claimed: "I did not kill my wife. I never had a wife; my mother and father died when I was very young. Where was I to get the money to marry a wife? Whose wife Murrium was, I can't say, I know not who she was or who murdered her. I have come here having been told by the people to do so."[26] This complete about-face in the defendant's statements shocked the court, which requested that the physician of the insane asylum, William Abbot Green, be brought in and asked about the defendant's state of mind when he had been brought to the asylum and after his treatment. Green stated that he believed the defendant upon admission had been "quite insane," that his insanity was due to his suffering "from cholera and dysentery in November 1851," and that he was a regular marijuana *(gunjah)* smoker.[27] However, following a few months of treatment in the hospital, the defendant calmed down, and after two full years of observation, he was considered cured and released.

The court agreed with Green's observations and ordered that the defendant be acquitted. The appellate court criticized the process of the investigation but eventually concurred, stating: "Believing that when the prisoner killed his wife, he was in a state of mind which rendered him incapable of knowing that what he was doing was an act forbidden by law, and for which he cannot, therefore, be held responsible, I acquit him of the murder."[28]

The circumstances of this case reveal several important facts about how the British in India viewed instances of insanity. Although the M'Naughten rules had been in place in England for over a decade and used a legal definition of insanity that differed from the medical definition, the courts relied on the expertise of two health care providers (the medical officer of the court and Green from the insane asylum) to ascertain the defendant's mental status. His insanity was also determined to be temporary and curable, resulting from diseases and his repeated drug use—which had impaired his reason a few days before and during the commission of the crime. Finally, although the defendant had become more obviously insane during his second interrogation when he denied even having a wife, the vital point to determine was whether he was insane when he committed the crime, not after it.

Although the opinion of a mufti was not sought and a British judge and local jury reached the final ruling, the outcome of the case would have been mainly the same had the matter been subject to the understandings of Hanafi *fiqh*, with only one important additional consideration. The loss of reason due to intentional intoxication—the defendant's continued voluntary use of marijuana—would not be considered a legitimate excuse for the crime in Hanafi *fiqh*. This would have caused a Muslim judge to pause. However, the presence of other illnesses and the fact that the defendant clearly and of his own admission committed the crime when he was not in his proper state of mind would have confirmed the presence of insanity and rendered him innocent, although he would have been required to pay blood money to the victim's family.

The Indian Penal Code

Article 84 of the IPC stated, "Nothing is an offence which is done by a person who, at the time of doing it, by reason of unsoundness of mind, is incapable of knowing the nature of the act, or that he is doing what is either wrong or contrary to law."[29] In the explanation of this article, the M'Naughten rules were cited and the term "unsoundness of mind" was considered to include "whether the want of capacity is temporary or permanent, natural or supervening, whether it arises from disease or exists from the time of birth. . . . Thus an idiot who is a person without understanding from his birth, a lunatic who has intervals of reason, and a person who is mad or delirious, are all persons of 'unsound mind.'"[30]

In 1864, following the implementation of the code, a barber named Tota from a village near the city of Aligarh was charged with the murder of his daughter. According to the testimony of witnesses, the defendant appeared to be of unsound mind because he had stopped working for the past two years and "goes about in a careless way with his head uncovered." One day, he felt that death was better than life, and he took his five–year-old daughter in his arms and jumped into a well near the outskirts of his village. Once in the water, he got scared and shouted for help. Other villagers pulled him out and brought him home, but Tota did not mention his daughter to his rescuers. When it became clear that she was missing from the home, he confessed that she had been in the well with him, and she was later found to have died from drowning. The jury found the defendant innocent by reason of insanity, but the sessions judge disagreed, believing that if he had been of sound enough mind to call for help, he should have known the likely fate of his daughter and that he had showed no signs of insanity when he was brought in front of the court. Therefore, the judge called for a verdict of guilty and sentenced the defendant to life in prison.

The appellate court judges were divided in the case, with two (W. Roberts and D. Simson) believing that the defendant was not insane. Roberts commented: "I do not think that he was in a state of unconsciousness as to his act, or of the nature of his acts, but rather that he is of a morbid temperament; that at the time of the act, owing to his family having left him, he was worked up to a state of excitement. He seems to have been in the same state at the time of committing the act, as he now is, which certainly does not show an aberration of mind amounting to insanity as defined in Section 393, Criminal Procedure Code."[31] Two other judges (J. H. Batten and W. Edwards) believed that no evidence of the defendant's insanity had been presented, with Batten remarking:

> The medical evidence in this case amounts to *nil*. The Sessions Judge uses this remarkable expression in his judgment: 'The main evidence, however, of insanity is the act itself with which the prisoner is charged.' The Judge then, after declaring his inability to give a 'certain opinion' as to the insanity of the prisoner, goes on to say 'granting that he was then insane, it cannot be allowed that he was insane when drawn out of the well.' If he was sane enough to have saved, or to have 'attempted to save, his daughter.' I entirely fail to see the force of this reasoning; after years of insanity, did one plunge into a well *cure* him? ... If the prisoner had any spite against the child, and if he had threatened to make away with her, or if he had told his neighbors that he could no longer support his daughter, then his allowing her to stay in the well from which he was himself rescued, might, perhaps, be considered a deliberate act; but there is nothing of the kind in evidence.[32]

A final judge (A. Ross) issued the deciding opinion for acquittal, stating:

> Medical evidence there is none, pro or con, as to the prisoner's state of mind when he committed the act. There is a considerable weight of general evidence as to the accused having been for a long time past of weak mind, and it is difficult to say whether he had at the time of committing the act such soundness of mind as to render him "capable of knowing the nature of the act charged, or that he was doing what was wrong or contrary to law." His conduct subsequent to his rescue, I think, on the whole, rather favors the conclusion that he had not. I observe, too, that suicide or attempt to commit suicide is generally taken to afford presumption of insanity. Under these circumstances, I would give the prisoner the benefit of the doubt, and acquit him on the ground of insanity.[33]

The wording and the subsequent application of the IPC in cases of homicide created a mixture of the views of common law and local custom—in this case, Islamic law. The M'Naughten rules had been established as the primary test for insanity, and all individuals were assumed to be sane. Thus, insanity had to be proven for a person to receive an acquittal. Insanity was connected to a person's ability to know that their actions were wrong or illegal at the time they were committed. In addition, the act committed could not be considered proof of insanity no matter how odd or irrational it might seem, as clarified by Batten's opinion. Instead, it was the defendant's state of mind before and during the commission of the act that must be judged.

The primary difference between Islamic *fiqh* and the IPC with respect to the definition of insanity was that in the latter, the state of insanity was not absolute, and individuals under some perceived delusion could be held responsible for their actions. In the explanation of the IPC, an example of this was given wherein a person's "delusion was, that the deceased had inflicted some injury on him or had caused the death of his relations, etc., and he killed him in revenge for such supposed injury."[34] Such an individual would be considered insane and therefore not responsible for his actions in the Islamic perspective, whereas under the IPC, such a defendant would be held liable for punishment at the judge's discretion.

Ottoman and Egyptian Codes

In the Egyptian code, the concept of insanity was discussed under the excuse of idiocy (*'atah*) and explained in article 63: "The person accused of a felony or misdemeanor is excused from the punishment passed upon him by law if it is proven that he was an idiot during the time of its commission." The explanation also stated that the general category of idiocy included "all elements which infect reason," including "insanity (*junun*), confusion (*balah*), and all of the other mental disorders."[35] Similar to its discussion of juvenile offenders, the Egyptian code described idiocy exactly as the Hanafi school did—that is, either permanent (*mutbaq*) or temporary (*ghayr mutbaq*) and either a fault placed by God (*khuluqi*) or the result of an event (*hadith*).

The same approach was taken in the Ottoman code, with article 41 stating, "If it is established that a criminal committed a crime in the state of insanity (*junun*), he is pardoned from the legally prescribed punishment."[36] Later the explanation of this article stated that a person was to be considered insane based on the testimony or certification of a medical expert. This was justified as the standard practice in Istanbul, where a doctor certified by the Ministry of Health issued reports on whether an individual was insane at the time they had committed a crime. The code stated that similar steps should be taken outside of the capital and that the advice of a reputable local medical professional should be sought out.[37]

Additionally, the Ottoman code made a point of emphasizing that the removal of reason carried out voluntarily, such as by drinking alcohol or taking drugs, did not constitute a valid excuse of insanity and would not mitigate criminal responsibility.[38]

Thus, the legal changes made by the new codes reflected the problems of each system and the difficulty the codes' creators and judges had in defining insanity. In the Hanafi school, which never established a legal definition of insanity, doctors were relied upon to determine the perpetrator's state of mind during the commission of a crime. This created a significant degree of uncertainty and meant that each case had to be judged individually. For common law, even though the M'Naughten rules had been established in the 1840s and created a strict legal definition of insanity, it was still unclear exactly when a person could be acquitted based on the defense of insanity. Therefore, the IPC and its subsequent application in Indian courts created a balance, using the M'Naughten rules as a test for insanity but continuing to rely on specialist testimony as in the Hanafi school. The Ottoman and Egyptian codes made no change to the definition of insanity in the classical approach, continuing to rely upon the expertise of doctors.

Shared Criminal Responsibility

In cases of homicide, Islamic legal theorists attempted to seek out the person who was directly responsible for the death and subject only that person to execution, while other accomplices were required to pay a share of punitive blood money (al-arsh). In an example that was first found in the work of al-Tahawi (and was often cited by jurists), "If a man assaulted another and sliced open his stomach, bringing out his insides, then [another] man came and struck his throat with a sword intentionally, then the killer who must face execution is the one who struck the throat and not the other."[39] This rule led Rudolph Peters to state: "Islamic criminal law is based on the principle of individual responsibility. Persons are punished for their own acts. Collective punishment is not allowed, although there are exceptional cases of collective liability, such as in the Hanafite *Qasāma* doctrine, where the inhabitants of a house or village can be held liable for the financial consequences of a homicide with an unknown perpetrator, committed in the house or village."[40]

An example of this type of individual responsibility can be found in cases of the second half of the nineteenth century in Egypt. In one case from 1861, two brothers (Ahmad and 'Umar al-Dawwa) were charged with the murder of a man named 'Ali walad Hamid. 'Umar had entered the home where the victim was sleeping and cursed him, accusing him of adultery. The victim woke up and chased 'Umar outside. There the victim was ambushed and beaten on the head by the two brothers with bamboo clubs, and he died a few days later from his injuries. Although both defendants were convicted and had clearly cooperated in the crime, the mufti ruled in his fatwa that in this case, only one of the defendants could be held wholly responsible for the death. He came to this conclusion because the witnesses' statements did not specify the defendants' cooperation and "had each beating been taken independently, it [would have] led to death. Death likely occurred from only one of the beatings."[41]

However, in *fiqh* works as well as most fatwa collections from the Hanafi school, legal scholars did accept the concept of shared criminal responsibility, known popularly as the idea of killing a group for the right of one (*qatl al-jama'a bi-l-wahid*). This was based on a case adjudicated by the second Caliph 'Umar. According to *al-Fatawa al-tatarkhaniya*, "If a group killed one person, then the [entire] group is to be killed, based on the consensus (*ijma'*) of the Prophet's Companions, and it is related that seven killed one in the city of San'a'. 'Umar executed all of the defendants involved and stated, 'If all the people of San'a' had come together (*tamala'*) [in the crime], then I would have executed them all.'"[42] Elsewhere in the same collection, a hypothetical case was presented: "If a man gravely injures another (*jiraha muthkhana*) from which [injury] it is not expected that he will live, and another injures him as well, then the murderer is the one who made [the] grave injury. This is if the two injuries are subsequent [to one another], but if they were in cooperation [with one another] (*mu'awin*), then they are both the murderers. This is also the case if one injures multiple times and the other only once, then they are both the murderers."[43]

The two terms that were used in these rules established the conditions for joint criminal responsibility in *fiqh* works were coming together (*tamalu'*) and cooperation (*ta'awun*). If one of these two conditions was met, then all involved could suffer the punishment of execution. The same opinions were mentioned in the *al-Fatawa al-'alamgiriya* and the *al-Fatawa al-anqarawiya*.[44] The latter also noted, citing Abu Bakr b. Mas'ud al-Kasani, that if multiple individuals participated in the commission of a crime but only one carried out the actual homicide, then the other participants should be judged independently and punished according to their actions.[45] Thus, although Islamic law attempted to identify the primary person responsible for the crime and apply the most extreme punishment only to the individual who took the life of the victim, if multiple persons either came together or cooperated in the commission of the crime, then they could all be held responsible—either being executed as a group or having their crimes judged independently according to the respective severity of each act leading up to the actual crime.

In another case, from Egypt in 1862, three villagers were charged with the murder of a man named Ahmad Farghali. A fight between a larger group of villagers was in progress when the victim joined to stop the fight and was beaten by the three defendants. He died a few days later. Two of the defendants confessed, and there was no evidence presented against the third. The two who confessed were convicted by the court of wrongful homicide, as there was no intent to kill, and the court ruled that they each were responsible for paying the full blood money *(diya)*. The mufti stated in his ruling that this punishment was inappropriate and argued that the blood money should have been divided into equal thirds among all those involved in the death, as the strikes occurred "subsequently *('ala al-ta'aqub)*" and all three men had participated in the killing.[46]

In common law, the people who participated in the commission of a crime were known as "accomplices" or "principals in the second degree." According to William Blackstone (d. 1780), principals of the second degree were people who were "present, aiding, and abetting the fact to be done."[47] They did not have to participate directly in the commission of the crime directly and could, for example, be standing guard and protecting the individual who was committing the actual crime. Typically, accomplices were subject to the same punishment as the principal perpetrator.

The people who aided in the commission of the crime but who were not actually present were known as "accessories," defined by Blackstone in this way: "he who is not the chief actor in the offense, nor present at its performance, but is someway concerned therein, either before or after the fact committed." Blackstone then defined two types of accessories: a person before the fact, who "being absent at the time of the crime committed, does yet procure, counsel, or command another to commit a crime," and a person after the fact, who "knowing a felony to have been committed, receives, relieves, comforts, or assists the felon."[48] Blackstone did not provide a punishment for accessorie. However, the much later Accessories and Abettors Act of 1861 stated that any accessory before the fact "may be indicted, tried, convicted, and punished in all respects as if he were a principal Felon," while accessories after the fact were subject to a punishment of up to two years in prison, with or without hard labor.[49]

Not until close to the end of the nineteenth century would a new case in common law start to establish a precedent for shared criminal responsibility, coming from the United States in 1893, with *State v. Tally*. A judge in Alabama named John Tally was removed from office for aiding and abetting in the murder of a man named Robert Ross. A family known as the Skeltons was chasing the defendant in revenge for his relationship with a relative (who was the wife of the judge), and Ross's relatives had sent him a telegram warning him that the Skeltons were on their way to kill him. Tally sent telegrams of his own to the town where Ross was taking refuge, ordering the telegraph company employee not to let Ross get away and to say nothing regarding any warnings received earlier. As a result, the Skeltons killed Ross. Initially, Tally was acquitted of the charge of murder. Upon appeal, he was found guilty of the murder because although he did not have absolute knowledge of the murderous intentions of the Skeltons when they set out, his subsequent actions and the telegrams he sent meant that he was "constructively present" at the time of the murder and therefore shared the guilt of those who committed the murder.[50]

Thus, both common law and Islamic law held that if there was a form of direct cooperation between the parties to a crime, they could in principle share in the guilt and punishment. In the nineteenth century, this meant that regardless of the jurisdiction, shared criminal responsibility could constitute either the same punishment issued to all the parties involved or different sentences for each participant depending upon the degree of their involvement.

British India

In Bareilly in 1853, three men (named Chait Ram, Purma, and Doolee) were charged with the willful murder of a seventeen-year-old boy named Gunga. His body was found in a field close to where he and the defendants had worked during the day, and "there was a string round the neck, and marks of fingers on the throat."[51] He had been wearing silver arm rings and gold earrings, which were missing. The jewelry was found in a shed belonging to Chait Ram, and when asked about the murder, the three defendants began accusing each other of killing Gunga.

At the police station, each defendant produced a confession that witnesses confirmed. Doolee stated that "Chait Ram and Purma got on the breast of the deceased, and were beating him. After the beating, Chait Ram gave him the rings, enjoining silence."[52] Purma stated that "Doolee compressed the neck of the deceased and took off his earrings. Chait Ram held the hands of the deceased and took off his arm rings; then Doolee and Chait Ram took up and carried away the body; he followed." Chait Ram stated "that he went to see his field. Dolee and Purma were with him; perceived a man cutting the crop; Purma seized his legs and then caught hold of his neck; cried out thief. Purma then compressed the throat of the man, and he died immediately; he and the two others took up the body and cast it in the field of Bhowane. Purma took off the ornaments and gave them to Doolee; said after that Doolee killed deceased from spite."[53]

In court, each defendant pleaded not guilty and claimed that they had been tortured into confessing by the police. Two of the three jury members convicted all prisoners, while the third had reservations about Chait Ram and acquitted him. The sessions judge sided with the majority of the jury and requested death sentences for all three defendants. The appellate judges (S. S. Brown and H. B. Harington) looked at the confessions and believed that the defendants knew what they were doing in providing contradictory stories and, in their admissions, "charged each other with being the principals and endeavored to present themselves as merely aiding and abetting." Ultimately, the court found fault with the confession of Chait Ram, believed his claim of torture, and decided to acquit him. Purma and Doolee were found guilty and sentenced to death.[54] In this case, two defendants were found to have cooperated in the murder and committed the crime together. As a result, they were both subject to capital punishment—a ruling that would have been the same had it been conducted in an Islamic setting, as the two fulfilled the requirements of a coming together (*tamalu'*) and cooperation (*ta'awun*) to commit the crime.

In a case from Bengal in 1854, five defendants were charged with the murder of Nundlal Singh, which had occurred as the result of a large fight between two groups (the cause of the fight is not mentioned in the records). In his fatwa, the mufti convicted the five men of being "guilty of affray with severe wounding," and the sessions judge agreed, sentencing each of the prisoners to four years in prison and ordering that each pay a fine of 50 rupees. Three of the defendants appealed their sentence, and the appellate court rejected their appeal based on the presence of eyewitnesses who had readily identified all those involved. In this case, no one person could be identified as the killer, and all those involved in the fight were sentenced to lighter punishments.[55] Had this crime been tried in an Islamic setting, the outcome would have been the same. As there was no evident cooperation between them, each defendant would have been required to pay a portion of the blood money *(diya)* and be subject to discretionary punishment *(ta'zir)* that could have included imprisonment.

The Indian Penal Code

Articles 34–38 of the IPC defined the participation of multiple parties in a crime:

Article 34: When a criminal act is done by several persons, each of such persons is liable for that act in the same manner as if the act were done by him alone.

Article 35: Whenever an act, which is criminal only by reason of its being done with a criminal knowledge or intention, is done by several persons, each of such persons, who joins in the act with such knowledge or intention is liable for the act in the same manner as if the act were done by him alone with that knowledge or intention.

Article 36: Wherever the causing of a certain effect, or an attempt to cause that effect by an act or by an omission, is an offence, it is to be understood that the causing of that effect partly by an act and partly by an omission is the same offence.

Article 37: When an offence is committed by means of several acts, whoever intentionally co-operates in the commission of that offence by doing any one of those acts, either singly, or jointly with any other person, commits that offence.

Article 38: Where several persons are engaged or concerned in the commission of a criminal act, they may be guilty of different offences by means of that act.[56]

The language of article 37 that defines cooperation is the most pertinent for the current discussion. Islamic discussions also used the term "cooperation" *(ta'awun)*, stipulating that as long as two individuals were proven to have worked together in the commission of a crime, they could be held fully responsible for the crime as if they had worked alone. Additionally, article 38 opened the door for other participants in the crime to be charged with more minor offenses.

In 1865 three people named Benee, Pirtheepal, and Bunsee were charged with the murder of two victims, named Sheobhuruth and Sewuk. This was a bizarre case, reportedly occurring because a village of fishermen had received letters from the Muslim holy cities of Mecca and Medina "calling upon them to break up their ornaments, burn their nets, abstain from eating fish and drinking wine, and to become Bhuguts."[57] After the letters had circulated among the villagers for a few days, the residents came together and held a carnival to celebrate their new religious importance. During the celebrations, the victims were accused of being demons from a former world, and it was believed that they would eat the other villagers. As a result, they were tied to a tree and beaten to death by the defendants. Witnesses and medical evidence proved to the initial judge and assessors that the three defendants were guilty, as they had all tied up the victims and caused their final, fatal wounds. The sessions judge believed "it is quite clear that these three *co-operated* in murdering the two."[58] However, the judge determined that one of the defendants, Bunsee, should not be held entirely responsible for the murder as another defendant, Benee, had threatened him with death if he refused to assist him in the murder. The judge sentenced Benee and Pirtheepal to execution by hanging and Bunsee to life in prison. Eleven other defendants were also brought to trial for the lesser charge of abetment, as they had taken part in the carnival and did nothing to prevent the crime that was taking place in front of them. After reviewing the case, the appellate court confirmed the death sentences but believed that the other eleven defendants "were no more than spectators on the occasion and seem to have been taken by surprise by the ultimate acts of extreme violence of the three men above named, and therefore they can be held to have been *merely passively* consenting to the murder committed, but not to have been guilty of abetment thereof."[59] As a result, the court acquitted the eleven offenders of abetment and ordered their immediate release. This case highlighted every aspect of shared criminal responsibility discussed in the IPC and shows how the court viewed both the concept of participants in the crime as well as abetment. The two defendants who were sentenced to death cooperated in committing the act, working together to tie the victims to the tree and cause their death. The third defendant, who had his sentence reduced to life in prison, had an excuse because he felt compelled to participate in the murder after a threat to his life. This was not enough to completely remove his responsibility, as article 94 of the IPC limited the use of such an excuse in situations of bodily harm or homicide. For the others, the simple fact that they were present during the crime was not sufficient to hold them criminally liable as their actions were merely passive. To be considered as having abetted the murder, they needed to have actively assisted the murderers by providing aid to them in some manner or refusing to come to the aid of those being murdered. This was not proven in the case, so those defendants were released after the case was reviewed.

The understanding of shared criminal responsibility developed under the IPC, therefore, closely followed the understanding of *fiqh* requiring that for a punishment to be issued, each participant had to be either actively cooperating with each other (thus, the participants would be understood as accomplices in common law) or to have come together (understood as abetting) to carry out the murder.

Ottoman and Egyptian Codes

Concerning participants in the same crime (*al-ishtirak fi al-jarima*), the Egyptian code stated in article 64 that "all those who participate with another in the act of a felony or a misdemeanor are to be punished in the same manner as the principal actor, as long as there is not a contradictory text in the law."[60] Later, in article 214, the code provided a lesser punishment in cases of homicide, stating that "[Other] participants in a homicide, for which a [primary] perpetrator is sentenced to death, are punished with life in prison with hard labor."[61]

In his explanation of the code, al-Bustani mentioned that this was one of the most challenging areas of criminal law and that legal scholars around the world differed in their approach to shared criminal responsibility. "If a group commits a singular crime as participants," he wrote, "it immediately comes to mind that they are not at the same level of participation and that there must be major differences between them."[62] However, he asked:

> Is there a definition for judges of limited power, as stated by one of the great jurists, that sets and confirms these multiple degrees and shades of participation so that he [the judge] may subsequently enforce a punishment based upon it? Are there also definitions for the judiciary's power that it may rely upon and specific texts it may reference? With this in mind, it is not shocking [to observe] what the Egyptian legislator has decided upon, following the French legislation, in placing an absolute rule of judgment, equal in its pillars,

[that] encompasses the doers of the crime and the [equal] participants in it with a single punishment.[63]

The Ottoman code spoke of the same difficulty in determining shared
responsibility and provided an outline of the concept in article 45: "The
shared perpetrators of a crime are to be punished as if they were acting
alone unless specifically mentioned in the [relevant] section."[64] Rashad Bek,
an explainer of the code, gave the example of several individuals who gath-
ered around a person and stabbed him with knives until he died. If each
stab could be determined through medical reports to have independently
caused the victim's death, they should be treated equally. In Rashad Bek's
opinion, the Ottoman code did not provide any significant detail regarding this point, but he believed that the example he gave would fit within
article 45. Khalil Rif'at, another explainer of the code, mentioned that this
was a problematic area of the law because it was taken directly from the
French Code's article 59. Significant work on expanding this area of the
law was left to the Ottoman jurists and legal experts. In particular, Rif'at
criticized the code for not fully encompassing the different levels of participation in a single act: "In its articles regarding the punishment of criminals,
the law did not specify differing degrees of participation . . . [I]t is not a
requirement that [a judge] rule upon each defendant with a single degree
[of punishment]. Rather, it is permissible to aggravate or mitigate the ruling considering what aggravating and mitigating circumstances appear for
each individual at trial."[65]

To see how these different degrees of participation would work in practice, consider a case from Salonica in 1880. Six defendants were accused of
attacking and killing a trader and injuring many of his employees following
Friday prayers. The investigation determined that only three defendants
(Mustafa, Dilli Isma'il, and Hasan b. Husayn Efendi) were responsible for
the crime, and the other three defendants were released. Mustafa was later
identified as the primary actor, but he died in prison from injuries sustained
in the fight. The remaining two defendants were sentenced to fifteen and
five years of hard labor, respectively.[66] In this case, the Ottoman judges
held all three defendants responsible for a single homicide and punished
them according to their degree of participation in the crime. Thus, although
the Ottoman code required active participants to receive identical punishment, in both the explanation of the code and practice, judges had significant

discretion to alter the severity of punishment depending upon each party's degree of participation.

When it came to abetment, article 175 of the Ottoman code used the terminology of the Hanafi school to state that "Whoever comes together (*yumali'*) or cooperates (*yu'awun*) with a murderer in the commission of a homicide shall be placed in prison for a period of time."[67] According to Rif'at, this required that an individual knew that the perpetrator intended to kill when cooperating with them by "directly handing them a weapon, directing them to where a weapon could be found, or preventing the victim from escaping."[68] Interestingly, although this article explicitly mentioned the Hanafi concepts of cooperation and coming together, they were utilized in a different manner. As mentioned above, these concepts were used by the Hanafi school to enhance the punishment of participants in a crime, allowing them to take the same responsibility as the primary offender. In the Ottoman code, however, this concept was used to differentiate between those who actively supported the commission of the crime and those who merely supported it, allowing them to be punished less harshly.

The confusion found within the Ottoman and Egyptian codes shows another area where European influence conflicted with the existing legal discourse. In this area of the law, the French understanding was directly applied to the Ottoman and Egyptian context. Jurists in both jurisdictions realized this problem and worked to make room for differing degrees of participation, eventually creating a legal definition distinct from the limited ruling found in the code. The IPC's understanding of shared criminal responsibility was much closer to the classical Hanafi understanding: it incorporated the concept of cooperation as understood in earlier *fiqh* discourse. Although the sources did not present a motive for these changes, it is important to note that, despite the complexity of determining the punishment deserved by multiple people who participated in a crime, the Hanafi school, the IPC, and the Ottoman and Egyptian codes came to the same conclusion in practice: they each tried to measure the responsibility of each defendant according to their level of participation.

Conclusion

As observed in the explanation of the Egyptian Penal Code of 1883 regarding shared responsibility, defining a person's degree of criminal responsibility was one of the most complicated areas of criminal law. At what point does a child truly understand the consequences of their actions?

Where should the line be drawn between sanity and insanity? Can an insane person, who has clearly lost their connection to the world around them, still be held responsible for a crime as egregious as taking the life of another? And finally, can an individual who participates with another fully understand and share the murderous intent of the principal perpetrator to such a degree that they should face the same fate?

Islamic and Western legal theorists developed different and complex answers to these questions. For Muslim jurists, the answer was to be found in the religious concept of *taklif*, which governed responsibility for acts of worship and worldly affairs alike. People who were able to bear the burden of meeting their daily prayer requirements and to comprehend the message that God had given humanity were deemed capable of being held responsible for their acts in this world. For Western theorists, the focus was on the state of mind. If a person who committed a crime could be found to have been of sound mind and aware of the consequences of their actions at the time, they could be held criminally responsible.

Although these two approaches based their explanations on different sources and carved out very different paths in their legal development, they came to similar conclusions that were reflected in the new penal codes of the nineteenth century—especially when the codes were applied in the courts. The line between a child and an adult could no longer be left to a subjective understanding of puberty that differed from one person to another. Efforts were made to identify specific points at which all individuals would be considered adults. The IPC left the most room for judicial discretion and allowed each case to be judged on its merits. Insanity was also more clearly defined. Again, the IPC gave the judge more discretion, while the Ottoman and Egyptian codes chose to rely more upon the evidence of medical experts. Finally, a general rule was established that people who actively cooperated in the commission of a crime or homicide could, in principle, be punished equally. However, the codes and court practice modified this rule, particularly in the Egyptian and Ottoman jurisdictions, allowing for a balanced application of the law to punish accomplices according to the degree of their participation.

The question of criminal responsibility was by no means solved with the introduction of new penal codes alone, and subsequent laws, case precedents, and developments in medical science in both the Muslim world and the West continued to provide new answers. In the case of insanity, the United Kingdom continued to have significant difficulty in reconciling its

M'Naughten rules with medical definitions of insanity. As a result, individuals who would be identified as insane by a psychiatrist could still face considerable punishment since, according to the rules, they merely needed to comprehend that their act was wrong or contrary to the law. The gap between the legal and the medical approaches eventually caused Parliament to issue the Criminal Procedure (Insanity and Unfitness to Plead) Act of 1991, which requires the "written evidence of two or more registered medical practitioners at least one of whom is duly approved [by the relevant government authority]" for a jury to return a verdict of acquittal on the ground of insanity.[69]

The situation has been quite different in India, with no statutory changes made to article 84 of the IPC since its implementation, despite the Law Commission of India's recommendation to revisit the article.[70] The practice of the courts has also expressed problems in defining insanity, and although the testimony of psychiatrists is often accepted as evidence, the courts have consistently confirmed that the test for insanity is legal and not medical. Even people certified to be insane by medical professionals could be subject to criminal liability if they showed other evidence of culpability, such as hiding the murder weapon.[71]

During the implementation of the new penal codes in the nineteenth century, the answers given to the complex questions of defining criminal responsibility represented a coalescence of Islamic and Western legal approaches. Legal scholars and judges attempted to find solutions that would work within the new legal systems, accord judges a certain amount of leeway when assessing perpetrators' responsibility, and as a result come as close as possible to achieving the certainty of guilt given the circumstances of each case.

6

Changing Tides and Islamism

This book has so far sought to highlight the linkages and continuities between the codes and the understanding of law within the premodern Islamic tradition. Focusing on *siyasa*, the writers, translators, commentators, and legal practitioners of the nineteenth century worked to adapt the law of homicide to fit contemporary needs, integrating new understandings of older concepts (like insanity and the right of the victim's family) into the codes while maintaining legitimacy within the shari'a.

However, many Muslims working today in the jurisdictions discussed do not perceive this as having happened. For laypersons and jurists alike, the legal systems of the Muslim world are antithetical to what they understand as Islamic norms and values. For example, the Egyptian judge and legal historian Tariq al-Bishri (d. 2021) suggested that the reform movements of the nineteenth century had systematically displaced the shari'a and that Egypt's system was now thoroughly foreign:

> The typical [law] student is trained that the history of his law can be traced back to the Romans, then to European ecclesiastical law, then to the Napoleonic Codes. . . . The shari'a, however, is relegated to the field of personal status. We called the process of excising shari'a and introducing French legislation "legal and legislative reform." We were indeed in need of reform; however, in this, as in all other fields, we neither reformed nor modernized. Instead, we destroyed the structures and edifices [of our own system]. We then upheld aspects of the foreign imported [system] chosen for us and then imposed them upon ourselves.[1]

For most of his career, al-Bishri was a prominent member of the Council of State (Majlis al-Dawla), Egypt's highest administrative court. He played an important role in the country's legislative development in the second half of the twentieth century and was appointed by the Supreme Council of Armed Forces to head the committee to draft Egypt's new constitution following the fall of the regime of President Muhammad Hosni Mubarak in 2011. Al-Bishri's view that the law of Egypt is antithetical to the shari'a and an importation of French law is representative of the general sentiment of many members of the Egyptian legal community.

In the 1890s, Amin Afram al-Bustani noticed members of the Egyptian Parliament (Majlis Shura al-Qawanin) and religious scholars expressing opposition to the new codes as foreign and opposed to the shari'a. In a collection of his articles that was published in 1919, al-Bustani looked back on the 1883 code and suggested that the Egyptian government had gone too far in accepting French influence. Although he provided no specific examples, he did note that to avoid the complexities of adapting its previous legal system, Egypt had "relied in its entirety on the legislation of Europe, except in limited situations."[2] This position stands in stark contrast to his explanation of the 1883 code, in which he defended the right of the state instead of the victim's family (as part of the shari'a) to determine the fate of murderers, ending blood feuds and taking punishment out of the hands of individuals.[3]

The reason for al-Bustani's change of heart can partially be traced to growing sentiments of Egyptian nationalism. For example, he stated that developing laws with European influence was a problem because "not all that works in the West is suitable for us, as laws are built on the customs, practices, natures, and needs of their people. Therefore, it [the development of laws] is a national project and cannot be transferred from one nation to another like a consumer product."[4] Additionally, when a group of attorneys, judges, and jurists came together in 1933 to issue a volume celebrating the fiftieth anniversary of the establishment of the National Courts, the contribution of each scholar focused on the importance of the evolving Egyptian court system as a critical part of the nationalist project. The capitulations (agreements made between the Ottoman Empire and Europe to grant foreign citizens special status) and the Mixed Courts were described as an "infringement on Egypt's sovereignty," which was remedied by the development of the new national legal system.[5]

In India, too, by the end of the nineteenth century, the silence of many of the *'ulama'* on the IPC had begun to break. They had retreated from the centers of power, but this had changed with the reintroduction of Muslim institutions and individuals into the public sphere. As in Egypt, in India nationalism and a new desire for agency grew. An increasing number of scholars from religious institutions like Dar al-'Ulum Deoband and Nadwat al-'Ulama' and the British system alike began to express opposition to British power and call for change. For example, Sohaira Siddiqui has analyzed the judgments of the first Muslim appointed to the High Court of Allahabad, Justice Syed Mahmood, who worked to reject British colonial intervention in substantive points of Islamic law.[6]

Muhammad 'Abd al-Hayy penned his reservations to British legal influence near the end of his life. In one fatwa from 1881, in response to a question about whether accepting a job in the British legal system was religiously permissible, he said it was, as long as the purpose of that job was not to "implement non-Islamic or unjust laws."[7] In another fatwa from the same year, 'Abd al-Hayy suggested that the legal picture of India was more complex: "Although most judges are infidels and rules against the shari'a are applied, in many issues, the fatwas of Muslim scholars are also implemented, and their judicial rulings agree with the shari'a."[8]

These fatwas are representative of a change in the mainstream attitude among Indian Muslims and show that the connection of colonial laws like the IPC to the shari'a was being questioned. However, 'Abd al-Hayy was not prepared to completely dismiss the legal system as outside the realm of Islamic norms. He believed that the content of the law was important when, for example, he allowed Muslims to approach contemporary British courts. As this chapter shows, others believed that colonial influence had systematically displaced Muslim scholars. In their view, the only way forward was not to focus on the content of the law applied but for Muslim scholars to play a more significant role in the judiciary and other areas of public life.

As a result of these developments in both the Egyptian and Indian contexts, the environment of legal adaptation and continuity with the shari'a seen in the earlier chapters of this book dissipated. A new form of political and legal identity arose, one that saw Islam as a unique civilization separate from that of Europe. Scholars from the period and later have described this phenomenon as the rise of Islamism—or, more specifically, of the ideological movement of pan-Islamism. Of course, these are imperfect terms associated with a range of scholars, ideas, and movements. For the purposes of this book, the term "Islamism" is simply meant to denote the belief that "public and political life should be guided by a set of Islamic principles."[9] What these principles were and how their grounding in a new understanding of the shariʻa formed the core of this new form of identity are the main questions addressed in this chapter.

A Uniquely "Islamic" Civilization

An exploration of the changes at the beginning of the twentieth century begins with the formation of what Cemil Aydin has termed the "Muslim World."[10] In his view, during the nineteenth century, Muslims were confronted with narratives of a single Western civilization. Juxtaposed to that were equally singular images of Islam and Muslims as a race, with no distinctions made between various political, economic, cultural, and even sectarian backgrounds. Frequently, the Muslim race was considered a problem for many colonial powers and their economic projects, and at times a potential source of instability and rebellion.

This can be seen most clearly in British India, where the colonial government began defining Muslims as a unified group following the Uprising of 1857. For example, Ilyse Fuerst has traced how British narratives of the events of 1857 resulted in the "minoritization and racialization of Muslims [and] created a grammar in which to be Muslim meant one was a threat to the empire, and threats to the empire were connected to Muslims."[11]

To push back against this narrative and negotiate a more equal footing for Muslims within colonial contexts, Muslim reformers developed the idea of Islam as an all-encompassing civilization that was on a par with its European counterparts in terms of tolerance, reason, and enlightenment.[12] Separate from the concept of the general unity of Muslims expressed through the *umma*, which had been a concept in Islamic thought since the Prophet's time, the idea of an Islamic civilization would allow Muslims to "counter the racism that justified mistreatment" at the hands of the West.[13]

It is difficult to trace precisely when the idea of Islamic civilization arose. Aydin placed it at the end of the nineteenth century, during the rule of the Ottoman Sultan Abdül Hamid II (ruled 1876–1909) and his adoption of pan-Islamism. Faced with external conflicts with Russia and economic failures believed to be caused by the earlier policies of the *tanzimat* reforms, Abdül Hamid II sought to take advantage of the growing anticolonial sentiment among Muslim elites and realign the empire along ostensibly religious lines. He did so mainly by elevating the importance of the Ottoman caliphate as the global leader of Muslims.[14] This move proved to be largely symbolic, with internal Ottoman opposition movements criticizing Abdül Hamid II's legitimacy.[15]

In India, Azmi Özcan has suggested that the connection of pan-Islamism to the Ottoman sultan as the true leader of the Muslim community materialized as early as the aftermath of the Uprising of 1857. With the Mughals officially removed from power and European colonial authority at its peak, "the Ottoman Sultan Caliph appeared to be the natural focus for the emotional and spiritual attachment of the rank and file of Indian Muslims," and mosques in cities and small villages alike began mentioning the name of the sultan in their Friday sermons as early as 1862.[16] The educational reformer Syed Ahmad Khan (d. 1898), known for establishing the Muhammadan Anglo-Oriental College at Aligarh in 1875, provided evidence that this might have occurred even earlier. He wrote that immediately following the rule of the Mughal Emperor Shah Alam (who was dethroned by the British in 1803,) "in mosques in Bombay, Calcutta, and other major cities, it became popular to mention the name of the Ottoman sultan (*sultan-e rum*) [during their Friday sermons]."[17]

Following the losses of the Ottoman Empire in World War I and the division of the Empire's Arab and European territories among the Allies, pan-Islamist sentiments and attachment to the caliph in Istanbul developed into the Khilafat Movement (1919–24). Indian elites, looking for a symbol around which all Indian Muslims could rally, used the threatened position of the Ottoman caliphate to articulate a "pan-Indian Muslim" identity based on "symbols of solidarity: the community of believers, the *umma*; its symbolic head, the caliph; its central place of pilgrimage, Mecca; its scripture, the Qur'an; its sacred law, the shari'a; and its local reference point, the mosque."[18]

In the Egyptian context, calls for pan-Islamic unity were primarily connected to the life and works of Jamal al-Din al-Afghani (d. 1897).[19] While in exile in France in 1884, al-Afghani published a journal with Muhammad 'Abdu (d. 1905; a student of al-Afghani and a reformer in his own right) titled *The Strongest Bond (al-'Urwa al-Wuthqa)*. Although the periodical's life was short—it was banned by the British in Egypt and India after only eight months of publication—*The Strongest Bond* acted as a catalyst for pan-Islamic sentiments. In one of its articles, al-Afghani spoke of the need for the political unity of the Muslim world in opposition to Western influence: "I do not mean to suggest by my words here that the control of the situation [Islamic government] be in the hands of one individual. This would be quite difficult. Instead, I envision that the master of all [heads of Muslim governments] be the Qur'an, and the focus of their unity be the religion, and that their power be directed toward the preservation of one another as much as they can, as their lives and existence depend upon one another."[20]

It has been pointed out that al-Afghani's political activism resulted in little progress on the ground during his lifetime, with his thought caught between "traditional ideas of the Muslim philosophers . . . and more modern ideas of political opposition."[21] However, his and 'Abdu's writings about a unified Muslim political entity driven by the principles of Islam set the tone for future calls to view many of the changes that had taken place during the nineteenth century (particularly in the realm of the law) as against the rules of the religion.

Redefining the Shari'a as *Fiqh*

As the twentieth century progressed, scholars and activists who supported pan-Islamism rallied around calls to reapply the shari'a. Recent studies have suggested that these reformers were interested in the shari'a as a "concept" and not as "a body of laws and texts rooted in particular institutional methodologies."[22] While this might be true for political slogans used by groups such as the Muslim Brotherhood in Egypt during the second half of the twentieth century,[23] the literature and debates surrounding the shari'a at the beginning of the century show a more complex picture. For most Islamists, the content of the law and who was making it mattered a great deal. In their view, through the development of new codes, modern states had moved away from what they viewed as the divine law (*qanun ilahi*) and adopted positive or manmade law (*qanun wad'i*).

In his work on the reception of European law in Egypt, Leonard Wood found the earliest manifestation of these opposing legal systems in an article from the first year (1898) of the popular Islamist magazine *al-Manar*.[24] In this article, Rashid Rida began by lamenting that Muslim societies had "become wretched after prosperity, become enslaved after freedom, and debased after being uplifted." Muslim rulers, he argued, had "abandoned Your divine shari'a and sought to replace it with positive laws (*al-qawanin al-wad'iya*) and legislated that the greatest leader be granted sacred powers to abrogate what was legislated, make permissible what was forbidden, make forbidden what was permissible, and pardon those who would be punished."[25] Indeed, one of the most famous anecdotes emphasizing the European nature of Egyptian law, quoted by the lawyer and legal historian 'Aziz Khanki (d. 1956) and later reproduced by the revivalist Muhammad al-Ghazali (d. 1996), is also reported by Rida. According to

'Aziz Khanki, Rifa'a Rafi' al-Tahtawi, the leader of the translation movement of the nineteenth century, was called to the court of Khedive Isma'il (ruled 1863–1879). "Oh exalted one *(Ya Rufa'a),*" the khedive stated,

> You are an *Azhari*, raised and educated in al-Azhar, one of the most knowledgeable of its scholars and the most capable of convincing them of what we desire of you. Foreigners *(al-farinja)* have gained many rights and commercial interests in this country, and cases emerge between them and Egyptians. Many have complained to me that they [Egyptians] do not know whether claims will be judged in their favor or against them. Likewise, they do not know how to defend themselves [in the courts], as the books of jurisprudence *(fiqh)* that our scholars use to reach their judgments are complicated and full of differences of opinion. I, therefore, request that the scholars of al-Azhar create a single book on Islamic commercial rules *(al-ahkam al-madaniya al-shar'iya)* that is similar to books of law *(al-qanun)* in their description of articles and clarification of differences [in opinion], so the judgments of the courts do not waiver. If they do not, I will be forced to implement the Napoleonic Code.

Al-Tahtawi responded,

> My Lord, I have traveled to Europe, studied there, and served the government by translating many French texts and have grown old, reaching an advanced age, and no one has ever questioned my attachment to the religion. If you now officially request this of me, the scholars of al-Azhar will question my faith. I am afraid that they will say that 'Shaykh Rifa'a has become an apostate at the end of his life, desiring to change the books of the shari'a and make them like the books of positive law *(al-qawanin al-wad'iya)'.* . . . I implore my Lord to excuse me from facing this accusation so that it is not said that I died an infidel.[26]

It is doubtful that this statement can be traced to al-Tahtawi, as he agreed to head the team tasked with translating the French codes for use in the Mixed Courts (as mentioned in chapter 2). Additionally, the language of the anecdote reflects a crucial change in the concept of the shari'a that took place at the beginning of the twentieth century and was exemplified through the sentiments of Rida.

Throughout most of the nineteenth century, as shown in the first section of this book, scholars in each jurisdiction covered viewed the implementation of *siyasa* as an integral part of the shari'a. State intervention in the law, as it sought to stamp out corruption and bring about a greater application of justice, was in line with the purposes for which the shari'a had been revealed. However, for Rida and later Islamists, the shari'a was defined only as the rules produced by the jurists. For example, in the first decades of the twentieth century, the vision of the shari'a (now understood as the rules of *fiqh*, and as opposed to positive law) developed into an entire field of comparative legal theory. Dozens of works appeared showing that the legal systems of the time were in opposition to the true intention of God's law. In the realm of criminal punishments, the most important of these is the work of the Egyptian judge 'Abd al-Qadir 'Awda (d. 1954) titled *Islamic Criminal Law, in Comparison with Positive Law*. 'Awda wrote the book, which was first published in the 1930s, to "declare the merits of shari'a, its supremacy over positive law and precedence in establishing all of the principles of humanity, as well as over the scientific and sociological theories that the world neither came to know nor scholars were guided to until recently."[27] In the remainder of the book, 'Awda highlighted how each of the prescribed criminal punishments of Islam *(hudud)* had been established to protect both society and individual sanctity. One example given early in the text is the punishment for public drunkenness *(shurb al-khamr)*, whose evils had only recently been recognized in Western societies, such as the United States— which had passed prohibition laws.[28]

Amr Shalaqany has traced the impact of this definition of the shari'a on the histories of Islamic law produced by Western scholars such as Joseph Schacht (d. 1969) and Noel Coulson (d. 1986). For them, the story of Islamic law was "a legal historiography of and about jurists—not law as it was applied by courts, followed in customary practices, or administered and enforced by state representatives."[29] This led them to view the Islamic legal system as "the consummate *Other* of Western law, the former religious, immutable, and fundamentally a-historical, the latter secular, innovative and historical in the most liberal and progressive sense of the word."[30]

What Shalaqany did not include in his analysis was the fact that the historiography of Islamic law developed by Schacht and Coulson was a product of the intellectual environment in which they lived and worked. Their definition of the shariʻa was heavily influenced by the rise of Islamism and its redefinition as solely the product of jurists. For example, Schacht taught at the Egyptian University (now Cairo University) in 1934–39, after escaping the expanding Nazi regime in Europe.[31] He was also an intellectual successor of the Hungarian Orientalist Ignac Goldziher (d. 1921), who had traveled in Syria, Palestine, and Egypt and regularly interacted with students at al-Azhar.[32] Although Coulson spent his academic life at the School of Oriental and African Studies at the University of London, he was influenced by the work of Schacht and in 1967 became the Chair of Oriental Laws, a position that had previously been occupied by former members of the colonial administration in British India.[33]

The practice of comparing the fixed, divine law of Islam to positive, manmade law continues to this day, and in 2019 at least eight titles were published that made such comparisons in subjects as diverse as local administration, conditions in contracts, constitutional protection of citizens, and the concept of freedom.[34] In each of these texts, the opinions of premodern jurists (*fuqahaʼ*), working within the classical schools of thought, are placed next to laws developed by contemporary Arab legal systems. It is interesting to note that none of these works tackles the methodological issue of comparing the *fiqh* rulings of, say, the early nineteenth-century Hanafi scholar Muhammad Amin b. ʻAbidin with the output of legislatures in Egypt, Jordan, or Morocco in the twentieth century. Instead, all premodern rulings are seen to constitute parts of a single, complete, and Islamic legal system (the shariʻa) defined by jurists from the traditional schools (*madhahib*), and the rulings are divorced from their historical and societal context.

To illustrate how the redefined shariʻa took shape and impacted debates surrounding the law in the nineteenth century, this chapter now turns to two case studies from Egypt and British India. In Egypt, public discourse about the validity of an article of the Penal Code of 1883, together with the eventual move by the political authority away from the law as envisioned by premodern jurists, stirred debates about the connection of the law to the shariʻa. In contrast, in India the link to the shariʻa hinged on the presence of Muslim judges in British courtrooms. For political and legal activists, the fact that the British had systematically removed Muslims from the legislative and judicial process was a more pressing matter than the content of the law.

Egypt and the Fate of Article 32

When the original version of the Egyptian Penal Code of 1883 was passed, its article 32 stated, "No defendant shall be punished by execution for a crime that warrants it unless he has confessed to it or two witnesses saw him in the act of committing it."[35] The content of this article was taken directly from *fiqh* texts, as typically in cases of homicide or personal injury only a confession or eyewitness testimony was required to impose retaliation *(qisas)* or one of the prescribed punishments *(hudud)*.[36] Following the *fiqh* approach to doubt *(shubha*; discussed in chapter 3), one of the earliest explanations of the code, by Muhammad Yasin, stated, "With this article, the law intended that execution should not take place except after the establishment of absolute and explicit proof . . . because execution is a grave matter that cannot be adjudicated by only the collection of logical evidence *(dala'il 'aqliya)* that dismisses the presence of doubt *(shubha)*."[37] Article 32 created a problem for Egyptian courts and legal commentators alike in practice. Since it was constructed narrowly and accepted no other forms of evidence for execution, only a handful of felons would be subject to the ultimate form of punishment. As a result, many murderers, rapists, and others found their sentences automatically reduced to a period in prison. Under other circumstances, and even before the implementation of the 1883 code, these same crimes could have been punished with execution through discretionary punishment *(ta'zir)* or the will of the political authority *(siyasa)*.

Pressure built within the government and the judiciary to either alter or abolish article 32, with al-Bustani as one of its harshest critics. Writing in the pro-British periodical *al-Muqattam*, al-Bustani argued that this article was "an anomaly" and "extremism on the part of the lawmaker that overstepped all forms of extremism in every religious or national law." The shari'a, he continued, "while requiring the presence of witnesses, also accepted judgments based on clear physical evidence *(al-qarina al-qati'a)*."[38] In an article that appeared in the same publication a few days later, al-Bustani recognized that article 32 was taken directly from the *fiqh*, but that had been done "as if the creator of our penal code took a position of the shari'a and amputated it, adopting part of it and ignoring another. . . . If a man were to leave a residence with a bloody knife in his hand and people entered the house to find a murdered body and no one else, the shari'a, in this case, would have ruled against the man on strong circumstantial evidence and executed him." Al-Bustani derided those who supported the article because they believed that it protected innocent individuals by giving them the benefit of the doubt. He stated sarcastically that "the realm of doubt in the world of article 32 is still quite present: it is possible to understand from this situation that the Jinn had killed him and then burrowed into the ground or flew into space, escaping from the eyes of man."[39]

Coming to the article's defense was a series of opinion pieces published in the anti-British newspaper *al-Mu'ayyad*, written anonymously by "one of the respected conservatives *(ahad al-fudala' al-usuliyin)*"—perhaps a reference to the writer's affiliation with al-Azhar. In the writer's view, understanding the debate about article 32 required looking beyond the text of the article and into its broader purpose in the law. Egypt was made up of three religious groups (Muslims, Christians, and Jews), and all of them had the Torah in common. According to the writer, "Issuing an order for execution without the condition of obtaining a confession or two witnesses was antithetical to all those who believe in the Torah, which every member of this nation follows." Some might ask, he continued, "Why does French law, which is where we draw our legal system from, contain no such article? We say that our law has realized something [the French] did not and that this issue is for one nation and not another, as what is suitable for this nation is not for that."[40] Therefore, article 32 was necessary to preserve the national nature of the law, based upon the shari'a and its founding principle that only people convicted of homicide beyond a reasonable doubt deserved execution.

Continuing the argument and providing perhaps the most interesting defense of the article came not from Egyptian Muslims but from a French attorney named Eugene Clavel. He began his career in Algeria but moved to the Mixed Courts of Alexandria and eventually became a professor at the Khedival Law School in Cairo. Clavel believed that article 32 "preserved the shari'a" in requiring strict evidentiary requirements to execute an offender. In a letter published in *al-Mu'ayyad*, Clavel posed two questions regarding the discourse about the article: can the state can alter the shari'a and would such a change result in the nation's progress or enhance its security? The answer to the first question was simple, Clavel argued, as all ancient laws are subject to change according to the circumstances of the day. Islam (including the shari'a) is just as capable of development and modernization as any other civilization. The problem came with the second question. The shari'a accepts that a person may be punished, but that can be done only when the highest standards of proof are met. The judge at this stage "shows his utmost respect for human life that can only be touched when evidence presents itself that is so obvious that it cannot be questioned."[41] The British occupiers want to put more power in the hands of the judge, Clavel continued, "and make the law seek out execution rather than issuing a ruling for execution only if the evidence is provided beyond a reasonable doubt." He concluded: "We wish to speak to the readers about the possibility that a judge might err in his rulings, something entirely possible if the law is freed to this extent. Instead, we stand in defense of the shari'a, which would rather have several evildoers and thieves declared innocent than execute an innocent defendant."[42]

With significant experience with the Islamic system through his writings on family law in both Algeria and Egypt, Clavel saw the importance that classical jurists placed on the doubt canon. For him, their construction was the correct expression of the shari'a. If the law were to change, it could maintain its connection to the shari'a only by adhering to what had been constructed by classically trained jurists due to the underlying principles they created; in this case, limiting the application of punishment whenever there was a sense of doubt. Broader calls for the application of justice, like those of al-Bustani, stepped beyond the boundaries of the sacred law.

It is essential to note the context in which this debate took place. As noted above, al-Bustani, who supported annulling the article, was writing in a pro-British periodical. Those against the move, including Clavel, submitted their articles to an anti-British newspaper. (Even so, the anonymous writer in the latter periodical nodded to British authority by citing the English jurist Jeremy Bentham and stating that "Punishment must be subject to review if evidence appears that the judgment was incorrect."[43]) Therefore, advocating the annulment of article 32 carried with it implied support for British colonial policy, while supporting the article implied support for nationalism.

There is also evidence that the debate about article 32 was connected to a specific criminal case. On September 4, 1897 (a few months before these articles were published), in the Delta city of Kafr al-Dawar, a British engineer named Alexander Welch was found murdered along with an Egyptian man named Muhammad Ahmad. The case received unprecedented attention in the colonial administration, with consular employees and foreign security officials directly involved in the investigation.[44] Three unnamed Bedouins were eventually arrested for the crime, but the judges in the National Courts were unable to impose the death penalty because of article 32: there were no eyewitnesses, and none of the defendants had confessed to the crime.

The high-profile murder of a British colonial subject and the inability of the National Court system to satisfy British demands to make an example of the defendants through their execution were essential factors behind the suggestion that article 32 be annulled. One anonymous article in *al-Ahram*, against the article's removal, suggested just that: "These days the [colonial] political authority has reached the point of interfering in the laws, playing with them as the political circumstances see fit, legislating and calling themselves 'reformers' by annulling this article and removing the barrier between them and the execution of the murderers of Mr. Welch."[45] In another article in this newspaper, a person identified only as writing from Damanhur, pushed back against this suggestion and stated, "It is irrelevant that the government suggested the annulment of this article following the murder of the Englishman Mr. Welch, as long as this annulment is beneficial to general security."[46]

In December 1897, a royal decree annulled article 32. The article's removal was welcomed by al-Bustani, who called it a victory for "the hand of truth" and stated that "justice, the shari'a, and the wisdom of the judiciary are now at a consensus [that the article is abhorrent]."[47] He even suggested that earlier opposition had subsided. The anonymous author from Damanhur mentioned above also expressed his joy in *al-Ahram*, stating: "The greatest thing that the British occupation government has done was to abolish article 32 from the penal code. If only every day the government would do a similar thing to protect security, we would thank it for performing its rightful duty."[48]

In a final contribution to *al-Mu'ayyad* published following the annulment, the anonymous conservative writer lamented that the annulment meant that corruption would spread, particularly among local officials who would use their considerable influence to fabricate evidence and remove their political opponents. He also suggested that a move as drastic as the total annulment was not necessary. He noted that the Egyptian Parliament had proposed making an amendment "to add the acceptance of clear physical evidence *(al-qarina al-qati'a)*, but we do not know how this compromise was passed over, and a full removal of the article advocated." Finally, he made a comparison to the Ottoman Penal Code of 1858, in which retaliation "was entirely in the hands of the victim's family, [who could] forgive the murderer. No execution can take place unless the victim's descendants *(wali al-damm)* refuse to mitigate the sentence. . . . If our government gave the victim's family this right, with the acceptance of physical evidence, it would have been a most blessed turn."[49]

The debate about article 32, its eventual annulment, and its relevance to the colonial context exemplify the changes in the interpretation of the shari'a in the late nineteenth century. For al-Bustani and others who had supported the development of the new criminal code, article 32 was an affront to the goal of the shari'a: achieving justice by ensuring that murderers received their just punishment. It was the prerogative of the political authority (*siyasa*) to create the laws that achieved these goals. For those against the article's annulment, including Clavel and eventually Islamists in the twentieth century, the shari'a was limited to the understandings of the *fiqh*. Only through an examination of the rules produced by classical jurists and the purposes for which these rules were created could the shari'a's goals be realized. Anything done outside this framework, particularly state intervention, was by definition contradictory to the unchanging, God-made shari'a.

India and the Call for Muslim Leadership

For Muslims in India, the law's connection to the shari'a was framed by who was responsible for making and enforcing the law—judges, governors, and so on. As we have seen in chapter 3, in the first half of the nineteenth century, Muslim muftis often sat alongside British judges. They issued opinions that, in most cases, were followed in the final judgment and helped shape the classification of homicide in British-ruled territories. For example, in a sampling of 400 homicide cases from Bengal and the North-Western Provinces brought to the Nizamut Adawlut (the appellate court), 195 included the mufti's opinion. Even when there was a conflict between the mufti and the sessions judge—which happened in 53 of the 400 cases—the appellate court frequently supported the mufti in (in 29 of the 53 cases).[50]

However, beginning in 1859 the role of muftis, as well as Muslim judges (*qadis*), was brought into question by the colonial government. In a letter to the government, the lieutenant governor of the North-Western Provinces stated, "When the British Government first succeeded to the possession and administration of these territories, it may have been a measure of wisdom and expediency to recognize the position and the perquisites of those who were not only priests of the persuasion to which their former rulers belonged, but took at the same time no small part in the judicial business of their Government. The same considerations are no longer operative."[51] In 1862, the chief justice of the Bengal High Court suggested that the position of Muslim and Hindu law officer be removed. Two years later, act 11 of 1864 was passed, repealing all previous laws that had regulated the appointment and duties of Muslim and Hindu law officers and officially removing the position.[52]

This act did not mean the complete removal of Muslims from the British legal system. A survey of court reports from the following years found several Muslim names mentioned as court officials—for example, "Principal Sudder Amin (an arbitrator or civil judge)"—indicating that many muftis simply shifted roles to use their experience within the amended judiciary.[53] However, a British military officer named James O'Kinealy mentioned in an 1870 report to the government's Judicial Department that "the abolition of the Mahomedan law officers on the introduction of the Penal Code deprived Mussulmans of mostly all the remaining respectable appointments not requiring a knowledge of English. . . . A few Kazies received judicial appointments, but, as a Mussulman once said 'chupprassess [court officers], duftries [secretaries] and peons are the only Mussulman officers in Bengal.'"[54]

Opposition to the 1864 act began almost immediately after it was passed, with Muslim groups from the North-Western Provinces, Bengal, Madras, and Bombay filing petitions with the government to amend or repeal it. There is also evidence that these petitions found favor with the viceroy, Richard Bourke, 6th Earl of Mayo (Lord Mayo, in office 1869–1872). He wrote, "It is hardly possible to conceive that when it [the act] obtained the sanction of the [Legislature], it was known that a large portion of the Mahomedan community would understand that it actually deprived them of an institution which was in their view an essential part of their religion and social system."[55]

The primary concern of the Muslims protesting the act was the need for a Muslim judge to officiate in matters of personal law like marriage and divorce. In a paper presented in 1868 to the Bengal Social Science Association, the founder of the Mahomedan Literary Society, Nawab Abdul Latif, argued that the removal of the *qadis* had resulted in a lapse in the proper record keeping of Muslim marriages and divorces. He suggested that this could be remedied through the appointment of registrars, with whom Muslims would voluntarily register their marriages and divorces before filing them in the colonial courts.[56]

The petitions by Muslim groups and discussions within the government resulted in the creation of a new law, the Kazis Act of 1880, which gave local administrations the right to appoint Muslim judges (*qadis*) and vice judges (*na'ib qadis*). However, the exact roles and duties of these new judges were unclear. For example, the law was careful to state that it did not "confer any judicial or administrative powers to any Kazi or Naib Kazi appointed hereunder." It was also clear that the law would not make "the presence of a Kazi or Naib Kazi necessary at the celebration of any marriage or the performance of any rite or ceremony." The law's explanation mentioned that it had been passed as "but a reasonable concession to the wants of the Muhammadan population" and "in order to satisfy the wants of the Muhammadan community [it] provides for the appointment of Kazis by Government, leaving the position and duties of the Kazis, whatever these may be, as they now are."[57]

Therefore, as the new law provided Muslim judges with no actual legal authority, it did little to quell Muslim concerns about their position within the legal system in British India. For the rest of the nineteenth century and well into the twentieth, British and Muslim reformers alike continued to push for a greater role for the *qadis*.[58]

The frustration of Muslim elites with their place in the legal system can be seen in the writings of Husayn Ahmad Madani (d. 1957). A graduate of Dar al-'Ulum Deoband, Madani was one of the leading advocates for independence from British rule and a founder of the Council of Muslim Theologians (*Jam'iyat 'Ulama-e-Hind*) in 1919 and of Jamia Millia Islamia University in 1920. He is well-known for his stance against partition and the creation of Pakistan. His 1938 treatise *Composite Nationalism and Islam*, along with his support for Indian independence, won him the country's highest civilian honor, the Padma Bhushan, in 1954.[59]

While serving a prison sentence in Allahabad in 1942 for participating in the Quit India Movement, Madani wrote his autobiography, titled *Naqsh-e Hayat*. Throughout this work, he detailed the process of expanding British control over every aspect of Indian Muslim government and public life, a process he referred to as "The Methods of Destroying Muslims (*musulmanun ko barbad karne ke tariqa*)." In his analysis, Madani relied primarily on the writings and statistics of the Scottish historian and civil servant William Hunter (d. 1900), especially his *The Indian Musulmans: Are They Bound in Conscience to Rebel against the Queen?* Published in 1871, Hunter's work was one of the most popular British analyses of the events of 1857, discussing—and eventually rejecting—the idea that most of India's Muslims were religiously obligated to engage in jihad and should be perceived as a continuous threat to British rule.[60]

When speaking of law, Madani noted that Muslims had occupied the greatest proportion of government positions in the first fifty years of the rule of the British East India Company, but "in the next fifty years, the situation completely changed."[61] British and Hindus entered the civil service in greater numbers, owing primarily to the growing use of English in the courts—which pushed out Muslims who were better versed in Mughal Persian. This process continued into the nineteenth century, to the point at which Muslims were removed entirely from the legal service. This was also the case for attorneys. Madani mentioned that in 1838 there were roughly the same numbers of Muslim, Hindu, and British employees in the court system. By 1869, however, there was "only one Muslim advocate left" in the High Court.[62]

From the writings of Madani and the petitions of Muslims to the British government, it appears that Muslims in India were not interested in the relationship of the shari'a to the content of the laws in place. Instead, their primary concern was having a voice in the legal system and increasing the number and authority of Muslims in the courts. What the law said and how it was applied in practice were secondary. Indeed, there is evidence that scholars such as Madani were open to a more flexible interpretation of the shari'a to "meet all changing needs and circumstances," particularly the political changes presented by the British and the potential for a pluralistic, independent India.[63]

Therefore, increasing the role of the *'ulama* was understood as the primary way through which the shari'a could be applied at the end of the colonial period in India, as recent academic literature has thoroughly documented. For example, Muhammad Qasim Zaman noted that the discourse driven by the Deobandi scholar Ashraf Ali Thanavi (d. 1943) that led to the Dissolution of Muslim Marriages Act of 1939 represented a "mechanism to escape some of the effects of colonial rule on the practice of Islamic law" as well as "an effort to extend the influence of the 'ulama'."[64] Although Thanavi's efforts eventually failed to create special committees where British courts could rely on religious scholars or muftis to guide their decision regarding Muslim personal matters, the message of Indian Muslims in the early twentieth century was clear: the shari'a was the purview of classically trained scholars (*'ulama*), albeit not exclusively the jurists (*fuqaha'*). The push for the role of the *'ulama* in India stands in contrast to the discourse in Egypt and can be explained by the lack of participation of Muslims in the colonial government and the development of the law in the nineteenth century.

However, what these two case studies share is that the shariʻa was characterized as a fixed set of divine rules, understood and elaborated upon by premodern jurists. For scholars in the late colonial context, and indeed for postcolonial Muslims across jurisdictions, legal developments comply with the shariʻa only if they are applications of premodern juristic rules or created with the direct involvement or sanction of the ʻulama.

Conclusion and a Search for Continuity

This chapter sought to bridge the gap between the environment that created the new penal codes of the nineteenth century and current perceptions of the law and shariʻa. A push against colonialism through the development of the so-called Muslim World and a reified Islamic civilization saw the developments of the nineteenth century recast as mere importations of European laws and one of the greatest defeats of global Muslims at the hands of the colonizers. For the realm of criminal law, this meant that the increased power of the state to create laws that would stamp out corruption and ensure an equal and just application of the law to everyone in developing nation-states was now a lamentable abandonment of the shariʻa, as described by Rida.

It must also be acknowledged that the understanding of the shariʻa as part of Islamism had also undergone a fundamental change. No longer was it a balance between God's law and practical application, as elucidated by the classical scholars mentioned in chapter 1, such as Muhammad b. Qayyim al-Jawziya. Nor was it al-Bustani's view that article 32 of the Egyptian Penal Code should be abolished so that murders would receive the punishment they deserved. Now in Egypt and British India, the general view was that only through the rules created by premodern jurists, interpreted using the authority of members of the ʻulama clerical class, could shariʻa legitimacy be found. The prescribed punishments (*hudud*)—which some historical studies have argued were hardly ever applied in practice, particularly given the presence of the doubt canon—were now the hallmarks of the Islamic criminal system. Their absence was further evidence to scholars like ʻAwda of the distance of these new legal systems from the shariʻa.

Although most legal writers in the twentieth-century Muslim World sought to point out the stark differences between Islamic and Western law and extol the virtues and supremacy of the fixed shariʻa, others continued to believe in the ideas of the nineteenth century and continued to combine Western and Islamic approaches well into the twentieth century. In the development of civil law, scholars of the Khedival Law School, such as 'Abd al-Razzaq al-Sanhuri and Shafiq Shihata, synthesized the French and Egyptian systems of contract.[65] Al-Sanhuri's primary work of legislation, the Egyptian Civil Code of 1948, is considered the most significant development in Islamic civil law after the Ottoman *Mecelle* of 1877 and still forms the basis for civil law in numerous Arab countries today.[66]

In criminal law, Ridwan Shafi'i al-Mut'afi, introduced in chapter 3, described the categories of punishment within the Islamic system—*qisas*, *hudud*, and *ta'zir*—and argued that they each had a corresponding element within the modern Egyptian legal system:

> We find an apparent similarity between the spirit of modern legislation and the spirit of Islamic law in general. We [also] find that the rules of the shari'a are mentioned by the explainers of the Penal Code and that the articles of the Egyptian code and their explanation in both public and private matters, as well as in some of the laws of the European nations, [contain] what might almost be a transfer of meaning of the statements of [classical] Muslim jurists. We also observe that, although some explainers [of the Penal Code] rely on the statements of Jaro, Jarson, Dalwaz, and so on, we find [these statements] in some of the books of the four schools [of Sunni jurisprudence].[67]

The work of scholars at the Khedival Law School, most notably al-Sanhuri, emphasized the continuity between the shari'a and state law. Graduates of this school would go on to work in Egyptian courts and law departments at national universities, shaping the development of the law across the Arab world—including Bahrain, Libya, and Kuwait.[68]

Despite these examples of continuity, the language of most twentieth-century reformers was different from that of their nineteenth-century counterparts. Calls to reapply the shari'a, centered around the application of the rules of *fiqh*, took center stage. For example, the Egyptian jurist 'Ali 'Ali Mansur, who was invited in the 1960s by the government of Libya and in the 1970s the United Arab Emirates to create new legal codes, summarized his mission by stating that "with the coming of European colonialism, the Arab-Islamic states took their [Europe's] positive laws and fascist systems (*qawaninahu al-wad'iya wa nuzumahu al-fashiya*) that overwhelmed the shari'a under the guise of "civilization." . . . The time has now come for the Truth *(al-haqq)* to return to its rightful place. The shari'a, *with its various schools of fiqh*, should dominate and be the primary source of legislation and order in this republic [Libya]."[69]

As a result, the methodology of those who supported the continuity of the shari'a in national penal systems fell by the wayside. Islamic criminal law understood in the nineteenth century—and indeed in previous centuries—was reduced to a fixed system that resided in the societies and interpretive methods of the past. It could be revived only through a search for and the application of rules that had already been developed, and there was little to no room for change outside of the boundaries of the *fiqh*.

Conclusion
A Bridge between Systems

T he purpose of this book is to explore the "end of the shari'a" thesis through an examination of the criminal law on homicide during the introduction of penal codes in the Egyptian, Indian, and Ottoman contexts. According to the dominant narrative within the secondary literature of Islamic legal historiography, these codes replaced Islamic with European law. By observing the work of local actors and comparing the composite elements of the crime of homicide (the act, intent, and definition of criminal responsibility) in premodern Islamic law and the new codes, this book has attempted to show that the penal codes were not a divergence from the shari'a. Instead, they represented a development in the law in which Islamic legal norms converged with European influence and changing local circumstances. In each of these jurisdictions, the shari'a remained the dominant understanding, shaped by the concerns of a growing, centralized state.

Chapter 1 initiated this argument by exploring the political and legal environments of the nineteenth century. During this period, Muslim scholars in each jurisdiction called for the political authorities to expand upon the existing Islamic concept of political authority (*siyasa*) and create new laws that would bring justice to a system that had been thrown out of balance. In pre-IPC India, where non-Muslim colonial officers were in control of the legal system, Muslim actors who worked with the British, such as Siraj al-Din 'Ali Khan, praised the *fiqh* of British officials like John Herbert Harrington.[1] Khan further suggested that *siyasa* be used in every instance where the traditional categories of retaliation (*qisas*) and discretionary punishment (*ta'zir*) failed to deter criminals or permitted necessary punishment.[2]

For Muslim political writers in the Ottoman Empire and Egypt, the problems of their society rested on a failure of justice. In their view, instances of crime such as homicide were on the rise, and the legal system that had served them for centuries had become corrupt and could no longer meet their needs. For people like 'Abd Allah b. Hasan Barakat Zada, educated in the Ottoman system and working in Egypt as a head judge, the solution to these problems was a return to a balanced understanding and application of *siyasa* to allow the Ottoman sultan to rein in corrupt officials while remaining loyal to the principles and goals of Islamic law.[3] Much like Muhammad b. Qayyim al-Jawziya, who had made similar arguments centuries earlier, Barakat Zada believed that the true shari'a was wherever justice could be found.[4]

Chapter 2 focused on the new cadre of legal elites and institutions that would take up the task of creating this balance. In India, the Delhi College supplemented the traditional Nizamiya curriculum, focusing on the natural sciences and English and helping produce an upsurge in writing in Urdu. The new approach to combining Eastern and Western thought created scholars such as Nazeer Ahmed, who translated the new Indian Penal Code into Urdu and strengthened its connection to local Indian—and Islamic—legal customs. Meanwhile, in Egypt, an evolving translation movement backed by the khedival government grew up around Rifa'a Rafi' al-Tahtawi, one of the century's most prominent reformers. His School of Translators formed the basis for new law schools that would transform the way Egyptian law was understood and applied. One of the graduates of this school, Muhammad Qadri Basha, was assigned by the Khedives Isma'il and Tawfiq to create the codes that would govern the country's National Courts. His understanding of the law helped strike a balance between European and Islamic influences.

The most significant change introduced by the new codes was the shift from understanding homicide as a crime against the victim and their family in the Islamic category of retaliation (*qisas*) to viewing it as a crime against society prosecuted and punished by the state. Chapter 3 looked at the issue of classification and argued that the development of the theory of homicide was built on a conflict of interests between desires of the state to punish and hesitation on the part of jurists, described by Intisar Rabb as the "doubt canon."[5] The balance shifted to total state control of the prosecution of homicide during the nineteenth century, leaving victims' families with only limited options for requesting blood money (*diya*) or financial compensation through the civil courts.

The framers of the codes did not ignore the importance of the shift to state dominance or its implications for the broader criminal system. As chapter 3 highlighted, explanations of both the Ottoman and Egyptian codes provided detailed justifications for this shift, with Amin Afram al-Bustani's work on the Egyptian code being the most elaborate. In each of these explanations, the role of Islamic law was confirmed. Both legal scholars and judges believed that the state's taking complete control of the prosecution of murderers was the only way to achieve Islam's goal of justice and prevent the rise of chaos and personal blood feuds.

The penal codes of the nineteenth century also selected simplified definitions of homicide and expanded the category of murderers who could be subject to execution. This book identified the first inclusion of external influence in the classification of homicide, with the Ottoman and Egyptian codes adapting the understandings of the French Code of 1810 in some areas. Still, the influence of the French system should not be considered to have caused radical departures from the Islamic tradition, and jurists such as Muhammad Hasanayn b. Muhammad Makhluf al-Minyawi in Egypt produced works to show how these changes were compatible with the Maliki school of *fiqh*.

Chapter 4 moved to the establishment of intent, which worked in concert with the newly expanded categorization of homicide. From its beginning, the Hanafi school focused on the presence of a deadly weapon in defining homicide. Although the approaches of the school's founder, Abu Hanifa, and of his students Abu Yusuf and Muhammad al-Shaybani differed, later scholars who attempted to reduce the scope of intentional murder focused on the material from which the weapon was made. As the state gained more influence in the nineteenth century, the scope of homicide was expanded. This resulted in a slow (in India) or immediate (in Egypt) implementation of the minority opinion of the Hanafi school that considered all weapons that caused an injury (*jarh*) to be deadly. Therefore, the door was opened for the use of other methods of homicide not always accepted within Hanafi discourse, such as strangulation, to be included as intentional murder.

The new penal codes also introduced alternative methods for determining intent. In British India, colonial officers ordered courts to focus on the perpetrator's motive. In contrast, in the Ottoman Empire and Egypt, the focus turned to premeditation, to show that a person had planned—and therefore fully intended—the result of his actions. The introduction of premeditation in the Ottoman Empire and Egypt, a direct adoption of French law, was an attempt to move away from Hanafi approaches to the specific characteristics of the deadly weapon. Despite these new approaches, the presence of a deadly weapon remained the primary way to establish intent. Court practice in each jurisdiction showed that judges debated what constituted a deadly weapon and its connection to intent.

Chapter 5 focused on the concept of criminal responsibility, an extension of the Islamic religious concept of *taklif*. Beginning with the treatment of juvenile offenders, the penal codes of the nineteenth century moved away from the variable of puberty (which differed from person to person) and chose fixed ages within a gradually evolving scale of enhanced responsibility. Hanafi law had done the same centuries earlier, and in the nineteenth century, scholars such as Muhammad Amin b. 'Abidin relied primarily upon the idea of puberty by age (*al-bulugh bi-l-sinn*) to hold everyone over the age of fifteen responsible for their crimes. In British India, common law had allowed children as young as twelve to be publicly hanged for murder. When questions of mental capacity arose in the Indian courts in the first half of the nineteenth century, judges stuck to the concept of puberty but believed that the presumption of limited responsibility "weakens as the prisoner's age approaches puberty."[6] By the end of the century, the new codes adopted a fixed age (twelve in India and fifteen in the Ottoman Empire and Egypt) at which individuals would be considered adults and held criminally responsible for their actions. However, judges in India retained the ultimate power of discretion and could acquit older defendants who were determined to have only a child's mental capacity.

When it came to insanity, the Islamic system left significant discretion to judges and medical experts, like the situation in Europe. During the nineteenth century, several cases within the common-law system—coupled with evolving understandings of mental health—ushered in changes in the legal definition of insanity with the M'Naughten rules, which were eventually applied in colonies in India. However, common-law understandings were not used in the Ottoman Empire or Egypt. The broader Islamic definition of insanity remained dominant, as judges continued to rely on the presence of expert evidence. The question of insanity remained one of the more complicated areas of homicide cases. As demonstrated in the Indian case of *Government v. Tota* (1864), judges were divided on the question of how insanity was established and used as a defense to mitigate punishment for homicide, despite the existence of more precise definitions.[7]

Last, when discussing the responsibility of multiple participants in the same crime, Muslim jurists had developed two criteria: cooperation *(ta'awun)* and coming together *(tamalu')*. Once these criteria were met, the judge could decide to either punish all accomplices equally (including by execution) or impose different punishments on each offender according to their degree of involvement. During the nineteenth century, both Islamic and Western legal systems preferred holding all direct participants in a crime equally responsible, and this became the established standard as represented in the new penal codes. However, in practice, Ottoman and Egyptian courts regularly modified this approach, preferring instead to punish accomplices to homicide according to their degree of participation.

Chapter 6 showed how this historical moment ended at the beginning of the twentieth century through the creation of a unique Islamic civilization. Developed as a counternarrative to European colonialism, Islamic civilization was everything that Europe was—civilized, developed, and progressive—and at the same time bound to its centuries-old heritage. At the core of this new idea was a recasting of the shari'a, the holy law of Islam sent down by God to the Prophet Muhammad and interpreted with the guidance of classically trained jurists *(faqih)*. The terms "shari'a" and "*fiqh*" became wedded, and legitimate Islamic law could be implemented only in the presence of Muslim judges, as in India, or through a combing of the vast library of the classical juristic tradition and a direct application of the rules there.

The redefining of the shari'a as *fiqh* was not accepted by everyone involved. The continuity of law that developed during the nineteenth century appeared in civil law through further application and adaptation of the Ottoman *Mecelle-i Ahkam-ı Adliye*, exemplified by the school of the Egyptian 'Abd 'al-Razzaq al-Sanhuri. Continuity persisted in criminal law as well. However, most scholars believed that once the state's power to legislate independently had been cemented in the nineteenth century, the shari'a had been lost.

Colonialism and Local Actors

As outlined in the book's introduction, the current historiography of Islamic law relies on three points to argue that the penal codes of the nineteenth century represented a divergence from Islamic law: the process of codification, the sidelining of traditionally trained scholars, and the foreign content of the laws. Given that recent scholarship has brought the first two points into question, this book focused on the third point. Given the construction, political and legal environments, scholars who participated in their formulation, and content of the new penal codes of the nineteenth century, it is clear that they maintained a connection to the shari'a. Whether colonization was direct and long-standing (India), short-lived (Egypt), or functioning only as a cultural influence until the twentieth century (Ottoman Empire), the result was still recognizably Islamic. This is not to say that there was no change in the legal system, or that there was no importation of European ideas. However, legal scholars analyzed, processed, and thought out those ideas and worked them into new legal systems that maintained a connection to the past.

The criminal codes of the nineteenth century were made possible by the work of local actors. Whether through the work of classically trained jurists such as Muhammad 'Abd al-Hayy of India or that of legal specialists trained in Western systems like al-Bustani and Muhammad Qadri Basha of Egypt, a new generation of scholars took up the reins of Islamic legal discourse. They engaged in debates and discussions of European and Islamic understandings, synthesizing these legal systems to create the resulting legal thought embodied in the codes. Often, this work occurred outside institutions such as al-Azhar in Cairo (which was mired in administrative and pedagogical difficulties) and was made possible through institutions, teachers, and graduates who straddled multiple realms of thought. This does not mean that traditional scholars sat on the sidelines: other works have shown how the presence of traditional voices tempered debates in Egypt and India.[8] However, particularly in terms of the law, by the end of the nineteenth century, the discourse had moved out of traditional centers of learning and into new law schools and courthouses, where most *fiqh* scholars held only marginal sway. Despite reforms that occurred in places like al-Azhar at the beginning of the twentieth century at the hands of Muhammad 'Abdu, a gap formed between traditional Islamic legal education and the people working in the National Courts. This rift continued to grow throughout the century and remains painfully apparent to this day.

The importance of focusing on local actors and their impact on the development of the law helps observers understand the complexities facing Muslim societies during this period. Most academic work on the colonial period who have been cited throughout this book looked at the changes in the law from the colonizer's perspective. Whether the perspective is Wael Hallaq's "demolish and replace" or Radhika Singha's "despotism of law,"[9] the colonizer (or its agents working through modernizing reformers) does the work as the colonized sits silently by, allowed to take over only following independence.

This book attempts to add nuances to this discussion in concert with other emerging views of the colonial period. By including the work of local actors and observing how new penal codes in the nineteenth century shaped the realm of homicide, the book presents the colonial period as a bridge between systems. Although the influence of colonial powers on the law introduced unprecedented changes in India, Egypt, and the Ottoman Empire, it did not destroy or replace existing legal dynamics. Just as occurred centuries earlier when Greek philosophy affected the formative and classical periods of Islamic thought, the colonial period ushered in new ideas that Muslim scholars debated, theorized, and integrated into Islamic law—or sometimes rejected.[10] However, the power dynamics between Muslims and those working outside the tradition in nineteenth-century law were different from those between Greek philosophy and Islamic thought, and this difference remains the main point of contention in discussions between academics (as well as laypersons) about the influence and effect of colonization on Islamic law. This book argues that local actors developed, explained, and implemented the codes in full awareness of those power differences. The content of the codes exhibits that awareness. Power dynamics are important to consider but should not be regarded as the primary or only way to approach the colonial period.

In the first half of the nineteenth century in India, traditional scholars worked with British officers to help expand *siyasa* and *ta'zir* to enforce punishment. Muftis in the courts regularly sided with British judges to provide rulings that helped punish murderers, even when traditional understandings of *fiqh* would not have punished them. When the legislatures of Egypt and the Ottoman Empire undertook the significant step of formally transforming homicide from a crime against the individual to one against society and the state, they were backed by scholars who worked out how the new criminal system should function while keeping Islamic understandings in mind.

Redefining the Shari'a

In addition to being a work of colonial legal history, this book contributes to broader debates about the shari'a. For Islamists in the twentieth century and Western observers such as Joseph Schacht and Noel Coulson, the term "shari'a" was directly connected to the realm of jurisprudence. What constituted Islamic law was only what was discussed within the texts of *fiqh*.[11] In the more extreme view of Schacht, most Islamic criminal laws were either not applicable due to their impracticality or dismissed by political rulers who sought more practical applications of the law.[12]

In response to these views, Wael Hallaq argued that the shari'a was very much a reality on the ground. For Hallaq, the shari'a represents a "complex set of social, economic, cultural, and moral relations that permeated the epistemic structures of the social and political orders."[13] The jurist (*faqih*) guides these relations and has two goals: The first is to "provide an intellectual superstructure that positioned the law within the larger tradition that conceptually defined Islam, thereby constituting a theoretical link between metaphysics and theology on the one hand, and the social and physical world on the other." The second goal is "the infusion of legal norms within a given social and moral order, an infusion where the method of realization was not imposition but rather mediation."[14] This process is mediated by a socially engaged and moral judge (*qadi*) who, along with nonjudicial social forces, helped develop the system from the bottom up without the influence of the modern state's powers of coercion. As a result, the shari'a is far more than a legal system as understood in the terms of the late nineteenth and twentieth centuries.

The two approaches appear to be opposed to one another, yet rest on the same assumption: that the shari'a is a jurists' law, based on an engagement with the fundamental texts of the Qur'an and Sunna that ultimately can be understood only by the *faqih*. Even Hallaq, who recognizes nonjuristic forces within the system, continues to place the *faqih* at the core of his "matrix," directly impacting his view of the laws created in the colonial period and beyond.[15]

This book argues that the shari'a should be understood as a legal system, not unlike civil or common law. Like Hallaq's view, this understanding contains the rules created by the *fuqaha'*. However, those rules intersect with the interests of the state and local custom and are interpreted and modulated when applied within the courts—precisely what occurred during the development of penal codes in the colonial period. According to its original definition in Arabic, the shari'a is a path in the desert that leads to a water source—the water here being justice, salvation, and paradise. Paradise is not attainable in this world, but the path to it is. In contrast, *fiqh* is a snapshot of the interactions at work in interpreting a particular historical period, school of thought, or scholar's work. Critical to this expanded definition of the shari'a as a legal system is the acceptance of work by scholars such as Khaled Fahmy, who argued that we should view *"siyāsa* and *qānūn,* not only *qaḍā'* and *fiqh,* as central to our understanding of Islamic law."[16]

External influence and change are alien neither to the shari'a nor to other legal systems. To take the example of codification, there were projects to codify the common-law systems of England and the United States throughout the nineteenth and early twentieth centuries. The staunchly codified French civil-law system in the same period experimented with the introduction of juries and greater judicial discretion.[17] No scholars suggested that the use of juries in the French system constituted the end of civil law, nor is the project of the Field Codes in the United States held to be demolishing and replacing common law. And in the unique case of Canada, both the common- and civil-law systems exist, with criminal matters governed by a criminal code first enacted in 1892 and primarily influenced by English common-law theorists and British attempts to codify their criminal law and procedure in the 1860s and 1870s.[18]

In the specific case of the shari'a in the nineteenth century and beyond, the primary sticking point for observers and practitioners is external colonial influence. The changes listed above in the common- and civil-law systems were viewed as locally produced, while the changes in the shari'a are seen as the result of a foreign colonial project. However, when the work of local actors is considered and the content and application of the new laws are analyzed, the picture begins to change. Some shifts within the new codes had their origins before the introduction of colonial influence. For example, transferring the prosecution of homicide from the victim's family and to the hands of the state began with the Indian *razinama* or the Egyptian view that the ruler or judge could be seen as the father of a victim and take the family's place.

Implications and Limitations

The argument of this book has implications not only for academics but also for those studying and practicing law in Muslim jurisdictions. For most of the twentieth century, legal change in the Muslim world has been a matter of extracting pragmatic opinions from within the *fiqh,* a process described through the legal terms *"takhayyur"* (selection) and *"talfiq"* (patching). In *takhayyur,* a school's minority opinion or an opinion from outside a region's dominant tradition is chosen from the library of extant *fiqh* opinions and brought into the system. Many scholars cite the *Mecelle-i Ahkam-ı Adliye* as the most significant case of *takhayyur* in the nineteenth century. In *talfiq*, elements from two or more schools are brought together to create a new form of the law. An example of this type of reform would be the changes made to Egyptian divorce and child custody laws with Decree/Law 25 of 1929. This law augmented the Hanafi divorce system by accepting the general Maliki principle of allowing a woman to obtain a judicial divorce if she can claim that the husband has done her harm, which could include taking a second wife.[19]

Contemporary scholars such as Hallaq have considered *takhayyur* and *talfiq* to be ineffective and symptomatic of the problems of modern Islamic law. According to Hallaq, the selection of single opinions removed the "*ijtihadic* plurality" inherent within the law and "did the bidding of the state in absorbing the Islamic legal tradition into its well-defined structures of codification."[20] Additionally, Hina Azam has pointed out that the use of *talfiq* in the rape laws of Pakistan, combining Maliki evidentiary requirements with the Hanafi system of prosecution, has led to the unjust imprisonment of countless women for adultery because they failed to meet the evidentiary requirements for rape. In her view, "More specifically problematic is that in the process of this *talfiq*, the substantive, evidentiary, and procedural instruments developed in Mālikī jurisprudence that could help rape victims are consistently ignored in modern legislation in favor of the simplistic and highly problematic approach of Ḥanafī jurisprudence, while the few protections that are afforded by Ḥanafī jurisprudence are conversely dismissed."[21]

Both views are correct in presenting the problems of legislation in modern Muslim states. However, the use of *takhayyur* and *talfiq* as the primary vehicles for legal reform, although present in the premodern literature, is a product of a new approach in the twentieth century that sees the shari'a as limited to the opinions constructed by *fiqh*. This is an assumption shared by many contemporary scholars of Islamic law, but as seen throughout this book, it was not universally adopted by legal scholars of the mid-nineteenth century. When explaining the Egyptian code of 1883, for example, al-Bustani commented, "The Egyptian legislature followed its [the French Code's] path, taking from it and *building upon it*."[22] Therefore, he was well aware of the French understanding but did not view the shari'a as a collection of *fiqh* rules from which to select the better option. Instead, al-Bustani and others sought out broader principles of the shari'a and found—as noted in the more general discussion of justice and state power in chapter 1—that for the application of the shari'a to be appropriately realized, the state must intervene in the prosecution of murderers.

Using this book as a historical analysis of legal evolution can help explain the changes in the twentieth century and show how the problems pointed out by Hallaq and Azam continue to perplex Muslims today. For example, following the partition of India in 1947, the newly created states of Pakistan and Bangladesh supplemented the Indian Penal Code with new elements such as the Pakistani Hudud, Qisas, and Diyat Ordinances following the military coup led by General Muhammad Zia-ul-Haq in 1977. The new elements were meant to be a part of a process to reintroduce the shari'a to what the Pakistani government felt were the non-Islamic laws promulgated by the British. These ordinances should be analyzed in the same way as the codes in this book, considering the role of local actors and changing intellectual circumstances (such as Islamism) that influenced their content. If the IPC—incorporated as the Pakistan Penal Code at partition—was mainly in line with Hanafi understandings and not a divergence from the shari'a, what purpose did the new ordinances serve? Perhaps they represented a new interpretation of, and a clearer deviation from, shari'a compared to the IPC created by the British—and thus in effect served the postcolonial ideology of Islamism.

Additionally, adopting the view of the mid-nineteenth century to understand the shari'a as not exclusively bound to the body of *fiqh* rules could provide a better path for future legal reformers. To take a recent application, in 2019 the president of the United Arab Emirates (UAE) set the amount of blood money *(diya)* to be paid to the families of victims who had died as a result of unintentional killing *(khata')* at 200,000 dirhams (approximately $54,400), regardless of whether the victim was male or female. This decree resulted from a question about the judicial interpretation of the term "deceased" *(mutawaffa)*, which had meant only men since the payment of blood money had been created as an option for criminal courts in 1991. The Dubai Court of Cassation, the highest appellate court in the emirate, was the first to suggest this more inclusive reading of the term.[23] The local court then elevated the case to the federal level, as the UAE constitution does not give the courts in each of the seven emirates the right to interpret vague terms without federal intervention. The resulting presidential decree confirmed the Dubai court's interpretation and applied it across the board.[24] The UAE was not the first country to equalize the amount of blood money paid for men and women: Iran had enacted similar legislation as part of its penal code in 2013.[25]

The presidential decree in the UAE and the equality of blood money for the families of men and women in Emirati and Iranian law runs contrary to the understandings of *fiqh*, as scholars from the earliest periods of Islamic law have always understood the blood money for a woman to be half that of a man.[26] The action of the UAE government was one of *siyasa*, and if the view of the shari'a developed in the twentieth century and the view of most current academic literature are to be accepted, then the actions of the UAE and Iranian governments run contrary to the very nature of the shari'a.

Suppose the argument of this book is accepted. In that case, there will be few obstacles preventing Western academics and Muslim legal scholars from viewing these laws as part of the continuity of the shari'a in the modern period. Although the state may issue rulings that go against the majority understanding of the *fiqh*, it is merely continuing to perform the role that materialized during the nineteenth century and was supported as an implementation of the purpose of the shari'a: to create a greater sense of justice in light of changing circumstances. For example, as mentioned by one legal commentator following the UAE decree, "the descendants of a woman may be in great need of the [full] blood money, particularly if they are children or if the deceased was a widow or divorcee."[27]

However, an important question remains: how far can the methodology of this book be extended? Would it be possible for a state to do anything, as long as it was justified as a broad application of principles of the shari'a? Therefore, is there a realm where an expanded understanding of the shari'a beyond the confines of premodern *fiqh* discourse could be placed, discussed, and even bound? Sherman Jackson has provided perhaps the most salient solution in his idea of the "shari'a secular," or the existence of "a realm that is beyond the religious *law*" but "not the same as . . . one that is beyond the *religion*."[28] This view, based on his analysis of the writings of the Maliki jurist Shihab al-Din al-Qarafi (d. 684/1285), suggests that the shari'a can limit both others (in that it restrains the ability of people to act without considering God's law) and itself (in that it delineates the areas of the law that exist beyond it). Secular rules for the modern world, such as the example of adhering to speed limits given by Jackson, can be guided by the ethical framework of the shari'a or what he defines as "God consciousness," yet at the same time they can exist beyond the creations of the *fuqaha'*.

Therefore, gender equality of blood money payments in the UAE could fall into this new realm.

The acceptance of this point will undoubtedly be an uphill battle, given the current view among most academics in the West and the Muslim world that the shari'a is bound to the *fiqh*. However, understanding what happened to the law during the colonial period, in this book's limited example of the realm of homicide, provides a historical application of Jackson's approach. When faced with a modernizing state and European influence, local actors worked to find a path through which a God-conscious view of the law could guarantee a continuity of the shari'a.

Notes

Introduction

1 Following judicial reforms initiated by Warren Hastings (the British governor-general of India in 1773–1785), a criminal prosecution was usually first assessed by a local magistrate in cooperation with the police. They would either issue a ruling that could be appealed or, particularly if the crime was relatively serious, prepare reports of evidence and testimony for the case to be heard in a sessions court presided over by a single judge. Following that court's ruling, if the defendants wished to appeal their case, there was a conflict between court consultants (assessors, juries, Muslim muftis, or Hindu pandits) and the sessions judge, or the judge was unsure about an element of the case, it could then be sent to the appellate court known as the Nizamut Adawlut.

2 Walter Morgan and Arthur George Macpherson, *The Indian Penal Code with Notes* (Calcutta: G. C. Hay, 1863), 258.

3 Culpable homicide is roughly equivalent to manslaughter and is used in several contemporary jurisdictions. It refers to the unlawful killing of one human being by another without the presence of premeditation, or malice aforethought. See Bryan Garner, ed., *Black's Law Dictionary* 9th ed. (St. Paul, MN: Thomson Reuters, 2009), 1049.

4 *Queen v. Aman and Nund Kishore* (1873) HC Nwp 1 Banda 130.

5 Morgan and Macpherson, *The Indian Penal Code with Notes*, 271.

6 Morgan and Macpherson, *The Indian Penal Code with Notes*, 258.

7 Morgan and Macpherson, *The Indian Penal Code with Notes*, 85.

8 Vigilantism is specifically prohibited in Islamic law by a hadith. The Companion Sa'd b. 'Ubada asked the Prophet, "If I find a man sleeping with my wife, should I leave him alone until I come with four witnesses?" The Prophet responded, "Yes." Sa'd was angered by this response and said "Never! By the One who sent you with the Truth if it happened to me then I would have quickly struck him with a sword." The Prophet then responded, "Listen to your friend as he has a sense of honor, [but] I have a greater sense of honor than him and God has a greater sense of honor than me" (Muslim b. al-Hajjaj al-Nisaburi, *Sahih Muslim* [Vaduz, Liechtenstein: Thesaurus Islamicus, 2000], 2:636, no. 3834).

9 This is one of the prescribed punishments *(hudud)* found in the Qur'an (see Qur'an, 5:33).

10 Scott Kugle, "Framed, Blamed, and Renamed: The Recasting of Islamic Jurisprudence in Colonial South Asia," *Modern Asian Studies* 35, no. 2 (2001): 258.

11 Radhika Singha, *A Despotism of Law: Crime and Justice in Early Colonial India* (Delhi: Oxford University Press, 1998), vii.

12 Wael Hallaq, "Can the Shari'a Be Restored?," in *Islamic Law and the Challenges of Modernity*, ed. Yvonne Haddad and Barbara Stowasser (Walnut Creek, CA: AltaMira Press, 2004), 24.

13 Wael Hallaq, *An Introduction to Islamic Law* (New York: Cambridge University Press, 2009), 117.

14 Rudolph Peters, *Crime and Punishment in Islamic Law: Theory and Practice from the Sixteenth to the Twenty-First Century* (New York: Cambridge University Press, 2005), 103.

15 This debate was sparked by the work of Cesare Beccaria (d. 1794), who argued for a criminal justice system based on the idea of reforming and deterring criminals, as opposed to one relying on the idea of retribution that had dominated European discourse until the Enlightenment. See Cesare Beccaria, *On Crimes and Punishments*, ed. and trans. Georg Koopmann (New York: Routledge, 2009).

16 Rudolph Peters, "From Jurists' Law to Statute Law or What Happens When the Shari'a Is Codified," *Mediterranean Politics* 7, no. 3 (2002): 86; Brinkley Messick, *The Calligraphic State: Textual Domination and History in a Muslim Society* (Berkeley: University of California Press, 1992), 3–4.

17 The statement "Differences [between] my nation is a mercy *(ikhtilaf al-umma rahma)*" is often cited as a *hadith*, although no chain of transmission *(sanad)* connecting it to the Prophet has ever been established. However, its content is still widely considered as consistent with Islamic principles and is found in numerous discussions of comparative legal methodologies throughout Islamic legal history. See Jalal al-Din al-Suyuti, *Jam' al-jawami'*, 2 vols. (Cairo: Dar al-Sa'ada li-l-Taba'a, 2005), 1:202.

18 Wael Hallaq, *Sharī'a: Theory, Practice, Transformations* (New York: Cambridge University Press, 2009), 448.

19 Hallaq, "Can the Shari'a Be Restored?," 22.

20 Mohammad Fadel, "The Social Logic of Taqlīd and the Rise of the Mukhtaṣar," *Islamic Law and Society* 3, no. 2 (1996): 193–233.

21 Ahmed Fekry Ibrahim, "The Codification Episteme in Islamic Juristic Discourse between Inertia and Change," *Islamic Law and Society* 22, no. 3 (May 2015): 157–220.

22 Anver Emon, "Codification and Islamic Law: The Ideology behind a Tragic Narrative," *Middle East Law and Governance* 8, nos. 2–3 (2016): 309.

23 Avi Rubin, "Modernity as a Code: The Ottoman Empire and the Global Movement of Codification," *Journal of the Economic and Social History of the Orient* 59, no. 5 (2016): 833.

24 Hallaq, "Can the Sharī'a Be Restored?," 1.

25 Avi Rubin, *Ottoman Nizamiye Courts: Law and Modernity* (New York: Palgrave Macmillan, 2011), 28.

26 The shariʿa courts of Egypt continued to operate, albeit with their jurisdiction reduced to cases of Muslim personal status, until their full integration into the National Courts in 1956. See Leonard Wood, *Islamic Legal Revival: Reception of European Law and Transformations in Islamic Legal Thought in Egypt, 1875–1952* (Oxford: Oxford University Press, 2016), 25.

27 Guy Burak, *The Second Formation of Islamic Law: The Ḥanafī School in the Early Modern Ottoman Empire* (New York: Cambridge University Press, 2015), 18.

28 Samy Ayoub, "The Sultan Says: State Authority in the Late Hanafi Tradition," *Islamic Law and Society* 23, no. 3 (2016): 239.

29 Kristen Stilt, *Islamic Law in Action: Authority, Discretion, and Everyday Experiences in Mamluk Egypt* (Oxford: Oxford University Press, 2012), 207.

30 Khaled Fahmy, *In Quest of Justice: Islamic Law and Forensic Medicine in Modern Egypt* (Oakland: University of California Press, 2018), 124.

31 Wael Hallaq, *A History of Islamic Legal Theories: An Introduction to Sunni usul al-fiqh* (New York: Cambridge University Press, 1997), 1.

32 See, for example, Ahmed Fekry Ibrahim, "Customary Practices as Exigencies in Islamic Law," *Oriens* 46, nos. 1/2 (2018): 222–61.

33 Gabriel Baer, "The Transition from Traditional to Western Criminal Law in Turkey and Egypt," *Studia Islamica* 45 (1977), 158.

34 Peters, *Crime and Punishment in Islamic Law*, 131.

35 Peters, *Crime and Punishment in Islamic Law*, 141.

36 Tobias Heinzelmann, "The Ruler's Monologue: The Rhetoric of the Ottoman Penal Code of 1858," *Die Welt des Islams* 54, nos. 3–4 (2014): 292. See also Avi Rubin, "Ottoman Judicial Change in the Age of Modernity: A Reappraisal," *History Compass* 7, no. 1 (2009): 119–140.

37 Khaled Fahmy, "The Anatomy of Justice: Forensic Medicine and Criminal Law in Nineteenth-Century Egypt," *Islamic Law and Society* 6, no. 2 (1999): 226.

38 Joseph Schacht, *An Introduction to Islamic Law* (Oxford: Oxford University Press, 1982), 96.

39 Michael R. Anderson, "Islamic Law and the Colonial Encounter in British India," in *Institutions and Ideologies: A SOAS South Asia Reader*, ed. David Arnold and Peter Robb (London: Curzon Press, 1993), 170.

40 Bernard Cohn, *Colonialism and Its Forms of Knowledge* (Princeton, NJ: Princeton University Press, 1996), 75.

41 *Navtej Singh Johar & Others v. Union of India* (2018) SCC 76, Part C, 13.

42 Iza Hussin, *The Politics of Islamic Law: Local Elites, Colonial Authority, and the Making of the Muslim State* (Chicago: University of Chicago Press: 2016), 15.

43 Hussin, *The Politics of Islamic Law*, 19.

44 Hussin, *The Politics of Islamic Law*, 103.

45 Singha, *A Despotism of Law*, 9–10.

46 The influence of the Ottoman imposition of the Hanafi school has been the subject of recent scholarship. Most importantly, Reem Meshal has documented how Hanafi interpretations were forcefully implemented on the ground in Egypt (*Sharia and the Making of the Modern Egyptian: Islamic Law and Custom in the Courts of Ottoman Cairo* [Cairo: American University in Cairo Press, 2014]).

47 Rudolph Peters, "'For His Correction and as a Deterrent Example for Others': Meḥmed ʿAlī's First Criminal Legislation (1829–30)," in "The Legal History of Ottoman Egypt," *Islamic Law and Society* 6, no. 2 (1999): 164–92.

48 Latifa Muhammad Salim has documented in detail how these courts functioned and mentions that, during the second half of the nineteenth century, the Mixed Courts often interpreted their jurisdiction much more widely than originally intended and at times intervened in cases in which a foreign interest (not simply the presence of a foreign party) was in play. However, the Mixed Courts only rarely dealt with criminal cases, and it was only with the establishment of the Native Courts in 1883 that a unified criminal system for all Egyptians was introduced. See Latifa Muhammad Salim, *al-Nizam al-qadaʾi al-misri al-hadith* (Cairo: Dar al-Shuruq, 2010).

49 Thomas Babington Macaulay, "Minute on Education," in *Selections from Educational Records, Part I (1781–1839)*, ed. H. Sharp (Delhi: National Archives of India, 1965), 116.

50 For more on the ʿUrabi revolution, see Juan Cole, *Colonialism and Revolution in the Middle East: Social and Cultural Origins of Egypt's Urabi Movement* (Princeton, NJ: Princeton University Press, 2001).

51 See Timothy Mitchell, *Colonising Egypt* (Berkeley: University of California Press, 1988).

52 The historical search for the origins of the term "shariʿa" was the subject of a recent article. See Mohammad Omar Farooq and Nedal El-Ghattis, "In Search of the Shari'ah," *Arab Law Quarterly* 32, no. 4 (2018): 315–54.

53 Wael Hallaq, "What Is Shari'a?," *Yearbook of Islamic and Middle Eastern Law Online* 12, no. 1 (2005): 152.

54 Mathias Rohe, *Islamic Law in Past and Present* (Leiden, the Netherlands: Brill, 2015), 3.

55 Rohe, *Islamic Law in Past and Present*, 5.

56 Muhammad Ahmad Serag, *Fi usul al-nizam al-qanuni al-islami Dirasa muqarana li-ʿilm usul al-fiqh wa tatbiqatihi al-fiqhiya wa-l-qanuniya* (Beirut: Markaz Nuhud li-l-Dirasat wal-Nashr, 2020), 29.

57 Peters, *Crime and Punishment in Islamic Law*, 189.

58 Wael Hallaq, *The Impossible State: Islam, Politics, and Modernity's Moral Predicament* (New York: Columbia University Press, 2013), 26.

59 Hallaq, *The Impossible State*, 25.

60 Peters, *Crime and Punishment in Islamic Law*, 189.

61 Hallaq, *The Impossible State*, 12.

62 Fahmy, *In Quest of Justice*, 279.

63 In this statement, Fahmy is also challenging the work of others such as Talal Asad, who argued that the secularization of Egyptian law also meant the disconnection of the law from its moral roots (*Formations of the Secular: Christianity, Islam, Modernity* [Stanford, CA: Stanford University Press, 2003]).

64 For example, in his description of the integration of forensic medicine into the nineteenth-century Egyptian penal system, Fahmy suggested that a closer observation of the views behind the initial resistance of the *ʿulama'* to autopsies would show that their objections came not from a *shar'i* opposition

but rather were based on the Egyptian family's concerns about family honor and the trauma of seeing their loved one dissected in the name of science. In the latter decades of the century, these local concerns abated, and Egyptians themselves sought autopsies of their dead relatives to find out the true cause of death and seek justice. See Fahmy, *In Quest of Justice*, 63.

Chapter 1. Establishing Justice through State Law

1   Muhammad 'Abd al-Hayy, *Khulasat al-fatawa*, 4 vols. (Lucknow, India: Munshi Nawal Kishor, n.d.), 4:3.

2   The term "infidel" (*kafir*) could also include Hindus and other non-Muslims. However, it is rare to see Hindus referred to using this term, and during the nineteenth century it was most commonly used to refer to the British colonial officers—as they were not only non-Muslim but foreign to the Indian system. See, for example, Yohanan Friedmann, "Islamic Thought in Relation to the Indian Context," in *India's Islamic Traditions, 711–1750*, ed. Richard Eaton (New Delhi: Oxford University Press, 2003), 52.

3   'Abd al-Hayy, *Khulasat al-fatawa*, 4:2.

4   Muhammad 'Abd al-Hayy, *Majmu'-e fatawa*, 3 vols. (Lucknow, India: Yusufi Press, 1911), 3:21.

5   See, for example, Roderic Davison, "Tanẓīmāt," in *Encyclopaedia of Islam*, 2nd ed., ed. P. Bearman, Th. Bianquis, C. E. Bosworth, E. van Donzel, and W. P. Heinrichs, eds., 2012, http://dx.doi.org/10.1163/1573–3912_islam_COM_1174.

6   See, for example, Niyazi Berkes, *The Development of Secularism in Turkey* (Montreal: McGill University Press, 1964).

7   See, for example, Avi Rubin, "Was There a Rule of Law in the Late Ottoman Empire?" *British Journal of Middle Eastern Studies* 46, no. 1 (2019): 123–138.

8   Butrus Abu-Manneh, "The Islamic Roots of the Gülhane Rescript," *Die Welt des Islams* 34, no. 2 (1994): 174.

9   *Düstur* (Istanbul: Matba'-e Amire, 1873), 4.

10 The attachment to the shari'a in the rhetoric of the declaration has been discussed by Tobias Heinzelmann ("The Ruler's Monologue: The Rhetoric of the Ottoman Penal Code of 1858," *Die Welt des Islams* 54, nos. 3–4 [2014]: 292–321).

11 In personal law, for example, Tarek Elgawhary has shown that in Egypt the opposition to the process of codification developed only in the late nineteenth and early twentieth centuries, with the works of figures such as Muhammad Rashid Rida (d. 1935) and Ahmad Shakir (d. 1958) ("Restructuring Islamic Law: The Opinions of the 'Ulama' towards Codification of Personal Status Law in Egypt," PhD diss., Princeton University, 2014).

12 Introduction to 'Ali b. Abi Bakr al-Marghinani, *The Hedaya, or Guide: A Commentary on the Mussulman laws*, trans. Charles Hamilton, 4 vols. (London: T. Bensley, 1791), 1:iv.

13 Hafiz Muhammad 'Ali Haydar, *Tadhkira-e mashahir-e Kakuri* (Lucknow, India: Asah al-Matabi', 1927), 432–33.

14   Quoted in Haydar, *Tadhkira-e mashahir-e Kakuri*, 433.

15   Salamat 'Ali Khan, *Islami qanun-e faujdari, tarjuma-e kitab al-ikhtiyar* (Azamgarh, India: Matba'-e Ma'arif, n.d.).

16   Quoted in Muhammad Qasim Zaman, *The Ulama in Contemporary Islam: Custodians of Change* (Princeton, NJ: Princeton University Press, 2002), 21.

17   Salamat 'Ali Khan, "al-Ikhtiyar," Ms. 2060, Khuda Baksh Library, Patna, India.

18   Najm al-Din 'Ali Khan, "Kitab-e jinayat," Ms. 3829, Khuda Baksh Library, Patna, India.

19   Siraj al-Din 'Ali Khan, *Jami' al-ta'zirat min kutub al-thiqat* (Hyderabad, India: Matba' 'Ayn al-'Ayan, 1820), 2–3.

20   See Wael Hallaq, "Was the Gate of Ijtihad Closed?," *International Journal of Middle East Studies* 16, no. 1 (1984): 3–41.

21   Abu Sa'id Zuhur al-Din, "Hirat al-fuqaha' wa hujjat al-quda'," Ms. 2669, Khuda Baksh Library, Patna, India.

22   Quoted in M. S. Naravane, *Battles of the Honourable East India Company: Making of the Raj* (Delhi: Ashish Publishing House, 2006), 77.

23   Jadunath Sarkar, *Fall of the Mughal Empire* (Calcutta: M. C. Sarkar and Sons, 1950), 4:335.

24   Shah 'Abd al-'Aziz Muhaddith Dahlawi, *Fatawa 'azizi* (Karachi, Pakistan: H. M. Sa'id Company, 1967), 454–55.

25   See, for example, 'Abd al-Hayy, *Majmu'-e fatawa*, 2:287–88.

26   Muhammad Mushtaq Ahmad, "The Notions of Dār Al-Ḥarb and Dār al-Islām in Islamic Jurisprudence with Special Reference to the Ḥanafī School," *Islamic Studies* 47, no. 1 (2008): 8–9.

27   Ayesha Jalal, *Partisans of Allah* (Cambridge, MA: Harvard University Press, 2010), 59–66.

28   For a detailed listing of the relevant fatwas, see Faysal Ahmad Nadwi Bhatkali, *Tahrik-e azadi main 'ulama' ka kardar* (Lucknow, India: Majlis-e Tahqiqat wa Nashriyat-e Islam, 2018).

29   Francis Robinson, *The 'Ulama of Farangi Mahall and Islamic Culture in South Asia* (London: C. Hurst, 2001), 186–187.

30   Brannon Ingram, *Revival from Below: The Deoband Movement and Global Islam* (Oakland: University of California Press, 2018), 18.

31   Usha Sanyal, *Ahmad Riza Khan Barelwi: In the Path of the Prophet* (Oxford: Oneworld Publications, 2005), 28–29.

32   Fariba Zarinebaf, *Crime and Punishment in Istanbul: 1700–1800* (Berkeley: University of California Press, 2010), 113.

33   Zarinebaf, *Crime and Punishment*, 176.

34   Mustafa Muhammad, "al-Ijram fi Misr," in *al-Kitab al-dhahabi li-l-mahakim al-ahliya*, 2 vols. (Bulaq, Egypt: al-Matba'a al-Amiriya, 1933), 2:40.

35   Joe Hicks and Grahame Allen, "A Century of Change: Trends in UK statistics since 1900," UK House of Commons Research Paper 99/111, 21 December 2019; A. Joan Klebba, "Homicide Trends in the United States, 1900–74," *Public Health Reports* 90, no. 3 (May-Jun 1975), 196.

36   Khaled Fahmy, *All the Pasha's Men: Mehmed Ali, His Army and the Making of Modern Egypt* (Cairo: American University in Cairo Press, 2002).

37 Rudolph Peters, "'For His Correction and as a Deterrent Example for Others': Meḥmed ʿAlī's First Criminal Legislation (1829–30)," *Islamic Law and Society* 6, no. 2, The Legal History of Ottoman Egypt (1999): 164–192.

38 Michael Gasper, *The Power of Representation: Publics, Peasants, and Islam in Egypt* (Stanford, CA: Stanford University Press, 2009).

39 ʿAbd al-Rahman b. Hasan al-Jabarti, *Mazhar al-taqdis bi-zawal dawlat al-fransis* (Cairo: Dar al-Kutub al-Misriya, 1998), 2–3.

40 Ahmad Fathi Zaghlul, *al-Muhama* (Cairo: Dar al-Kutub wa-l-Watha'iq al-Qawmiya, 2015), 223.

41 Zaghlul, *al-Muhama*, 240–41.

42 Muhammad Labib ʿAtiya, "Tatawwur qanun al-ʿuqubat fi Misr min ʿahd insha' al-mahakim al-ahliya," in *al-Kitab al-dhahabi li-l-mahakim al-ahliya*, 2 vols. (Bulaq, Egypt: al-Matbaʿa al-Amiriya, 1933), 2:6.

43 Khaled Fahmy, "Rudolph Peters and the History of Modern Egyptian Law," in *Legal Documents as Sources for the History of Muslim Societies: Studies in Honour of Rudolph Peters*, ed. Maaike van Berkel (Leiden, the Netherlands: Brill, 2017), 16.

44 Fahmy, "Rudolph Peters and the History of Modern Egyptian Law," 16–17.

45 ʿAbd al-Rahman al-Kawakibi, *al-Aʿmal al-kamila*, ed. Muhammad ʿImara (Cairo: Dar al-Shuruq, 2019), 181.

46 ʿAbd Allah b. Hasan Barakat Zada was a Turkish judicial official who began his career as a scribe under the Ottoman Shaykh al-Islam Seyit Mehmed Sadettin Efendi (in office 1858–1863). He reached the position of chief scribe and was then appointed as a judge in Beirut and an inspector in Syria. Later he became the chief judge of Egypt and Anatolia. However, he remained a resident of Cairo until his death in 1900, and he was buried close to the mausoleum of al-Shafiʿi. See introduction to ʿAbd Allah b. Hasan Barakat Zada, *al-Siyasa al-sharʿiya fi huquq al-raʿi wa saʿadat al-raʿiya* (Cairo: Matbaʿat al-Taraqqi, 1900), 4–6.

47 Barakat Zada, *al-Siyasa*, 49.

48 Barakat Zada, *al-Siyasa*, 56.

49 See, for example, Ahmad al-Barzanji al-Husayni, *al-Nasiha al-ʿamma li-muluk al-Islam wa-l-ʿamma* (Damascus: n.p., 1890); Muhammad Bayram al-Khamis, *Mulahizat siyasiya ʿan al-tanzimat al-lazima li-l-dawla al-ʿuliya* (n.p.: n.p., 1880).

50 Quoted in Peters, "'For His Correction and as a Deterrent Example for Others,'" 172.

51 al-Kawakibi, *al-Aʿmal al-kamila*, 291.

52 Baber Johansen, "Signs as Evidence: The Doctrine of Ibn Taymiyya (1263–1328) and Ibn Qayyim al-Jawziyya (d. 1351) on Proof," *Islamic Law and Society* 9, no. 2 (2002): 168–93. For more on the movement of Taqi al-Din Ahmad b. Taymiya, see Ovamir Anjum, *Politics, Law, and Community in Islamic Thought: The Taymiyyan Movement* (New York: Cambridge University Press, 2012).

53 Muhammad b. Qayyim al-Jawziya, *al-Turuq al-hukmiya fi al-siyasa al-sharʿiya* (Beirut: Maktabat al-Muʾayyad, 1989), 13.

54 Ibn Qayyim al-Jawziya, *al-Turuq al-hukmiya*, 13.

55 Ibn Qayyim al-Jawziya, *al-Turuq al-hukmiya*, 4.
56 Ibn Qayyim al-Jawziya, *al-Turuq al-hukmiya*, 13.
57 Halil İnalcık, *Osmanlı'da Devlet, Hukuk ve Adalet* (Istanbul: Kronik Yayıncılık, 2016).
58 Siraj al-Din 'Ali Khan, *Jami'*, 108–109.
59 'Abd al-Hayy, *Majmu'-e fatawa*, 2:221.
60 *Gov. v. Baij Roy* (1853) NA Ben 2 Shahabad 955.
61 *Gov. v. Sooltan Bhueemya* (1853) NA Ben 2 Backergunge 480.
62 'Abd al-Hayy, *Majmu'-e fatawa*, 2:226.
63 Barakat Zada, *al-Siyasa*, 8.
64 Barakat Zada, *al-Siyasa*, 37.
65 Barakat Zada, *al-Siyasa*, 48.
66 Khaled Fahmy, "The Anatomy of Justice: Forensic Medicine and Criminal Law in Nineteenth-Century Egypt," *Islamic Law and Society* 6, no. 2 (1999): 226.
67 Fahmy, "Anatomy of Justice," 252–53.
68 Fahmy, "Anatomy of Justice," 264.
69 Quoted in Fahmy, "Anatomy of Justice," 266.

Chapter 2. New Elites Shaping the Law

1   See, for example, Leonard Wood, *Islamic Legal Revival: Reception of European Law and Transformations in Islamic Legal Thought in Egypt, 1875–1952* (Oxford: Oxford University Press, 2016).
2   Robert Hefner, *Schooling Islam: The Culture and Politics of Modern Muslim Education* (Princeton, NJ: Princeton University Press, 2010), 14.
3   Francis Robinson, *The 'Ulama of Farangi Mahall and Islamic Culture in South Asia* (London: C. Hurst, 2001), 53.
4   Introduction to Shah Wali Allah Dahlawi, *The Conclusive Argument from God*, trans. Marcia Hermansen (Leiden, the Netherlands: Brill, 1996), xxix–xxx.
5   William Dalrymple, "Transculturation, Assimilation, and Its Limits: The Rise and Fall of the Delhi White Mughals, 1805–57," in *The Delhi College: Traditional Elites, the Colonial State, and Education before 1857*, ed. Margrit Pernau (Delhi: Oxford University Press, 2006), 98–101.
6   Dalrymple, "Transculturation, Assimilation, and Its Limits," 98–101.
7   Ebba Koch, "The Madrasa of Ghaziu'd-Din Khan at Delhi," in *The Delhi College: Traditional Elites, the Colonial State, and Education before 1857*, ed. Margrit Pernau (Delhi: Oxford University Press, 2006), 38.
8   Introduction to *The Delhi College: Traditional Elites, the Colonial State, and Education before 1857*, ed. Margrit Pernau (Delhi: Oxford University Press, 2006), 1–2.
9   Gail Minault, "The Perils of Cultural Mediation: Master Ram Chandra and Academic Journalism at Delhi College," in *The Delhi College: Traditional Elites, the Colonial State, and Education before 1857*, ed. Margrit Pernau (Delhi: Oxford University Press, 2006), 190.
10 Mushirul Hasan, "Maulawi Zaka Ullah: Sharif Culture and Colonial Rule," in *The Delhi College: Traditional Elites, the Colonial State, and Education before 1857*, ed. Margrit Pernau (Delhi: Oxford University Press, 2006), 282.

11   Hasan, "Maulawi Zaka Ullah," 274.
12   See Peter Hill, *Utopia and Civilisation in the Arab Nahda* (Cambridge: Cambridge University Press, 2019), 50.
13   Ibrahim b. Muhammad b. Duqmaq, *Description de l'Égypte* (Cairo: Matba'at al-Bulaq, 1893). For the impact on the *Description* on European interest in Egypt, see Andrew Bednarski. *Holding Egypt: Tracing the reception of the Description de l'Égypte in nineteenth-century Great Britain* (London: Golden House Publications, 2005).
14   Ibrahim Abu-Lughod, *The Arab Rediscovery of Europe: A Study in Cultural Encounters* (Princeton, NJ: Princeton University Press, 1963), 6.
15   Quoted in Jamal al-Din al-Shayyal, *Tarikh al-tarjuma wa-l-haraka al-thiqafiya fi 'asr Muhammad 'Ali* (Cairo: Dar al-Fikr al-'Arabi, 1951), 121.
16   Quoted in Jamal al-Din al-Shayyal, *Rifa'a Raf' al-Tahtawi* (Cairo: Dar al-Ma'arif, 1958), 25.
17   Quoted in al-Shayyal, *Rifa'a Raf' al-Tahtawi*, 33.
18   Rudolph Peters, "'For His Correction and as a Deterrent Example for Others': Mehmed 'Ali's First Criminal Legislation (1829–30)," in "The Legal History of Ottoman Egypt," *Islamic Law and Society* 6, no. 2 (1999): 164–92.
19   Nubar Nubarian, *Mudhakkirat Nubar Basha*, trans. Jaru Rubayr Tabaqiyan (Cairo: Dar al-Shuruq, 2009).
20   Mark Hoyle, *Mixed Courts of Egypt* (London: Graham and Trotman, 1991).
21   al-Shayyal, *Rifa'a Raf' al-Tahtawi*, 46–47.
22   Wood, *Islamic Legal Revival*, 55.
23   Muhammad Ibrahim, "Athar Madrassat al-Huquq al-Khidawiya fi tatwir al-dirasat al-fiqhiya," MA thesis, Cairo University, 2015, 8.
24   al-Shayyal, *Rifa'a Raf' al-Tahtawi*, 21.
25   Indira Falk Gesink, *Islamic Reform and Conservatism: al-Azhar and the Evolution of Modern Sunni Islam* (London: I. B. Tauris, 2009), 7.
26   See, for example, his autobiography ('Ali Mubarak, *Hayati* [Cairo: Maktabat al-Adab, 1989]).
27   Quoted in Michael Reimer, "Contradiction and Consciousness in Ali Mubarak's Description of al-Azhar," *International Journal of Middle East Studies* 29, no. 1 (1997): 54.
28   Gesink, *Islamic Reform and Conservatism*, 41–42.
29   Shibli Nu'mani, *Safarnama-e Rum wa Misr wa Sham* (Delhi: Qawmi Press, 1901), 150–151.
30   Gesink, *Islamic Reform and Conservatism*, 56.
31   'Ali Mubarak, *al-Khitat al-Tawfiqiya al-jadida li-Misr al-Qahira wa muduniha wa biladiha al-qadima wa al-shahira*, 14 vols. (Bulaq, Egypt: al-Matba'a al-Amiriya, 1887), 4:27.
32   Mubarak, *al-Khitat*, 4:27.
33   Nu'mani, *Safarnama*, 167–168.
34   Nu'mani, *Safarnama*, 67–68.
35   Nu'mani, *Safarnama*, 58.
36   Barbara Metcalf, *Islamic Revival in British India: Deoband, 1860–1900* (Princeton, NJ: Princeton University Press, 1982), 87.

37 Muhammad Qasim Zaman, *Ashraf 'Ali Thanawi: Islam in Modern South Asia* (Oxford: Oneworld, 2007), 1.

38 Zaman, *Ashraf 'Ali Thanawi*, 107–108.

39 Tàwfiq Iskaru, "Muhammad Qadri Basha," *al-Muqtataf* 48, no. 3 (March 1916): 253–63.

40 Muhammad Qadri Basha, *Murshid al-hayran ila ma'rifat ahwal al-insan fi al-mu'amalat al-shar'iya 'ala madhhab al-Imam al-A'zam Abi Hanifa al-Nu'man*, ed. Muhammad Ahmad Siraj (Cairo: Dar al-Salam, 2011).

41 'Abd al-Razzaq al-Sanhuri, *Masadir al-haqq fi al-fiqh al-islami*, 2 vols. (Cairo: Ma'had al-Buhuth wa-l-Dirasat al-'Arabiya, 1967–1968).

42 Muhammad Qadri Basha, "The Application of What Is Found in the French Civil Code in Agreement with the School of Abu Hanifa (*Tatbiq ma wujida fi al-qanun al-madani—al-faransi—muwafiqan li-madhhab Abi Hanifa*)," Ms. 48119, Dar al-Kutub, Cairo.

43 Muhammad Qadri Basha, "Application."

44 Art. 28 C. civ. 1804.

45 See, for example, Qur'an 4:11–12 and 176.

46 'Aziz Khanki, *al-Mahakim al-mukhtalata wa-l-mahakim al-ahliya: Madiuha, hadiruha, wa mustaqbaluha* (Cairo: al-Matba'a al-'Asriya, 1939), 92–93.

47 Muhammad 'Abd al-Mun'im Khafaji and 'Ali 'Ali Subh, *al-Azhar fi alf 'am*, 6 vols. (Cairo: al-Maktaba al-Azhariya li-l-Turath, 2011), 3:96–97.

48 Khanki, *al-Mahakim al-mukhtalata wa-l-mahakim al-ahliya*, 93. See also Jakob Skovgaard-Petersen, *Defining Islam for the Egyptian State: Muftis and Fatwās of the Dār al-Iftā'* (Leiden, the Netherlands: Brill, 1997), 100.

49 Rudolph Peters, "Muḥammad al-'Abbāsī al-Mahdī (d.1897), Grand Mufti of Egypt, and His 'al-Fatāwā al-Mahdiyya,'" *Islamic Law and Society* 1, no. 1 (1994), 82.

50 Quoted in 'Ali 'Ali Mansur, *Khatwa ra'ida nahw tatbiq ahkam al-shari'a al-islamiya fi al-Jumhuriya al-'Arabiya al-Libiya* (Tripoli, Libya: Dar al-Turath al-'Arabi, 1972), 32.

51 Mansur, *Khatwa*, 31.

52 Yuaqim Mikha'il, *Tarikh al-qanun fi Misr* (Cairo: Matba'at Misr, 1899), 91.

53 Christopher King, *One Language, Two Scripts: The Hindi Movement in Nineteenth Century North India* (Delhi: Oxford University Press, 1995).

54 Sir William Muir (d. 1905) was a Scottish Orientalist who came to India in 1837 and worked in various positions for the colonial administration until his retirement from public service in 1903. During his career, he wrote a number of works on Islamic history and theology. See Avril Powell, *Scottish Orientalists and India: The Muir Brothers, Religion, Education, and Empire* (Rochester, NY: Boydell Press, 2010).

55 Muhammad Mahdi, *Tadhkira shams al-'ulama' Hafiz Nazir Ahmad marhum* (n.p., n.d.).

56 Babu Kunj Bihari Lal and Munshi Muhammad Nazir, *Sharh majmu'-e qawanin-e ta'zirat-e Hind* (Fatehpur: Matba' Nasim-e Hind, 1885), 1.

57 Mahdi, *Tadhkira*, 9.

58　Carter Findley, *The Turks in World History* (New York: Oxford University Press, 2005), 160–161.

59　Avi Rubin, *Ottoman Nizamiye Courts: Law and Modernity* (New York: Palgrave Macmillan, 2011), 81.

60　Khaled Fahmy, *In Quest of Justice: Islamic Law and Forensic Medicine in Modern Egypt* (Oakland: University of California Press, 2018), 126.

61　Shaden Tageldin, *Disarming Words: Empire and the Seductions of Translation in Egypt* (Berkeley: University of California Press, 2011), 10.

Chapter 3. The Classification of Homicide

1　Ahmad b. Muhammad al-Tahawi, *Mukhtasar al-Tahawi* (Hyderabad, India: Lajnat Ihya' al-Ma'arif al-Nu'maniya, n.d.), 232–33.

2　Qur'an 4:92–93.

3　'Abd Allah b. Muhammad b. Abi Shayba, *al-Musannaf* (Beirut: Dar al-Taj, 1989), 5:436, no. 27763–67; 'Ali b. 'Umar al-Darqutni, *Sunan al-Darqutni* (Cairo: Dar al-Mahasin, 1966), 3:94, no. 47.

4　This incident is found in several major *hadith* collections. See, for example, Muhammad b. Isma'il al-Bukhari, *al-Jami' al-musnad al-sahih* (Vaduz, Liechtenstein: Thesaurus Islamicus, 2000), 3:1394, no. 6996; Muslim b. al-Hajjaj al-Nisaburi, *Sahih Muslim* (Vaduz, Liechtenstein: Thesaurus Islamicus, 2000), 2:729, no. 4483.

5　Abu Bakr b. Mas'ud al-Kasani, *Bada'i' al-sana'i' fi tartib al-shara'i'*, 10 vols. (Beirut: Dar al-Kutub al-'Ilmiya, 2003), 10:234–35.

6　Francis Robinson, *The 'Ulama of Farangi Mahall and Islamic Culture in South Asia* (London: C. Hurst, 2001), 240–51.

7　Muhammad Amin b. 'Abidin, *Radd al-muhtar 'ala al-durr al-mukhtar*, 10 vols. (Riyadh: Dar 'Alim al-Kutub, 2003), 10:155.

8　al-Kasani, *Bada'i'*, 10:237, emphasis added.

9　Intisar Rabb, *Doubt in Islamic Law: A History of Legal Maxims, Interpretation, and Islamic Criminal Law* (New York: Cambridge University Press, 2015), 1–3.

10　Rabb, *Doubt in Islamic Law*, 333–47.

11　*Family of Fatuma bt. Isma'il Agha Saghuli v. Abu Iltija' Abi Zayd* (1861) FM 6 Damanhur 78.

12　Ibn 'Abidin, *Radd al-muhtar*, 10:197.

13　Qur'an 2:179.

14　Muhammad b. Jarir al-Tabari, *Jami' al-bayan 'an ta'wil ay al-Qur'an* (Beirut: Mu'assasat al-Risala, 1994), 1:483–184.

15　Muhammad al-Tahir b. 'Ashur, *Tafsir al-tahrir wa-l-tanwir* (Tunis: al-Dar al-Tunisiya li-l-Nashr, 1984), 2:144–145.

16　al-Bukhari, *al-Jami'*, 3:1385, nos. 6952–6953.

17　Christian Lange, *Justice, Punishment, and the Medieval Muslim Imagination* (New York: Cambridge University Press, 2008), 53.

18　Ahmet Mumcu, *Osmanlı Devletinde Siyaseten Katl* (Ankara: Ajans-Türk Matbaası, 1963).

19　*Gov. v. Upoorbokisto Mundul* (1854) NA Ben 1 24–Pergunnahs 517.

20 *Rumjoo Khan and Gov. v. Gowhur Ally* (1854) NA Ben 1 Behar 230.

21 *Gov. v. Sobow* (1854) NA Ben 1 Sarun 281.

22 *Gov. v. Kirtinarain Shaha* (1853) NA Ben 2 Tipperah 416.

23 Chapter 5 compares the concept of insanity in Islamic and common law.

24 *Gov. v. Sooltan Bhueemya* (1853) NA Ben 2 Backergunge 480.

25 Muhammad b. Husayn al-Anqarawi, *al-Fatawa al-anqarawiya*, 2 vols. (Bulaq, Egypt: n.p., 1865), 1:178.

26 *Bunsee Singh v. Goolzar* (1853) NA Ben 2 Tirhoot 487.

27 *Gov. v. Nusseeruddeen* (1854) NA Ben 1 24–Pergunnahs 72.

28 This is not a universally accepted opinion, although it is a commonly understood concept within traditional Islamic law that a father is not to be held criminally liable for the murder of his children based on the *hadith* "prescribed punishments are not to be carried out in mosques and a father is not to be killed for [the sake of his] son." See 'Alim b. al-'Ala' al-Andarpati, *al-Fatawa al-tatarkhaniya*, 20 vols. (Deoband, India: Maktabat Zakariya, 2010), 19:22.

29 *Gov. v. Mussumat Oodee* (1853) NA Nwp 1 Delhi 646.

30 al-Andarpati, *al-Fatawa al-tatarkhaniya*, 19:18.

31 See Scott Kugle, "Framed, Blamed, and Renamed: The Recasting of Islamic Jurisprudence in Colonial South Asia," *Modern Asian Studies* 35, no. 2 (2001): 300–301.

32 Quoted in Walter Morgan and Arthur George Macpherson, *The Indian Penal Code with Notes* (Calcutta: G. C. Hay, 1863), 222.

33 Quoted in Morgan and Macpherson, *The Indian Penal Code with Notes*, 223.

34 Ibn 'Abidin, *Radd al-muhtar*, 10:155.

35 Morgan and Macpherson, *The Indian Penal Code with Notes*, 226–27.

36 al-Anqarawi, *al-Fatawa al-anqarawiya*, 1:176–177.

37 Morgan and Macpherson, *The Indian Penal Code with Notes*, 226.

38 al-Andarpati, *al-Fatawa al-tatarkhaniya*, 19:10.

39 Lisa Surridge, "On the Offenses against the Person Act, 1828," BRANCH: Britain, Representation and Nineteenth-Century History, January 2013, http://www.branchcollective.org/?ps_articles=lisa-surridge-on-the-offenses-against-the-person-act-1828; Homicide Act 1957, 5 & 6 Eliz. 2, c. 11, § 1(1).

40 See, for example, *R. v. Mitchell* (1983) 2 All ER 427.

41 IPC, Article 300.

42 Morgan and Macpherson, *The Indian Penal Code with Notes*, 239.

43 Ibn 'Abidin, *Radd al-muhtar*, 10:155–156.

44 al-Tahawi, *Mukhtasar*, 234; *al-Fatawa al-'alamgiriya*, 6 vols. (Bulaq, Egypt: al-Matba'a al-Amiriya, 1892), 6:6.

45 *al-Fatawa al-'alamgiriya*, 6:5.

46 Siraj al-Din 'Ali b. 'Uthman al-Tanimi, *al-Fatawa al-sirajiya* (Beirut: Dar al-Kutub al-'Ilmiya, 2011), 566.

47 Quoted in Morgan and Macpherson, *The Indian Penal Code with Notes*, 271–72.

48 See, for example, Uriel Heyd, *Studies in Old Ottoman Criminal Law* (Oxford: Clarendon Press of Oxford University Press, 1973), 105.

49 Quoted in Heyd, *Studies in Old Ottoman Criminal Law*, 106.

50 Irene Schneider, "Imprisonment in Pre-Classical and Classical Islamic Law," *Islamic Law and Society* 2, no. 2 (1995): 157–173.

51 Barry Wright, "Macaulay's Indian Penal Code: Historical Context and Originating Principles," in *Codification, Macaulay and the Indian Penal Code: The Legacies and Modern Challenges of Criminal Law Reform*, ed. Wing-Cheong Chan, Barry Wright, and Stanley Yeo (London: Routledge, 2016), 44.

52 Keith John Michael Smith, *Lawyers, Legislators, and Theorists: Developments in English Criminal Jurisprudence 1800–1957* (Oxford: Clarendon Press of Oxford University Press, 1998), 159.

53 Quoted in Khalil Rif'at, *Kulliyat sharh al-jaza'* (Beirut: al-Matba'a al-'Umumiya, 1886), 177.

54 Quoted in Rif'at, *Kulliyat*, 182.

55 Rif'at, *Kulliyat*, 202.

56 Rif'at, *Kulliyat*, 193.

57 Egyptian Penal Code, article 213.

58 Egyptian Penal Code, article 216.

59 Egyptian Penal Code, article 215.

60 Rif'at, *Kulliyat*, 177.

61 French Penal Code of 1810, articles 295–8 and 319.

62 Quoted in al-Andarpati, *al-Fatawa al-tatarkhaniya*, 19:11.

63 Reem Meshal, *Sharia and the Making of the Modern Egyptian: Islamic Law and Custom in the Courts of Ottoman Cairo* (Cairo: American University in Cairo Press, 2014), 8.

64 Ahmed Fekry Ibrahim, *Pragmatism in Islamic Law: A Social and Intellectual History* (Syracuse, NY: Syracuse University Press, 2015), 129.

65 A. Ibrahim, *Pragmatism*, 63–104.

66 Leonard Wood, *Islamic Legal Revival: Reception of European Law and Transformations in Islamic Legal Thought in Egypt, 1875–1952* (Oxford: Oxford University Press, 2016), 107.

67 Wood, *Islamic Legal Revival*, 108.

68 Wood, *Islamic Legal Revival*, 108.

69 Muhammad Hasanayn b. Muhammad Makhluf al-Minyawi, *Tatbiq al-qanun al-Faransawi al-madani wa-l-jina'i 'ala madhhab al-Imam Malik* (Cairo: Dar al-Salam, 1999).

70 'Abd Allah 'Ali Husayn, *al-Muqaranat al-tashri'iya bayn al-qawanin al-wad'iya al-madaniya wa-l-tashri' al-islami* (Cairo: Dar al-Salam, 2001).

71 Rudolph Peters, *Crime and Punishment in Islamic Law: Theory and Practice from the Sixteenth to the Twenty-First Century* (New York: Cambridge University Press, 2005), 39.

72 Radhika Singha, *A Despotism of Law: Crime and Justice in Early Colonial India* (Delhi: Oxford University Press, 1998), 9.

73 Rif'at, *Kulliyat*, 179.

74 Quoted in Rif'at, *Kulliyat*, 202.

75 Rif'at, *Kulliyat*, 179.

76 Rif'at, *Kulliyat*, 179.

77 *State v. Muhammad b. 'Uthman* (1880) CM 79 Istanbul, 3.

78 Amin Afram al-Bustani, *Sharh qanun al-'uqubat al-misri* (Cairo: Matba'at al-Mahrusa, 1894), 11.

79 al-Bustani, *Sharh*, 11.

80 al-Bustani, *Sharh*, 11–12.

81 Quoted in al-Bustani, *Sharh*, 12.

82 al-Bustani, *Sharh*, 15.

83 Quoted in al-Bustani, *Sharh*, 15–16.

84 al-Bustani, *Sharh*, 16–17.

85 See Muslim b. al-Hajjaj al-Nisaburi, *Sahih Muslim* (Vaduz, Liechtenstein: Thesaurus Islamicus, 2000), 2:636, no. 3834; Yavuz Aykan, "A Legal Concept in Motion: The 'Spreader of Corruption *(sāʿī bi'l-fesād)*' from Qarakhanid to Ottoman Jurisprudence," *Islamic Law and Society* 26, no. 3 (2019): 252–71.

86 *State v. Muhammad walad Sahib al-Sam'awi* (1861) FM 6 Kurdafan, 72.

87 Quoted in *State v. Ibrahim Agha al-Sirsawi* (1861) FM 6 Kurdafan, 69–70.

88 Ridwan Shafi'i al-Muta'afi, *al-Jinayat al-muttahida fi al-qanun wa-l-shari'a* (Cairo: al-Matba'a al-Salafiya, 1930), 133–135.

89 al-Muta'afi, *al-Jinayat*, 141.

90 al-Muta'afi, *al-Jinayat*, 143–145.

Chapter 4. Establishing Criminal Intent

1 This *hadith* is considered one of the most reliable within the Islamic canon, as it contains the strongest chain of narrators connecting it to the Prophet. See Muhammad b. Isma'il al-Bukhari, *al-Jami' al-musnad al-sahih* (Vaduz, Liechtenstein: Thesaurus Islamicus, 2000), 1:2, no. 1.

2 Paul Powers, *Intent in Islamic Law: Motive and Meaning in Medieval Sunnī Fiqh* (Leiden, the Netherlands: Brill, 2006), 170.

3 Quoted in 'Ali b. Abi Bakr al-Marghinani, *al-Hidaya sharh bidayat al-mubtadi*, commentary by 'Abd al-Hayy Luknawi (Karachi, Pakistan: Idarat al-Qur'an wa-l-'Ulum al-Islamiya, 1996), 8:3.

4 Walter Oberer, "The Deadly Weapon Doctrine: Common Law Origin," *Harvard Law Review* 75, no. 8 (1962): 1573.

5 Muhammad b. Mukarram b. Manzur, *Lisan al-'arab*, 15 vols. (Beirut: Dar Sadir, 1993), 2:486.

6 Quoted in 'Abd al-Ghani al-Ghanimi al-Maydani, *al-Lubab fi sharh al-kitab*, 4 vols. (Beirut: al-Maktaba al-'Ilmiya, n.d.), 3:141–142.

7 Quoted in Ahmad b. Muhammad al-Tahawi, *Mukhtasar al-Tahawi* (Hyderabad, India: Lajnat Ihya' al-Ma'arif al-Nu'maniya, n.d.), 234.

8 al-Tahawi, *Mukhtasar*, 234.

9 al-Maydani, *al-Lubab*, 3:141–142, emphasis added.

10 This opinion is first found in the work of al-Shafi'i. See Muhammad b. Idris al-Shafi'i, *al-Umm*, 8 vols. (Beirut: Dar al-Ma'rifa, n.d.), 7:329–30.

11 Abu Bakr b. Mas'ud al-Kasani, *Bada'i' al-sana'i' fi tartib al-shara'i'*, 10 vols. (Beirut: Dar al-Kutub al-'Ilmiya, 2003), 10:233–34.

12 al-Kasani, *Bada'i'*, 10:233–34. The term for metallic rocks *(al-maru)* referred to a "white, shiny rock used to make fire" and took its name from a mountain in Mecca. It is unlikely that this stone contained any amount of iron. However

al-Kasani probably understood the rock as being either metallic or containing iron ore because of its physical qualities. See Muhammad b. Ya'qub al-Firuzabadi, *al-Qamus al-muhit* (Beirut: Mu'assasat al-Risala, 2005), 1334.

13　al-Kasani, *Bada'i'*, 10:233–34.

14　'Alim b. al-'Ala' al-Andarpati, *al-Fatawa al-tatarkhaniya*, 20 vols. (Deoband, India: Maktabat Zakariya, 2010), 19:5.

15　Muhammad b. Husayn al-Anqarawi, *al-Fatawa al-anqarawiya*, 2 vols. (Bulaq, Egypt: n.p., 1865), 1:164–165; Muhammad Amin b. 'Abidin, *Radd al-muhtar 'ala al-durr al-mukhtar*, 10 vols. (Riyadh: Dar 'Alim al-Kutub, 2003), 10:157.

16　*al-Fatawa al-'alamgiriya*, 6 vols. (Bulaq, Egypt: al-Matba'a al-Amiriya, 1892), 6:3.

17　Muhammad b. Ahmad al-Sarakhsi, *al-Mabsut*, 30 vols. (Beirut: Dar al-Ma'rifa, n.d.), 27:87–90.

18　al-Andarpati, *al-Fatawa al-tatarkhaniya*, 19:5; *al-Fatawa al-'alamgiriya*, 6:5; Ibn 'Abidin, *Radd al-muhtar*, 10:156.

19　Intisar Rabb, *Doubt in Islamic Law: A History of Legal Maxims, Interpretation, and Islamic Criminal Law* (New York: Cambridge University Press, 2015), 121. Emphasis added.

20　al-Andarpati, *al-Fatawa al-tatarkhaniya*, 19:16; al-Anqarawi, *al-Fatawa al-anqarawiya*, 1:179.

21　Quoted in Radhika Singha, *A Despotism of Law: Crime and Justice in Early Colonial India* (Delhi: Oxford University Press, 1998), 52–53.

22　Quoted in Singha, *Despotism*, 51.

23　Quoted in Singha, *Despotism*, 51.

24　*Gov. v. Hulkara Singh* (1853) NA Ben 2 Behar 544.

25　*Gov. v. Nokory Bagdee* (1853) NA Ben 2 Hooghly 987.

26　*Gov. v. Mussumat Mohuree* (1854) NA Nwp 1 Saugor 468.

27　Walter Morgan and Arthur George Macpherson, *The Indian Penal Code with Notes* (Calcutta: G. C. Hay, 1863), 230.

28　Morgan and Macpherson, *The Indian Penal Code with Notes*, 231 (emphasis added).

29　Morgan and Macpherson, *The Indian Penal Code with Notes*, 244.

30　Offences against the Persons Act 1861, 24 & 25 Vict c. 100, §6.

31　*Queen v. Girdharee Singh* (1873) NA Nwp Allahabad 26. Emphasis added.

32　*Queen v. Girdharee Singh* (1873) NA Nwp Allahabad 26.

33　"Qatl az Bandaqa Rasasiya," in *Decisions of the Majlis-e 'Aliya-e 'Adalat* (Hyderabad: Matba'-e Muqannin-e Dakkan, 1887), 91.

34　Khaled Fahmy, "The Police and the People in Nineteenth-Century Egypt," *Die Welt des Islams* 39, no. 3 (November 1999): 355.

35　*Family of Muhammad Gharif v. Ahmad b. al-Hajj al-Daqsabi* (1860) FM 6 Danqla 47.

36　*Family of 'Ali Hijazi v. al-Shaykh Muhammad al-Habishi* (1860) FM 6 Baltim 58.

37　*State v. Amin Rafiq & Hasan* (1880) CM 31 Sarokhan 2.

38　Khalil Rif'at, *Kulliyat sharh al-jaza'* (Beirut: al-Matba'a al-'Umumiya, 1886), 177.

39　Rif'at, *Kulliyat*, 178.

40　Rif'at, *Kulliyat*, 177.

41　Rif'at, *Kulliyat*, 177.

42 Muhammad Yasin, *Sharh qanun al-'uqubat* (Cairo: Matba'at al-Sadiq, 1886), 221–22.
43 Yasin, *Sharh*, 225; Code Penal, 1810, article 297.
44 Yasin, *Sharh*, 226; Code Penal, 1810, article 298.
45 Yasin, *Sharh*, 226.
46 Yasin, *Sharh*, 223. Emphasis added.
47 *Family of Zanuba bt. Muhammad v. Sayyid 'Abd al-Muta'al* (1888) FB Fayum 318.
48 Muhammad 'Arafa al-Dusuqi, *Hashiyat al-Dusuqi 'ala al-sharh al-kabir* (Cairo: Dar Ihya' al-Kutub al-'Arabiya, n.d.), 4:238.
49 Rif'at, *Kulliyat*, 178.
50 Yasin, *Sharh*, 226.

Chapter 5. Criminal Responsibility
1 Ahmad b. Muhammad al-Tahawi, *Mukhtasar al-Tahawi* (Hyderabad, India: Lajnat Ihya' al-Ma'arif al-Nu'maniya, n.d.), 229.
2 Qur'an, 2:185–6 and 4:101–102.
3 Muhammad Amin b. 'Abidin, *Radd al-muhtar 'ala al-durr al-mukhtar*, 10 vols. (Riyadh: Dar 'Alim al-Kutub, 2003), 1:308.
4 Rudolph Peters, *Crime and Punishment in Islamic Law: Theory and Practice from the Sixteenth to the Twenty-First Century* (New York: Cambridge University Press, 2005), 21.
5 "Execution of a 12 Year Old Boy," British Library, 1829, http://www.bl.uk /learning/timeline/item102910.html.
6 *Sumadhan v. Roopun* (1853) NA Nwp 1 Bareilly 311.
7 *Shaik Monee on the part of Gov. v. Mathur Bewa* (1853) NA Ben 2 Assam 57.
8 Walter Morgan and Arthur George Macpherson, *The Indian Penal Code with Notes* (Calcutta: G. C. Hay, 1863), 59.
9 Khalil Rif'at, *Kulliyat sharh al-jaza'* (Beirut: al-Matba'a al-'Umumiya, 1886), 48–49.
10 Rif'at, *Kulliyat*, 47.
11 Amin Afram al-Bustani, *Sharh qanun al-'uqubat al-misri* (Cairo: Matba'at al-Mahrusa, 1894), 175.
12 al-Bustani, *Sharh*, 176. Emphasis added.
13 al-Bustani, *Sharh*, 178–80.
14 See Khaled Fahmy, *All the Pasha's Men: Mehmed Ali, His Army and the Making of Modern Egypt* (Cairo: American University in Cairo Press, 2002).
15 *The Penal Code of France, Translated into English* (London: H. Butterworth, 1819), 14–15.
16 Quoted in Homer D. Crotty, "History of Insanity as a Defence to Crime in English Criminal Law," *California Law Review* 12, no. 2 (1924): 112.
17 Quoted in Crotty, "History," 114. See also *R. v. Arnold* (1724) 16 How St. Tr. 765.
18 *R v. Hadfield* (1800) 27 How St. Tr. 765.
19 *M'Naughten's Case* (1843) All ER Rep 229.
20 See, for example, Michael Dols, *Majnūn: The Madman in Medieval Islamic Society* (Oxford: Clarendon Press of Oxford University Press, 1992), 434 and 439.

21 Khulud bt. 'Abd al-Rahman al-Muhayza', *Ahkam al-marid al-nafsi fi al-fiqh al-islami* (Riyadh: Dar al-Sami'i, 2013), 75–76.

22 Ernst Cassirer, *The Philosophy of the Enlightenment* (Princeton, NJ: Princeton University Press, 1951), 7.

23 Muhammad b. Mukarram b. Manzur, *Lisan al-'arab*, 15 vols. (Beirut: Dar Sadir, 1993), 13:92.

24 *Gov. v. Kunhai Chung* (1853) NA Ben 2 Backergunge 835.

25 *Gov. v. Abool Hossein* (1853) NA Ben 2 Backergunge 258, 258–59.

26 *Gov. v. Abool Hossein* (1853) NA Ben 2 Backergunge 258, 260.

27 *Gov. v. Abool Hossein* (1853) NA Ben 2 Backergunge 258, 261.

28 *Gov. v. Abool Hossein* (1853) NA Ben 2 Backergunge 258, 262.

29 Morgan and Macpherson, *The Indian Penal Code with Notes*, 60.

30 Morgan and Macpherson, *The Indian Penal Code with Notes*, 60–61.

31 *Gov. v. Tota* (1864) NA Nwp 1 Aligarh 211, 213.

32 *Gov. v. Tota* (1864) NA Nwp 1 Aligarh 211, 214.

33 *Gov. v. Tota* (1864) NA Nwp 1 Aligarh 211, 216.

34 Morgan and Macpherson, *The Indian Penal Code with Notes*, 62.

35 al-Bustani, *Sharh*, 185–186.

36 Quoted in Rif'at, *Kulliyat*, 53.

37 Rif'at, *Kulliyat*, 55.

38 Rif'at, *Kulliyat*, 55.

39 al-Tahawi, *Mukhtasar*, 234.

40 Peters, *Crime and Punishment in Islamic Law*, 20.

41 *Family of 'Ali walad Hamid v. Ahmad & 'Umar al-Dawwa* (1861) FM 6 Kurdafan 103.

42 al-Andarpati, *al-Fatawa al-tatarkhaniya*, 19:26.

43 al-Andarpati, *al-Fatawa al-tatarkhaniya*, 19:19.

44 *al-Fatawa al-'alamgiriya*, 6 vols. (Bulaq, Egypt: al-Matba'a al-Amiriya, 1892), 6:5; Muhammad b. Husayn al-Anqarawi, *al-Fatawa al-anqarawiya*, 2 vols. (Bulaq, Egypt: n.p., 1865), 1:165.

45 al-Anqarawi, *al-Fatawa al-anqarawiya*, 1:165.

46 *Family of Ahmad Farghali v. Farhat Jawda* (1862) FM 6 Girga 127.

47 William Blackstone, *Commentaries on the Laws of England*, 4 vols. (Philadelphia, PA: J. B. Lippincott, 1908), 2:33.

48 Blackstone, *Commentaries on the Laws of England*, 2:36.

49 Accessories and Abettors Act 1861, 24 & 25 Vict. c. 94.

50 *State v. Tally* (1893) 102 Alabama 25.

51 *Untram v. Chait Ram* (1853) NA Nwp 3 Pillbheet 750.

52 *Untram v. Chait Ram* (1853) NA Nwp 3 Pillbheet 750, 751.

53 *Untram v. Chait Ram* (1853) NA Nwp 3 Pillbheet 750, 751.

54 *Untram v. Chait Ram* (1853) NA Nwp 3 Pillbheet 750, 752.

55 *Gov. v. Heeramun Singh, Kunchun Jha, Heera Singh, Chummun, and Gungadeen* (1854) NA Ben 1 Bhaugulpore 703.

56 Quoted in Morgan and Macpherson, *The Indian Penal Code with Notes*, 25–28.

57 *Gov. v. Benee and 12 others* (1865) NA Nwp 1 Benares 114.

58 *Gov. v. Benee and 12 others* (1865) NA Nwp 1 Benares 114, 117. Emphasis added.
59 *Gov. v. Benee and 12 others* (1865) NA Nwp 1 Benares 114, 120. Emphasis added.
60 Quoted in al-Bustani, *Sharh*, 206.
61 Quoted in Muhammad Yasin, *Sharh qanun al-'uqubat* (Cairo: Matba'at al-Sadiq, 1886), 234–35.
62 al-Bustani, *Sharh*, 203.
63 al-Bustani, *Sharh*, 204–05.
64 Quoted in Rif'at, *Kulliyat*, 60.
65 Rif'at, *Kulliyat*, 60.
66 *State v. Mustafa* (1880) CM 33 Salonica 4.
67 Quoted in Rif'at, *Kulliyat*, 185–86.
68 Rif'at, *Kulliyat*, 186.
69 Criminal Procedure (Insanity and Unfitness to Plead) Act 1991, c. 25 § 1(1). See also Estella Baker, "Human Rights, M'Naughten and the 1991 Act," *Criminal Law Review* (February 1994): 84–92.
70 Suresh Bada Math, Channaveerachari Naveen Kumar & Sydney Moirangthem, "Insanity Defense: Past, Present, and Future," *Indian Journal of Psychological Medicine* 37, no. 4 (2015): 381–87.
71 See, for example, *Jai Lal v. Delhi Administration* (1969) AIR SC 15; *Sudhakaran v. State of Kerala* (2010) 10 SCC 582; *Surendra Mishra v. State of Jharkhand* (2011) 11 SCC 495.

Chapter 6. Changing Tides and Islamism

1   Tariq al-Bishri, *al-Haraka al-siyasiya fi Misr 1945–1953* (Cairo: Dar al-Shuruq, 2002), 50.
2   Amin Afram al-Bustani, *Mukhtarat Amin al-Bustani al-Muhami* (Cairo: Matba'at al-Hilal, 1919), 9.
3   Amin Afram al-Bustani, *Sharh qanun al-'uqubat al-misri* (Cairo: Matba'at al-Mahrusa, 1894), 11.
4   al-Bustani, *Mukhtarat*, 8.
5   Enid Hill, "The Golden Anniversary of Egypt's National Courts," in *Historians in Cairo: Essays in Honor of George Scanlon*, ed. Jill Edwards (Cairo: American University in Cairo Press, 2002), 209–210.
6   Sohaira Siddiqui, "Navigating Colonial Power: Challenging Precedents and the Limitation of Local Elites," *Islamic Law and Society* 26, no. 3 (2018): 3.
7   Muhammad 'Abd al-Hayy, *Majmu'-e fatawa*, 3 vols. (Lucknow, India: Yusufi Press, 1911), 2:198.
8   'Abd al-Hayy, *Majmu'*, 2:198.
9   Emin Poljarevic, "Islamism," in *The Oxford Encyclopedia of Islam and Politics*, 2015, http://www.oxfordislamicstudies.com/article/opr/t342/e0252.
10 Cemil Aydin, *The Idea of the Muslim World: A Global Intellectual History* (Cambridge, MA: Harvard University Press, 2017).
11 Ilyse R. Morgenstein Fuerst, *Indian Muslim Minorities and the 1857 Rebellion: Religion, Rebels, and Jihad* (London: I. B. Tauris, 2017), 5.

12 Aydin, *The Idea of the Muslim World*, 229–30.

13 Aydin, *The Idea of the Muslim World*, 231.

14 Donald Quataert, *The Ottoman Empire, 1700–1922* (New York: Cambridge University Press, 2005), 84.

15 Kamal Soleimani, *Islam and Competing Nationalisms in the Middle East, 1876–1926* (New York: Palgrave Macmillan, 2016), 3.

16 Azmi Özcan, *Pan-Islamism: Indian Muslims, the Ottomans and Britain (1877–1924)* (Leiden, the Netherlands: Brill, 1997), 19.

17 Sir Syed Ahmad Khan, "Khutba main Badshah ka nam," in *Tahdhib al-Akhlaq*, edited by Muhammad Fadl al-Din, 2 vols. (Lahore, Pakistan: Matba'a Mustafa'i, 1895), 400.

18 Gail Minault, *The Khilafat Movement: Religious Symbolism and Political Mobilization in India* (Delhi: Oxford University Press, 1982), 3.

19 Albert Hourani, *Arabic Thought in the Liberal Age, 1798–1939* (New York: Cambridge University Press, 2013), 107–108.

20 Jamal al-Din al-Afghani and Muhammad 'Abdu, "al-Wihda al-islamiya," in *al-'Urwa al-wuthqa* (Beirut: Dar al-Kitab al-'Arabi, n.d.), 112.

21 Nikki Keddie, *An Islamic Response to Imperialism: Political and Religious Writings of Sayyid Jamāl al-Dīn "al-Afghānī"* (Los Angeles: University of California Press, 1968), 39.

22 Rachel Scott, *Recasting Islamic Law* (Ithaca, NY: Cornell University Press, 2021), 36.

23 Kristen Stilt, "'Islam Is the Solution': Constitutional Visions of the Egyptian Muslim Brotherhood," *Texas International Law Journal* 46, no. 1 (Fall 2010): 73–108.

24 Leonard Wood, *Islamic Legal Revival: Reception of European Law and Transformations in Islamic Legal Thought in Egypt, 1875–1952* (Oxford: Oxford University Press, 2016), 58.

25 Rashid Rida, "Rabbana inna ata'na sadatana wa-kubara'ana fa-adalluna al-sabila," *al-Manar* 32 (October 1898): 606.

26 Quoted in 'Aziz Khanki, *al-Mahakim al-mukhtalata wa-l-mahakim al-ahliya: Madiuha, hadiruha, wa mustaqbaluha* (Cairo: al-Matba'a al-'Asriya, 1939), 93; see also Muhammad al-Ghazali, *Qadha'if al-haqq* (Damascus: Dar al-Qalam, 1997), 190–91.

27 'Abd al-Qadir 'Awda, *al-Tashri' al-jina'i al-islami muqarinan bi-l-qanun al-wad'i*, Rev. ed. (Cairo: Dar al-Hadith, 2009), 3.

28 The United States banned the manufacture, transportation, and sale of alcoholic beverages with the passing of the Eighteenth Amendment to the Constitution in 1920. However, that amendment was repealed in 1933 with the ratification of the Twenty-First Amendment. The United States was not the first or the only country to enact such laws, and Christian movements across Europe and North America had worked throughout the early twentieth century to pass similar laws, which had been either modified or abolished by the second half of the century.

29 Amr Shalaqany, "Islamic Legal Histories," *Berkeley Journal of Middle Eastern & Islamic Law* 1, no. 1 (2008): 6.

30 Shalaqany, "Islamic Legal Histories," 8. Emphasis added.

31 Jeanette Wakin, *Remembering Joseph Schacht (1902–1969)* (Cambridge, MA: Harvard Islamic Legal Studies Program, 2003), 4.

32 Hinrich Biesterfeldt, "Goldziher as a Contemporary of Islamic Reform," in *Kleine Schriften*, ed. Josef van Ess (Leiden, the Netherlands: Brill, 2018), 497–511.

33 Ian Edge, "Obituary: Noel Coulson," *Bulletin of the School of Oriental and African Studies, University of London* 50, no. 3 (1987): 532–35.

34 See, for example, Huda Muhammad 'Abd al-Rahman Sayyid, *Kafa'at al-idara al-mahaliya fi al-qanun al-wad'i wa-l-fiqh al-islami: Dirasa muqarana* (Amman: al-Manhal li-l-Nashr al-Iliktruni, 2019); Inas Muhammad Ibrahim Jad al-Haqq, *al-Shart al-mani' min al-tasarruf: Dirasa muqarana bayn al-Qanun al-wad'i wa-l-fiqh al-islami* (Amman: al-Manhal li-l-Nashr al-Iliktruni, 2019); Ahmad Isma'il Muhammad Mash'al, *al-Himaya al-dusturiya wa-l-qada'iya li-l-muwatana: Dirasa muqarana bayn al-qanun al-wad'i wa-l-shari'a al-islamiya* (Alexandria, Egypt: Maktabat al-Wafa' al-Qanuniya, 2019).

35 Muhammad Yasin, *Sharh qanun al-'uqubat* (Cairo: Matba'at al-Sadiq, 1886), 29.

36 Rudolph Peters, *Crime and Punishment in Islamic Law: Theory and Practice from the Sixteenth to the Twenty-First Century* (New York: Cambridge University Press, 2005), 12–13.

37 Muhammad Yasin, *Sharh*, 29.

38 Amin Afram al-Bustani, "al-Madda 32," *al-Muqattam*, November 26, 1897.

39 Amin Afram al-Bustani, "'Awda li-l-Madda 32," *al-Muqattam*, November 30, 1897.

40 Ahad al-Fudala' al-Usuliyin, "Mashru' al-tawassu' fi al-da'm bi-ilgha' al-madda 32 min qanun al-'uqubat," *al-Mu'ayyad*, December 4, 1897.

41 Eugene Clavel, "Mashru' al-tawassu' fi al-i'dam: al-Madda 32 min qanun al-'uqubat al-misri," *al-Mu'ayyad*, December 8, 1897.

42 Clavel, "Mashru'."

43 Ahad al-Fudala' al-Usuliyin, "Mashru'."

44 Shana Minkin, *Imperial Bodies: Empire and Death in Alexandria, Egypt* (Stanford, CA: Stanford University Press, 2019), 73–74.

45 "al-Tawassu' fi 'uqubat al-qatl," *al-Ahram*, December 6, 1897.

46 Hadarat Makatibuna al-Damanhuri, "al-Madda 32 wa-l-amn al-'amm," *al-Ahram*, December 14, 1897.

47 Amin Afram al-Bustani, "Khitam al-kalam 'ala al-madda 32," *al-Muqattam*, December 18, 1898.

48 Hadarat Makatibuna al-Damanhuri, "al-Madda 32."

49 Ahad Afadil al-Kuttab al-Usuliyin, "al-Madda 32 (min qanun al-'uqubat al-misri)," *al-Mu'ayyad*, December 15, 1897.

50 Brian Wright, "Islamic Law for the Colonists: Muftis in Nineteenth-Century British India," *Islamic Studies* 58, no. 3 (2019): 377–80.

51 Quoted in Uma Yaduvansh, "Decline of the Qazis (1793–1876)," *Indian Journal of Political Science* 28, no. 4 (October–December 1967): 217.

52 See *A Collection of the Acts Passed by the Governor General of India in Council in the Year 1864* (Calcutta: O. T. Cutter, Military Orphan Press, 1865).

53   Brian Wright, "Islamic Law for the Colonists," 400.

54   Quoted in Yaduvansh, "Decline of the Qazis," 223.

55   Quoted in Yaduvansh, "Decline of the Qazis," 225.

56   Muhammad Yusuf Abbasi, *Muslim Politics and Leadership in South Asia, 1876–92* (Islamabad: Institute of Islamic History, Culture, and Civilization, 1981), 110–112.

57   The Kazis Act, 1880.

58   See Robert Imervee, "Shari'at and Muslim Community in Colonial Punjab, 1865–1885," *Modern Asian Studies* 48, no. 4 (2014): 1068–1095.

59   Muhammad Qasim Zaman, *The Ulama in Contemporary Islam: Custodians of Change* (Princeton, NJ: Princeton University Press, 2002), 36–37; Husayn Ahmad Madani, *Muttahida qawmiyyat aur Islam* (Lahore, Pakistan: Maktaba Mahmudiyya, 1975).

60   William Wilson Hunter, *The Indian Musulmans: Are They Bound in Conscience to Rebel against the Queen?* (London: Trübner and Company, 1871).

61   Husayn Ahmad Madani, *Naqsh-e Hayat* (Lahore, Pakistan: al-Mizan, 2013), 362.

62   Madani, *Naqsh-e Hayat*, 365–66.

63   Zaman, *The Ulama in Contemporary Islam*, 33.

64   Qasim Zaman, *Ashraf 'Ali Thanawi*, 31.

65   See, for example, Chafik Chehata, *Essai d'une théorie générale de l'obligation en droit musulman* (Paris, Dalloz: 2005); 'Abd al-Razzaq al-Sanhuri, *Masadir al-haqq fi al-fiqh al-islami* (Cairo: Ma'had al-Buhuth wa-l-Dirasat al-'Arabiya, 1967–68).

66   Nabil Saleh. "Civil Codes of Arab Countries: The Sanhuri Codes," *Arab Law Quarterly* 8, no. 2 (1993): 161–67.

67   Ridwan Shafi'i al-Muta'afi, *al-Jinayat al-muttahida fi al-qanun wa-l-shari'a* (Cairo: al-Matba'a al-Salafiya, 1930), 3.

68   'Abd al-Razzaq al-Sanhuri, *al-Khilafa wa tatawwuruha ila 'asabat umam sharqiya*, ed. Kamal Jad Allah, Sami Mandur, and Ahmad Lashin (Beirut: Markaz Nuhud li-l-Dirasat wa-l-Nashr, 2019), 50–52.

69   'Ali 'Ali Mansur, *Khatwa ra'ida nahw tatbiq ahkam al-shari'a al-islamiya fi al-Jumhuriya al-'Arabiya al-Libiya* (Tripoli: Libya: Dar al-Turath al-'Arabi, 1972), 11 (emphasis added).

Conclusion. A Bridge between Systems

1   Siraj al-Din 'Ali Khan, *Jami' al-ta'zirat min kutub al-thiqat* (Hyderabad, India: Matba' 'Ayn al-'Ayan, 1820), 2–3.

2   Siraj al-Din 'Ali Khan, *Jami'*, 108–109.

3   'Abd Allah b. Hasan Barakat Zada, *al-Siyasa al-shar'iya fi huquq al-ra'i wa sa'adat al-ra'iya* (Cairo: Matba'at al-Taraqqi, 1900), 37.

4   Barakat Zada, *al-Siyasa*, 8.

5   Intisar Rabb, *Doubt in Islamic Law: A History of Legal Maxims, Interpretation, and Islamic Criminal Law* (New York: Cambridge University Press, 2015), 1–3.

6   *Shaik Monee on the part of Gov. v. Mathur Bewa* (1853) NA Ben 2 Assam 57, 61.

7   *Gov. v. Tota* (1864) NA Nwp 1 Aligarh 211.

8   See, for example, Indira Falk Gesink, *Islamic Reform and Conservatism: al-Azhar and the Evolution of Modern Sunni Islam* (London: I. B. Tauris, 2009); Muhammad Qasim Zaman, *The Ulama in Contemporary Islam: Custodians of Change* (Princeton, NJ: Princeton University Press, 2002), 1–2.

9   Wael Hallaq, "Can the Shari'a Be Restored?," in *Islamic Law and the Challenges of Modernity*, ed. Yvonne Haddad and Barbara Stowasser (Walnut Creek, CA: Altamira Press, 2004), 24; Radhika Singha, *A Despotism of Law: Crime and Justice in Early Colonial India* (Delhi: Oxford University Press, 1998), vii.

10 Frank Griffel, *The Formation of Post-Classical Philosophy in Islam* (Oxford: Oxford University Press, 2021).

11 Noel Coulson, *A History of Islamic Law* (Edinburgh: Edinburgh University Press, 1964), 1–2.

12 Joseph Schacht, *An Introduction to Islamic Law* (Oxford: Oxford University Press, 1982), 50 and 77.

13 Wael Hallaq, "What Is Shari'a?," *Yearbook of Islamic and Middle Eastern Law Online* 12, no. 1 (2005): 151–80.

14 Hallaq, "What Is Shari'a?," 160.

15 Hallaq, "What Is Shari'a?," 175. Hallaq's corollation between the role of the *faqih* and the Islamic nature of a legal system has been articulated by Anver Emon ("Codification and Islamic Law: The Ideology behind a Tragic Narrative," *Middle East Law and Governance* 8, nos. 2–3 [2016]: 275–309).

16 Khaled Fahmy, *In Quest of Justice: Islamic Law and Forensic Medicine in Modern Egypt* (Oakland: University of California Press, 2018), 27.

17 See, for example, James M. Donovan, *Juries and the Transformation of Criminal Justice in France in the Nineteenth and Twentieth Centuries* (Chapel Hill: University of North Carolina Press, 2010); Stephen C. Thaman, "The Model Penal Code and the Dilemma of Criminal Law Codification in the United States," in *Codification in International Perspective*, ed. Wen-Yeu Wang (New York: Springer, 2014): 165–83.

18 Desmond Haldane Brown, *The Genesis of the Canadian Criminal Code of 1892* (Toronto: University of Toronto Press, 1989).

19 For a detailed discussion of *takhayyur* and *talfiq*, see Muhammad Hashim Kamali, "Shari'ah and Civil Law: Towards a Methodology of Harmonization," *Islamic Law and Society* 14, no. 3 (2007): 391–420.

20 Wael Hallaq, *Sharī'a: Theory, Practice, Transformations* (New York: Cambridge University Press, 2009), 449.

21 Hina Azam, *Sexual Violation in Islamic Law: Substance, Evidence, and Procedure* (New York: Cambridge University Press, 2015), 243.

22 Amin Afram al-Bustani, *Sharh qanun al-'uqubat al-misri* (Cairo: Matba'at al-Mahrusa, 1894), 8 (emphasis added).

23 Salam al-Amir, "New Law Guarantees Equal Death Compensation Payments for Families of Men and Women," *National*, October 10, 2019, https://www.thenationalnews.com/uae/courts/new-law-guarantees-equal-death-compensation-payments-for-families-of-men-and-women-1.921280.

24 UAE Constitution, article 99, section 7.

25 Article 550 of the code declared the blood money paid for a woman to be half that paid for a man. However, article 551 suggested that "the difference between the amount of the blood money [for a woman] and the amount of blood money for a man shall be paid from the Fund for Compensation of Bodily Harm," meaning that in theory the total blood money paid to the family of a female victim would be equal to that paid to the family of a male victim. See Mohammad Tavana, "Three Decades of Islamic Criminal Law Legislation in Iran: A Legislative History Analysis with Emphasis on the Amendments of the 2013 Islamic Penal Code," *Electronic Journal of Islamic and Middle Eastern Law* 2 (2014): 36.

26 *al-Mawsu'a al-fiqhiya* (Kuwait City, Kuwait: Wizarat al-Awqaf wa-l-Shu'un al-Islamiya, 1992), 21:59.

27 Nura al-Amir, "Qanuniyun: Tahdid al-diya bi-200 alf dirham li-l-jinsayn yu'azziz huquq al-mar'a," *al-Bayan*, December 11, 2019.

28 Sherman Jackson, "Islamic Law, Muslims, and American Politics," *Islamic Law and Society* 22, no. 3 (2015): 285.

Bibliography

Abbasi, Muhammad Yusuf. *Muslim Politics and Leadership in South Asia, 1876–92.* Islamabad: Institute of Islamic History, Culture, and Civilization, 1981.

'Abd al-Hayy, Muhammad. *Khulasat al-fatawa.* 4 vols. Lucknow, India: Munshi Nawal Kishur, n.d.

———. *Majmu'-e fatawa.* 3 vols. Lucknow, India: Yusufi Press, 1911.

Abu-Lughod, Ibrahim. *The Arab Rediscovery of Europe: A Study in Cultural Encounters.* Princeton, NJ: Princeton University Press, 1963.

Abu-Manneh, Butrus. "The Islamic Roots of the Gülhane Rescript." *Die Welt des Islams* 34, no. 2 (1994): 173–203.

al-Afghani, Jamal al-Din, and Muhammad 'Abdu. "al-Wihda al-islamiya." In *al-'Urwa al-wuthqa.* Beirut: Dar al-Kitab al-'Arabi, n.d: 107–13.

Ahad Afadil al-Kuttab al-Usuliyin. "al-Madda 32 (min qanun al-'uqubat al-misri)." *al-Mu'ayyad* December 15, 1897.

Ahad al-Fudala' al-Usuliyin. "Mashru' al-tawassu' fi al-i'dam bi-ilgha' al-madda 32 min qanun al-'uqubat." *al-Mu'ayyad*, December 4, 1897.

Ahmad, Muhammad Mushtaq. "The Notions of Dār Al-Ḥarb and Dār al-Islām in Islamic Jurisprudence with Special Reference to the Ḥanafī School," *Islamic Studies* 47, no. 1 (2008): 5–37.

al-Amir, Nura. "Qanuniyun: tahdid al-diya bi-200 alf dirham li-l-jinsayn yu'azziz huquq al-mar'a." *al-Bayan*, December 11, 2019.

al-Amir, Salam. "New Law Guarantees Equal Death Compensation Payments for Families of Men and Women." *National*, October 10, 2019. https://www .thenationalnews.com/uae/courts/new-law-guarantees-equal-death-compen sation-payments-for-families-of-men-and-women-1.921280.

al-Andarpati, 'Alim b. al-'Ala'. *al-Fatawa al-tatarkhaniya.* 20 vols. Deoband, India: Maktabat Zakariya, 2010.

Anderson, Michael R. "Islamic Law and the Colonial Encounter in British India." In *Institutions and Ideologies: A SOAS South Asia Reader*, edited by David Arnold and Peter Robb, 165–85. London: Curzon Press, 1993.

Anjum, Ovamir. *Politics, Law, and Community in Islamic Thought: The Taymiyyan Movement.* New York: Cambridge University Press, 2012.

al-Anqarawi, Muhammad b. Husayn. *al-Fatawa al-anqarawiya.* 2 vols. Bulaq, Egypt: n.p., 1865.

Asad, Talal. *Formations of the Secular: Christianity, Islam, Modernity*. Stanford, CA: Stanford University Press, 2003.

'Atiya, Muhammad Labib. "Tatawwur qanun al-'uqubat fi Misr min 'ahd insha' al-mahakim al-ahliya." In *al-Kitab al-dhahabi li-l-mahakim al-ahliya*, 2:5–19. Bulaq, Egypt: al-Matba'a al-Amiriya, 1933.

'Awda, 'Abd al-Qadir. *al-Tashri' al-jina'i al-islami muqarinan bi-l-qanun al-wad'i*. Rev. ed.. Cairo: Dar al-Hadith, 2009.

Aydin, Cemil. *The Idea of the Muslim World: A Global Intellectual History*. Cambridge, MA: Harvard University Press, 2017.

Aykan, Yavuz. "A Legal Concept in Motion: The 'Spreader of Corruption *(sāʿī biʾl-fesād)*' from Qarakhanid to Ottoman Jurisprudence." *Islamic Law and Society* 26, no. 3 (2019): 252–71.

Ayoub, Samy. "The Sultan Says: State Authority in the Late Hanafi Tradition." *Islamic Law and Society* 23, no. 3 (2016): 239–78.

Azam, Hina. *Sexual Violation in Islamic Law: Substance, Evidence, and Procedure*. New York: Cambridge University Press, 2015.

Baer, Gabriel. "The Transition from Traditional to Western Criminal Law in Turkey and Egypt," *Studia Islamica* 45 (1977): 139–58.

Baker, Estella. "Human Rights, M'Naughten and the 1991 Act." *Criminal Law Review* (February 1994): 84–92.

Barakat Zada, 'Abd Allah b. Hasan. *al-Siyasa al-shar'iya fi huquq al-ra'i wa sa'adat al-ra'iya*. Cairo: Matba'at al-Taraqqi, 1900.

Beccaria, Cesare. *On Crimes and Punishments*. Edited and translated by Georg Koopmann. New York: Routledge, 2009.

Berkes, Niyazi. *The Development of Secularism in Turkey*. Montreal: McGill University Press, 1964.

Bhatkali, Faysal Ahmad Nadwi. *Tahrik-e azadi main 'ulama' ka kardar*. Lucknow, India: Majlis-e Tahqiqat wa Nashriyat-e Islam, 2018.

Biesterfeldt, Hinrich. "Goldziher as a Contemporary of Islamic Reform." In *Kleine Schriften*, edited by Josef van Ess, 497–511. Leiden, the Netherlands: Brill, 2018.

al-Bishri, Tariq. *al-Haraka al-siyasiya fi Misr 1945–1953*. Cairo: Dar al-Shuruq, 2002.

Blackstone, William. *Commentaries on the Laws of England*. 4 vols. Philadelphia, PA: J. B. Lippincott, 1908.

Brown, Desmond Haldane. *The Genesis of the Canadian Criminal Code of 1892*. Toronto: University of Toronto Press, 1989.

al-Bukhari, Muhammad b. Isma'il. *al-Jami' al-musnad al-sahih*. Vaduz, Liechtenstein: Thesaurus Islamicus, 2000.

Burak, Guy. *The Second Formation of Islamic Law: The Hanafi School in the Early Modern Ottoman Empire*. New York: Cambridge University Press, 2015.

al-Bustani, Amin Afram. "'Awda li-l-madda 32." *al-Muqattam*, November 30, 1897.

———. "Khitam al-kalam 'ala al-madda 32." *al-Muqattam*, December 17, 1897.

———. "al-Madda 32." *al-Muqattam*, November 26, 1897.

———. *Mukhtarat Amin al-Bustani al-Muhami*. Cairo: Matba'at al-Hilal, 1919.

———. *Sharh qanun al-'uqubat al-misri*. Cairo: Matba'at al-Mahrusa, 1894.

Cassirer, Ernst. *The Philosophy of the Enlightenment*. Princeton, NJ: Princeton University Press, 1951.

Chehata, Chafik. *Essai d'une théorie générale de l'obligation en droit musulman*. Paris, Dalloz: 2005.

Clavel, Eugene. "Mashru' al-tawassu' fi al-i'dam: al-madda 32 min qanun al-'uqubat al-misri." *al-Mu'ayyad*, December 8, 1897.

Cohn, Bernard. *Colonialism and Its Forms of Knowledge*. Princeton, NJ: Princeton University Press, 1996.

Cole, Juan. *Colonialism and Revolution in the Middle East: Social and Cultural Origins of Egypt's Urabi Movement*. Princeton, NJ: Princeton University Press, 2001.

A Collection of the Acts Passed by the Governor General of India in Council in the Year 1864. Calcutta: O.T. Cutter, Military Orphan Press, 1865.

Crotty, Homer D. "History of Insanity as a Defence to Crime in English Criminal Law." *California Law Review* 12, no. 2 (1924): 105–23.

Coulson, Noel. *A History of Islamic Law*. Edinburgh: Edinburgh University Press, 1964.

Dahlawi, Shah 'Abd al-'Aziz Muhaddith. *Fatawa 'azizi*. Karachi, Pakistan: H.M. Sa'id Company, 1967.

Dahlawi, Shah Wali Allah. *The Conclusive Argument from God*. Translated by Marcia Hermansen. Leiden, the Netherlands: Brill, 1996.

Dalrymple, William. "Transculturation, Assimilation, and Its Limits: The Rise and Fall of the Delhi White Mughals, 1805–57." In *The Delhi College: Traditional Elites, the Colonial State, and Education before 1857*, edited by Margrit Pernau, 60–101. Delhi: Oxford University Press, 2006.

al-Darqutni, 'Ali b. 'Umar. *Sunan al-Darqutni*. Cairo: Dar al-Mahasin, 1966.

Davison, Roderic. "Tanzīmāt." In *Encyclopaedia of Islam*, 2nd ed., edited by P. Bearman, Th. Bianquis, C.E. Bosworth, E. van Donzel, and W.P. Heinrichs, 2012, http://dx.doi.org/10.1163/1573–3912_islam_COM_1174.

Dols, Michael. *Majnūn: The Madman in Medieval Islamic Society*. Oxford: Clarendon Press of Oxford University Press, 1992.

Donovan, James M. *Juries and the Transformation of Criminal Justice in France in the Nineteenth and Twentieth Centuries*. Chapel Hill: University of North Carolina Press, 2010.

Düstur. Istanbul: Matba'-e Amire, 1873.

al-Dusuqi, Muhammad 'Arafa. *Hashiyat al-Dusuqi 'ala al-sharh al-kabir*. 4 vols. Cairo: Dar Ihya' al Kutub al-'Arabiya, n.d.

Edge, Ian. "Obituary: Noel Coulson." *Bulletin of the School of Oriental and African Studies, University of London* 50, no. 3 (1987): 532–35.

Elgawhary, Tarek. "Restructuring Islamic Law: The Opinions of the 'Ulamā' towards Codification of Personal Status Law in Egypt." PhD diss., Princeton University, 2014.

Emon, Anver. "Codification and Islamic Law: The Ideology behind a Tragic Narrative." *Middle East Law and Governance* 8, nos. 2–3 (2016): 275–309.

"Execution of a 12 Year Old Boy." British Library, 1829. http://www.bl.uk/learning/timeline/item102910.html.

Fadel, Mohammad. "The Social Logic of Taqlīd and the Rise of the Mukhtaṣar." *Islamic Law and Society* 3, no. 2 (1996): 193–233.

Fahmy, Khaled. *All the Pasha's Men: Mehmed Ali, His Army and the Making of Modern Egypt*. Cairo: American University in Cairo Press, 2002.

———. "The Anatomy of Justice: Forensic Medicine and Criminal Law in Nineteenth-Century Egypt." *Islamic Law and Society* 6, no. 2 (1999): 224–71.

———. *In Quest of Justice: Islamic Law and Forensic Medicine in Modern Egypt.* Oakland: University of California Press, 2018.

———. "The Police and the People in Nineteenth-Century Egypt." *Die Welt des Islams* 39, no. 3 (November 1999): 340–77.

———. "Rudolph Peters and the History of Modern Egyptian Law." In *Legal Documents as Sources for the History of Muslim Societies: Studies in Honour of Rudolph Peters*, edited by Maaike van Berkel, 12–35. Leiden, the Netherlands: Brill, 2017.

Farooq, Mohammad Omar, and Nedal El-Ghattis. "In Search of the Shari'ah." *Arab Law Quarterly* 32, no. 4 (2018): 315–54.

al-Fatawa al-'alamgiriya. 6 vols. Bulaq, Egypt: al-Matba'a al-Amiriya, 1892.

Findley, Carter. *The Turks in World History.* New York: Oxford University Press, 2005.

al-Firuzabadi, Muhammad b. Ya'qub. *al-Qamus al-muhit.* Beirut: Mu'assasat al-Risala, 2005.

Friedmann, Yohanan. "Islamic Thought in Relation to the Indian Context." In *India's Islamic Traditions, 711–1750*, edited by Richard Eaton, 50–63. New Delhi: Oxford University Press, 2003.

Fuerst, Ilyse R. Morgenstein. *Indian Muslim Minorities and the 1857 Rebellion: Religion, Rebels, and Jihad.* London: I. B. Tauris, 2017.

Garner, Bryan, ed. *Black's Law Dictionary.* 9th ed. St. Paul, MN: Thomson Reuters, 2009.

Gasper, Michael. *The Power of Representation: Publics, Peasants, and Islam in Egypt.* Stanford, CA: Stanford University Press, 2009.

Gesink, Indira Falk. *Islamic Reform and Conservatism: al-Azhar and the Evolution of Modern Sunni Islam.* London: I. B. Tauris, 2009.

al-Ghazali, Muhammad. *Qadha'if al-haqq.* Damascus: Dar al-Qalam, 1997.

Griffel, Frank. *The Formation of Post-Classical Philosophy in Islam.* Oxford: Oxford University Press, 2021.

Hadarat Makatibuna al-Damanhuri. "al-Madda 32 wa-l-amn al-'amm." *Al-Ahram*, December 14, 1897.

Hallaq, Wael. "Can the Shari'a Be Restored?" In *Islamic Law and the Challenges of Modernity*, edited by Yvonne Haddad and Barbara Stowasser, 21–53. Walnut Creek, CA: Altamira Press, 2004.

———. *A History of Islamic Legal Theories: An Introduction to Sunni usul al-fiqh.* New York: Cambridge University Press, 1997.

———. *The Impossible State: Islam, Politics, and Modernity's Moral Predicament.* New York: Columbia University Press, 2013.

———. *An Introduction to Islamic Law.* New York: Cambridge University Press, 2009.

———. *Sharī'a: Theory, Practice, Transformations.* New York: Cambridge University Press, 2009.

———. "Was the Gate of Ijtihad Closed?" *International Journal of Middle East Studies* 16, no. 1 (1984): 3–41.

———. "What Is Shari'a?" *Yearbook of Islamic and Middle Eastern Law Online* 12, no. 1 (2005): 151–80.

Hasan, Mushirul. "Maulawi Zaka Ullah: Sharif Culture and Colonial Rule." In *The Delhi College: Traditional Elites, the Colonial State, and Education before 1857*, edited by Margrit Pernau, 261–98. Delhi: Oxford University Press, 2006.

Haydar, Hafiz Muhammad 'Ali. *Tadhkira-e mashahir-e Kakuri*. Lucknow, India: Asah al-Matabi', 1927.

Hefner, Robert. *Schooling Islam: The Culture and Politics of Modern Muslim Education*. Princeton, NJ: Princeton University Press, 2010.

Heinzelmann, Tobias. "The Ruler's Monologue: The Rhetoric of the Ottoman Penal Code of 1858." *Die Welt des Islams* 54, nos. 3–4 (2014): 292–321.

Hermansen, Marcia, trans. Introduction to Shah Wali Allah Dahlawi, *The Conclusive Argument from God*. Leiden, the Netherlands: Brill, 1996.

Heyd, Uriel. *Studies in Old Ottoman Criminal Law*. Oxford: Clarendon Press of Oxford University Press, 1973.

Hicks, Joe, and Grahame Allen. "A Century of Change: Trends in UK Statistics since 1900." UK House of Commons Research Paper 99/111, December 21, 2019.

Hill, Enid. "The Golden Anniversary of Egypt's National Courts." in *Historians in Cairo: Essays in Honor of George Scanlon*, edited by Jill Edwards, 203–22. Cairo: American University in Cairo Press, 2002.

Hill, Peter. *Utopia and Civilisation in the Arab Nahda*. Cambridge: Cambridge University Press, 2019.

Hourani, Albert. *Arabic Thought in the Liberal Age, 1798–1939*. New York: Cambridge University Press, 2013.

Hoyle, Mark. *Mixed Courts of Egypt*. London: Graham and Trotman, 1991.

Hunter, William Wilson. *The Indian Musulmans: Are They Bound in Conscience to Rebel against the Queen?* London: Trübner and Company, 1871.

Husayn, 'Abd Allah 'Ali. *al-Muqaranat al-tashri'iya bayn al-qawanin al-wad'iya al-madaniya wa-l-tashri' al-islami*. Cairo: Dar al-Salam, 2001.

al-Husayni, Ahmad al-Barzanji. *al-Nasiha al-'amma li-muluk al-Islam wa-l-'amma*. Damascus: n.p., 1890.

Hussin, Iza. *The Politics of Islamic Law: Local Elites, Colonial Authority, and the Making of the Muslim State*. Chicago: University of Chicago Press, 2016.

Ibn Abi Shayba, 'Abd Allah b. Muhammad. *al-Musannaf*. Beirut: Dar al-Taj, 1989.

Ibn 'Abidin, Muhammad Amin. *Radd al-muhtar 'ala al-durr al-mukhtar*. 10 vols. Riyadh: Dar 'Alim al-Kutub, 2003.

Ibn 'Ashur, Muhammad al-Tahir. *Tafsir al-tahrir wa-l-tanwir*. 2 vols. Tunis: al-Dar al-Tunisiya li-l-Nashr, 1984.

Ibn Duqmaq, Ibrahim b. Muhammad. *Description de l'Égypte*. Cairo: Matba'at al-Bulaq, 1893.

Ibrahim, Ahmed Fekry. "The Codification Episteme in Islamic Juristic Discourse between Inertia and Change." *Islamic Law and Society* 22, no. 3 (May 2015): 157–220.

———. "Customary Practices as Exigencies in Islamic Law." *Oriens* 46, nos. 1/2 (2018): 222–61.

———. *Pragmatism in Islamic Law: A Social and Intellectual History*. Syracuse, NY: Syracuse University Press, 2015.

Ibrahim, Muhammad. "Athar Madrassat al-Huquq al-Khidawiya fi tatwir al-dirasat al-fiqhiya." MA thesis, Cairo University, 2015.

Imervee, Robert. "Shari'at and Muslim Community in Colonial Punjab, 1865–1885." *Modern Asian Studies* 48, no. 4 (2014): 1068–95.

İnalcık, Halil. *Osmanlı'da Devlet, Hukuk ve Adalet*. Istanbul: Kronik Yayıncılık, 2016.

Ingram, Brannon. *Revival from Below: The Deoband Movement and Global Islam*. Oakland: University of California Press, 2018.

Iskaru, Tawfiq. "Muhammad Qadri Basha." *al-Muqtataf* 48, no. 3 (March 1916): 253–63.

al-Jabarti, 'Abd al-Rahman b. Hasan. *Mazhar al-taqdis bi-zawal dawlat al-Fransis*. Cairo: Dar al-Kutub al-Misriya, 1998.

Jackson, Sherman. "Islamic Law, Muslims, and American Politics." *Islamic Law and Society* 22, no. 3 (2015): 253–91.

Jad al-Haqq, Inas Muhammad Ibrahim. *al-Shart al-mani' min al-tasarruf: Dirasa muqarana bayn al-qanun al-wad'i wa-l-fiqh al-islami*. Amman: al-Manhal li-l-Nashr al-Iliktruni, 2019.

Jalal, Ayesha. *Partisans of Allah*. Cambridge, MA: Harvard University Press, 2010.

al-Jawziya, Muhammad b. Qayyim. *al-Turuq al-hukmiya fi al-siyasa al-shar'iya*. Beirut: Maktabat al-Mu'ayyad, 1989.

Johansen, Baber. "Signs as Evidence: The Doctrine of Ibn Taymiyya (1263–1328) and Ibn Qayyim al-Jawziyya (d. 1351) on Proof." *Islamic Law and Society* 9, no. 2 (2002): 168–93.

Kamali, Muhammad Hashim. "Sharī'ah and Civil Law: Towards a Methodology of Harmonization." *Islamic Law and Society* 14, no. 3 (2007): 391–420.

al-Kasani, Abu Bakr b. Mas'ud. *Bada'i' al-sana'i' fi tartib al-shara'i'*. 10 vols. Beirut: Dar al-Kutub al-'Ilmiya, 2003.

al-Kawakibi, 'Abd al-Rahman. *al-A'mal al-kamila*. Edited by Muhammad 'Imara. Cairo: Dar al-Shuruq, 2019.

Keddie, Nikki. *An Islamic Response to Imperialism: Political and Religious Writings of Sayyid Jamal al-Din "al-Afghani."* Los Angeles: University of California Press, 1968.

Khafaji, Muhammad 'Abd al-Mun'im, and 'Ali 'Ali Subh. *al-Azhar fi alf 'am*. 6 vols. Cairo: al-Maktaba al-Azhariya li-l-Turath, 2011.

al-Khamis, Muhammad Bayram. *Mulahazat siyasiya 'an al-tanzimat al-lazima li-l-dawla al-'uliya*. N.p: n.p., 1880.

Khan, Najm al-Din 'Ali. *Kitab-e jinayat*. Ms. 3829, Khuda Baksh Library, Patna, India.

Khan, Salamat 'Ali. *al-Ikhtiyar*. Ms. 2060, Khuda Baksh Library, Patna, India.

———. *Islami qanun-e faujdari, tarjuma-e kitab al-ikhtiyar*. Azamgarh, India: Matba'-e Ma'arif, n.d.

Khan, Sir Syed Ahmad. "Khutba main Badshah ka nam." In *Tahdhib al-akhlaq*, edited by Muhammad Fadl al-Din, 399–403. 2 vols. Lahore: Pakistan, Matba'a Mustafa'i, 1895.

Khan, Siraj al-Din 'Ali. *Jami' al-ta'zirat min kutub al-thiqat*. Hyderabad, India: Matba' 'Ayn al-'Ayan, 1820.

Khanki, 'Aziz. *al-Mahakim al-mukhtalata wa-l-mahakim al-ahliya: Madiuha, hadiruha, wa mustaqbaluha*. Cairo: al-Matba'a al-'Asriya, 1939.

King, Christopher. *One Language, Two Scripts: The Hindi Movement in Nineteenth Century Northern India*. Delhi: Oxford University Press, 1995.

Klebba, A. Joan. "Homicide Trends in the United States, 1900–74," *Public Health Reports* 90, no. 3 (May–June 1975): 195–204.

Koch, Ebba. "The Madrasa of Ghaziu'd-Din Khan at Delhi." In *The Delhi College: Traditional Elites, the Colonial State, and Education before 1857*, edited by Margrit Pernau, 35–58. Delhi: Oxford University Press, 2006.

Kugle, Scott. "Framed, Blamed, and Renamed: The Recasting of Islamic Jurisprudence in Colonial South Asia." *Modern Asian Studies* 35, no. 2 (2001): 257–313.

Lal, Babu Kunj Bihari, and Munshi Muhammad Nazir. *Sharh majmu'-e qawanin-e ta'zirat-e Hind*. Fatehpur: Matba' Nasim-e Hind, 1885.

Lange, Christian. *Justice, Punishment, and the Medieval Muslim Imagination*. New York: Cambridge University Press, 2008.

Macaulay, Thomas Babington. "Minute on Education." In *Selections from Educational Records, Part I (1781–1839)*, edited by H. Sharp, 107–17. Delhi: National Archives of India, 1965.

Madani, Husayn Ahmad. *Muttahida qawmiyyat aur Islam*. Lahore, Pakistan: Maktaba Mahmudiyya, 1975.

———. *Naqsh-e hayat*. Lahore, Pakistan: al-Mizan, 2013.

Mahdi, Muhammad. *Tadhkira shams al-'ulama' Hafiz Nazir Ahmad marhum*. N.p., n.d.

al-Mahdi, Muhammad al-'Abbasi. *al-Fatawa al-mahdiya fi al-waqa'i' al-misriya*. 6 vols. Cairo: al Matba'a al-Misriya, 1883.

Mansur, 'Ali 'Ali. *Khatwa ra'ida nahw tatbiq ahkam al-shari'a al-islamiya fi al-Jumhuriya al-'Arabiya al-Libiya*. Tripoli, Libya: Dar al-Turath al-'Arabi, 1972.

Ibn Manzur, Muhammad b. Mukarram. *Lisan al-'Arab*. 15 vols. Beirut: Dar Sadir, 1993.

al-Marghinani, 'Ali b. Abi Bakr. *The Hedaya, or Guide: A Commentary on the Mussulman Laws*. Translated by Charles Hamilton. London: T. Bensley, 1791.

———. *al-Hidaya sharh bidayat al-mubtadi'*. 8 vols. Commentary by 'Abd al-Hayy Luknawi. Karachi, Pakistan: Idarat al-Qur'an wa-l-'Ulum al-Islamiya, 1996.

Mash'al, Ahmad Isma'il Muhammad. *al-Himaya al-dusturiya wa-l-qada'iya li-l muwatana: Dirasa muqarana bayn al-qanun al-wad'i wa-l-shari'a al-islamiya*. Alexandria, Egypt: Maktabat al-Wafa' al-Qanuniya, 2019.

Math, Suresh Bada, Channaveerachari Naveen Kumar, and Sydney Moirangthem. "Insanity Defense: Past, Present, and Future." *Indian Journal of Psychological Medicine* 37, no. 4 (2015): 381–87.

al-Mawsu'a al-fiqhiya. 45 vols. Kuwait City, Kuwait: Wizarat al-Awqaf wa-l-Shu'un al-Islamiya, 1992.

al-Maydani, 'Abd al-Ghani al-Ghanimi. *al-Lubab fi sharh al-kitab*. 4 vols. Beirut: al-Maktaba al-'Ilmiya, n.d.

Meshal, Reem. *Sharia and the Making of the Modern Egyptian: Islamic Law and Custom in the Courts of Ottoman Cairo*. Cairo: American University in Cairo Press, 2014.

Messick, Brinkley. *The Calligraphic State: Textual Domination and History in a Muslim Society*. Berkeley: University of California Press, 1992.

Metcalf, Barbara. *Islamic Revival in British India: Deoband, 1860–1900*. Princeton, NJ: Princeton University Press, 1982.

Mikha'il, Yuaqim. *Tarikh al-qanun fi Misr*. Cairo: Matba'at Misr, 1899.

Minault, Gail. *The Khilafat Movement: Religious Symbolism and Political Mobilization in India*. Delhi: Oxford University Press, 1982.

———. "The Perils of Cultural Mediation: Master Ram Chandra and Academic Journalism at Delhi College." In *The Delhi College: Traditional Elites, the Colonial State, and Education before 1857*, edited by Margrit Pernau, 189–202. Delhi: Oxford University Press, 2006.

Minkin, Shana. *Imperial Bodies: Empire and Death in Alexandria, Egypt*. Stanford, CA: Stanford University Press, 2019.

al-Minyawi, Muhammad Hasanayn b. Muhammad Makhluf. *Tatbiq al-qanun al-Faransawi al-madani wa-l-jina'i 'ala madhhab al-Imam Malik*. Cairo: Dar al-Salam, 1999.

Mitchell, Timothy. *Colonising Egypt*. Berkeley: University of California Press, 1988.

Morgan, Walter, and Arthur George Macpherson. *The Indian Penal Code with Notes*. Calcutta: G. C. Hay, 1863.

Mubarak, 'Ali. *Hayati*. Cairo: Maktabat al-Adab, 1989.

———. *al-Khitat al-Tawfiqiya al-jadida li-Misr al-Qahira wa muduniha wa biladiha al-qadima wa-l-shahira*. 14 vols. Bulaq, Egypt: al-Matba'a al-Amiriya, 1887.

Muhammad, Mustafa. "al-Ijram fi Misr." In *al-Kitab al-dhahabi li-l-mahakim al-ahliya*, 2:19–45. Bulaq, Egypt: al-Matba'a al-Amiriya, 1933.

al-Muhayza', Khulud bt. 'Abd al-Rahman. *Ahkam al-marid al-nafsi fi al-fiqh al-islami*. Riyadh: Dar al-Sami'i, 2013.

Mumcu, Ahmet. *Osmanlı Devletinde Siyaseten Katl*. Ankara: Ajans-Türk Matbaası, 1963.

Musa, Nifin Muhammad. *Mukhtarat min watha'iq al-ifta' al-misri fi al-qarn al-tasi' 'ashar*. Cairo: Dar al-Kutub wa-l-Watha'iq al-Qawmiya, 2013.

al-Muta'afi, Ridwan Shafi'i. *al-Jinayat al-muttahida fi al-qanun wa-l-shari'a*. Cairo: al-Matba'a al-Salafiya, 1930.

Naravane, M. S. *Battles of the Honourable East India Company: Making of the Raj*. Delhi: Ashish Publishing House, 2006.

al-Nisaburi, Muslim b. al-Hajjaj. *Sahih Muslim*. Vaduz, Liechtenstein: Thesaurus Islamicus, 2000.

Nubarian, Nubar. *Mudhakkirat Nubar Basha*. Translated by Jaru Rubayr Tabaqiyan. Cairo: Dar al-Shuruq, 2009.

Nu'mani, Shibli. *Safarnama-e Rum wa Misr wa Sham*. Delhi: Qawmi Press, 1901.

Oberer, Walter. "The Deadly Weapon Doctrine: Common Law Origin." *Harvard Law Review* 75, no. 8 (1962): 1565–76.

Özcan, Azmi. *Pan-Islamism: Indian Muslims, the Ottomans and Britain (1877–1924)*. Leiden, the Netherlands: Brill, 1997

The Penal Code of France, Translated into English. London: H. Butterworth, 1819.

Peters, Rudolph. *Crime and Punishment in Islamic Law: Theory and Practice from the Sixteenth to the Twenty-First Century*. New York: Cambridge University Press, 2009.

———. "'For His Correction and as a Deterrent Example for Others': Mehmed 'Ali's First Criminal Legislation (1829–30)." *Islamic Law and Society* 6, no. 2 (1999): 164–92.

————. "From Jurists' Law to Statute Law or What Happens When the Shari'a Is Codified." *Mediterranean Politics* 7, no. 3 (2002): 82–95.

————. "Muḥammad al-'Abbāsī al-Mahdī (d.1897), Grand Mufti of Egypt, and His 'al-Fatāwā al-Mahdiyya,'" *Islamic Law and Society* 1, no. 1 (1994): 66–82.

Poljarevic, Emin. "Islamism." In *The Oxford Encyclopedia of Islam and Politics*, 2015. http://www.oxfordislamicstudies.com/article/opr/t342/e0252.

Powell, Avril. *Scottish Orientalists and India: The Muir Brothers, Religion, Education, and Empire*. Rochester, NY: Boydell Press, 2010.

Powers, Paul. *Intent in Islamic Law: Motive and Meaning in Medieval Sunnī Fiqh*. Leiden, the Netherlands: Brill, 2006.

Qadri, Muhammad (Basha). *Murshid al-hayran ila ma'rifat ahwal al-insan fi al-mu'amalat al-shar'iya 'ala madhhab al-imam al-a'zam Abi Hanifa al-Nu'man*. Edited by Muhammad Ahmad Siraj. Cairo: Dar al-Salam, 2011.

————. *Tatbiq ma wujida fi al-qanun al-madani—al-faransi—muwafiqan li-madhhab Abi Hanifa*. Ms. 48119, Dar al-Kutub, Cairo.

"Qatl az Bandaqa Rasasiya." In *Decisions of the Majlis-e 'Aliya-e 'Adalat*, 91. Hyderabad, India: Matba'-e Muqannin-e Dakkan, 1887.

Quataert, Donald. *The Ottoman Empire, 1700–1922*. New York: Cambridge University Press, 2005.

Rabb, Intisar. *Doubt in Islamic Law: A History of Legal Maxims, Interpretation, and Islamic Criminal Law*. New York: Cambridge University Press, 2015.

Reimer, Michael. "Contradiction and Consciousness in Ali Mubarak's Description of al-Azhar." *International Journal of Middle East Studies* 29, no. 1 (1997): 53–69.

Rida, Rashid. "Rabbana inna ata'na sadatana wa-kubara'ana fa-adalluna al-sabila." *al-Manar* 32 (1898): 606–10.

Rif'at, Khalil. *Kulliyat sharh al-jaza'*. Beirut: al-Matba'a al-'Umumiya, 1886.

Robinson, Francis. *The 'Ulama of Farangi Mahall and Islamic Culture in South Asia*. London: C. Hurst, 2001.

Rohe, Mathias. *Islamic Law in Past and Present*. Leiden, the Netherlands: Brill, 2015.

Rubin, Avi. "Modernity as a Code: The Ottoman Empire and the Global Movement of Codification." *Journal of the Economic and Social History of the Orient* 59, no. 5 (2016): 828–56.

————. "Ottoman Judicial Change in the Age of Modernity: A Reappraisal." *History Compass* 7, no. 1 (2009): 119–40.

————. *Ottoman Nizamiye Courts: Law and Modernity*. New York: Palgrave Macmillan, 2011.

————. "Was There a Rule of Law in the Late Ottoman Empire?" *British Journal of Middle Eastern Studies* 46, no. 1 (2019): 123–38.

Saleh, Nabil. "Civil Codes of Arab Countries: The Sanhuri Codes." *Arab Law Quarterly* 8, no. 2 (1993): 161–67.

Salim, Latifa Muhammad. *al-Nizam al-qada'i al-misri al-hadith*. Cairo: Dar al-Shuruq, 2010.

al-Sanhuri, 'Abd al-Razzaq. *al-Khilafa wa tatawwuruha ila 'asabat umam sharqiya*. Edited by Kamal Jad Allah, Sami Mandur, and Ahmad Lashin. Beirut: Markaz Nuhud li-l-Dirasat wa-l-Nashr, 2019.

———. *Masadir al-ḥaqq fi al-fiqh al-Islami*. 2 vols. Cairo: Maʻhad al-Buhuth wa-l-Dirasat al-ʻArabiya, 1967–68.

Sanyal, Usha. *Ahmad Riza Khan Barelwi: In the Path of the Prophet*. Oxford: Oneworld Publications, 2005.

al-Sarakhsi, Muhammad b. Ahmad. *al-Mabsut*. 30 vols. Beirut: Dar al-Maʻrifa, n.d.

Sarkar, Jadunath. *Fall of the Mughal Empire*. 4 vols. Calcutta: M.C. Sarkar and Sons, 1950.

Sayyid, Huda Muhammad ʻAbd al-Rahman. *Kafaʼat al-idara al-mahaliya fi al-qanun al-wadʻi wa-l-fiqh al-islami: Dirasa muqarana*. Amman: al-Manhal li-l-Nashr al-Iliktruni, 2019.

Schacht, Joseph. *An Introduction to Islamic Law*. Oxford: Oxford University Press, 1982.

Schneider, Irene. "Imprisonment in Pre-Classical and Classical Islamic Law." *Islamic Law and Society* 2, no. 2 (1995): 157–73.

Scott, Rachel. *Recasting Islamic Law*. Ithaca, NY: Cornell University Press, 2021.

Serag, Muhammad Ahmad. *Fi usul al-nizam al-qanuni al-islami: Dirasa muqarana li-ʻilm usul al-fiqh wa tatbiqatihi al-fiqhiya wa-l-qanuniya*. Beirut: Markaz Nuhuḍ li-l-Dirasat wal-Nashr, 2020.

al-Shafiʻi, Muhammad b. Idris. *al-Umm*. 8 vols. Beirut: Dar al-Maʻrifa, n.d.

Shalaqany, Amr. "Islamic Legal Histories." *Berkeley Journal of Middle Eastern & Islamic Law* 1, no. 1 (2008): 2–82.

al-Shayyal, Jamal al-Din. *Rifaʻa Rafiʻ al-Tahtawi*. Cairo: Dar al-Maʻarif, 1958.

———. *Tarikh al-tarjuma wa-l-haraka al-thaqafiya fi ʻasr Muhammad ʻAli*. Cairo: Dar al-Fikr al-ʻArabi, 1951.

Siddiqui, Sohaira. "Navigating Colonial Power: Challenging Precedents and the Limitation of Local Elites." *Islamic Law and Society* 26, no. 3 (2018): 1–41.

Singha, Radhika. *A Despotism of Law: Crime and Justice in Early Colonial India*. Delhi: Oxford University Press, 1998.

Skovgaard-Petersen, Jakob. *Defining Islam for the Egyptian State: Muftis and Fatwās of the Dār al-iftāʼ*. Leiden, the Netherlands: Brill, 1997.

Skuy, David. "Macaulay and the Indian Penal Code of 1862: The Myth of the Inherent Superiority and Modernity of the English Legal System Compared to India's Legal System in the Nineteenth Century." *Modern Asian Studies* 32, no. 3 (1998): 513–57.

Smith, Keith John Michael. *Lawyers, Legislators, and Theorists: Developments in English Criminal Jurisprudence 1800–1957*. Oxford: Clarendon Press of Oxford University Press, 1998.

Soleimani, Kamal. *Islam and Competing Nationalisms in the Middle East, 1876–1926*. New York: Palgrave Macmillan, 2016.

Stilt, Kristen. "'Islam Is the Solution': Constitutional Visions of the Egyptian Muslim Brotherhood." *Texas International Law Journal* 46, no. 1 (Fall 2010): 73–108.

———. *Islamic Law in Action: Authority, Discretion, and Everyday Experiences in Mamluk Egypt*. Oxford: Oxford University Press, 2012.

Surridge, Lisa. "On the Offenses Against the Person Act, 1828." BRANCH: Britain, Representation and Nineteenth-Century History, January 2013. http://www.branchcollective.org/?ps_articles=lisa-surridge-on-the-offenses-against-the-person-act-1828.

al-Suyuti, Jalal al-Din. *Jam' al-jawami'*. 2 vols. Cairo: Dar al-Sa'ada li-l-Tiba'a, 2005.

al-Tabari, Muhammad b. Jarir. *Jami' al-bayan 'an ta'wil ay al-Qur'an*. 7 vols. Beirut: Mu'assasat al-Risala, 1994.

Tageldin, Shaden. *Disarming Words: Empire and the Seductions of Translation in Egypt*. Berkeley: University of California Press, 2011.

al-Tahawi, Ahmad b. Muhammad. *Mukhtasar al-Tahawi*. Hyderabad, India: Lajnat Ihya' al-Ma'arif al-Nu'maniya, n.d.

al-Tanimi, Siraj al-Din 'Ali b. 'Uthman. *al-Fatawa al-sirajiya*. Beirut: Dar al-Kutub al-'Ilmiya, 2011.

Tavana, Mohammad. "Three Decades of Islamic Criminal Law Legislation in Iran: A Legislative History Analysis with Emphasis on the Amendments of the 2013 Islamic Penal Code,. *Electronic Journal of Islamic and Middle Eastern Law* 2 (2014): 24–38.

"al-Tawassu' fi 'uqubat al-qatl." *al-Ahram*, December 6, 1897.

Thaman, Stephen C. "The Model Penal Code and the Dilemma of Criminal Law Codification in the United States." In *Codification in International Perspective*, edited by Wen-Yeu Wang, 165–83. New York: Springer, 2014.

Wakin, Jeanette. *Remembering Joseph Schacht (1902–1969)*. Cambridge, MA: Harvard Islamic Legal Studies Program, 2003.

Wood, Leonard. *Islamic Legal Revival: Reception of European Law and Transformations in Islamic Legal Thought in Egypt, 1875–1952*. Oxford: Oxford University Press, 2016.

Wright, Barry. "Macaulay's Indian Penal Code: Historical Context and Originating Principles." In *Codification, Macaulay and the Indian Penal Code: The Legacies and Modern Challenges of Criminal Law Reform*, edited by Wing-Cheong Chan, Barry Wright, and Stanley Yeo, 19–55. London: Routledge, 2016.

Wright, Brian. "Islamic Law for the Colonists: Muftis in Nineteenth-Century British India." *Islamic Studies* 58, no. 3 (2019): 377–402.

Yaduvansh, Uma. "Decline of the Qazis (1793–1876)." *Indian Journal of Political Science* 28, no. 4 (October–December 1967): 216–28.

Yasin, Muhammad. *Sharh qanun al-'uqubat*. Cairo: Matba'at al-Sadiq, 1886.

Zaghlul, Ahmad Fathi. *al-Muhama*. Cairo: Dar al-Kutub wa-l-Watha'iq al-Qawmiya, 2015.

Zaman, Muhammad Qasim. *Ashraf 'Ali Thanawi: Islam in Modern South Asia*. Oxford: Oneworld, 2007.

———. *The Ulama in Contemporary Islam: Custodians of Change*. Princeton, NJ: Princeton University Press, 2002.

Zarinebaf, Fariba. *Crime and Punishment in Istanbul: 1700–1800*. Berkeley: University of California Press, 2010.

Zuhur al-Din, Abu Sa'id. *Hirat al-fuqaha' wa hujjat al-quda'*. Ms. 2669, Khuda Baksh Library, Patna, India.

Index

siyasa 19, 26, 38–44, 64–65, 71, 78, 80, 156, 158, 162, 169–170, 175, 180

Stilt, Kristen 8–9

al-Tahtawi, Rifa'a Rafi' 50–52, 155, 170

taklif 121–122, 147

tanzimat 25–26

Tawfiq, Khedive 59, 61, 170

ta'zir 27, 39, 64, 78, 87, 95, 142, 158, 167, 169, 175

translation 40, 68, 92; British India 26–28, 48, 62, 63–64; Egypt 50–52, 58, 155, 170

Uprising of 1857 14, 24, 33, 49, 53, 57, 152–153, 164

'uqubat 81–82

vigilantism 1–2, 96, 183n8

waqf 4–5, 55

Wood, Leonard 53, 92, 154

Yasin, Muhammad 115–116, 158

Zaghlul, Ahmad Fathi 35–36

Zaman, Muhammad Qasim 165

Zarinebaf, Fariba 33–34

CPSIA information can be obtained
at www.ICGtesting.com
Printed in the USA
JSHW031530150123
36191JS00008BB/10/J